RICHARD JENKYNS

Classical Literature

A PELICAN INTRODUCTION

PELICAN
an imprint of
PENGUIN BOOKS

PELICAN BOOKS

Published by the Penguin Group

Penguin Books Ltd, 80 Strand, London
WC2R ORL, England

Penguin Group (USA) Inc., 375 Hudson
Street, New York, New York 10014, USA

Penguin Group (Canada), 90 Eglinton
Avenue East, Suite 700, Toronto, Ontario,
Canada M4P 2Y3 (a division of Pearson
Penguin Canada Inc.)

Penguin Ireland, 25 St Stephen's Green,
Dublin 2, Ireland (a division of Penguin
Books Ltd)

Penguin Group (Australia), 707 Collins
Street, Melbourne, Victoria 3008,
Australia (a division of Pearson
Australia Group Pty Ltd)

Penguin Books India Pvt Ltd,
11 Community Centre, Panchsheel Park,
New Delhi – 110 017, India

Penguin Group (NZ), 67 Apollo Drive,
Rosedale, Auckland 0632, New Zealand
(a division of Pearson New Zealand Ltd)

Penguin Books (South Africa) (Pty) Ltd,
Block D, Rosebank Office Park,
181 Jan Smuts Avenue, Parktown North,
Gauteng 2193, South Africa

Penguin Books Ltd, Registered Offices:
80 Strand, London WC2R ORL, England

First published in 2015
003

Copyright © Richard Jenkyns, 2015

Book design by Matthew Young
Set in 10/14.664 pt Freight Text Pro
Typeset by Jouve (UK), Milton Keynes
Printed in Great Britain by Clays Ltd,
St Ives plc

ISBN: 978-0-141-97735-5

www.pelicanbooks.com
www.penguin.com

Contents

ACKNOWLEDGEMENTS

Warm thanks to Laura Stickney, who commissioned and edited this book, Kit Shepherd, who copy-edited it, and James Morwood, who read the whole of it in draft. The advice of all of them has improved it. Needless to say, it is also greatly indebted to what I have read, to those who have taught me, and to those whom I have taught in turn. I should also acknowledge that I have sometimes borrowed from myself: where I have written about a topic before, and could think of no better way of putting what I wanted to say, I have been content to adapt some old ideas and phrases. Faults and mistakes, old and new, are all my own work.

PREFACE

This book is about the literature of ancient Greece and Rome. So it is, among other things, a story – an account of what Greek and Latin authors invented and imagined, of what they learned from one another, of how their literature grew and flowered and changed. It is a story of lasting importance, since western civilization was formed in classical antiquity by the Greeks, Romans and Jews, and in large part through what they thought and wrote. We need some appreciation of classical literature if we are fully to understand where our own culture came from and what it is.

But the subject is also compelling in itself. Classical literature includes some works that rank among the supreme achievements of the human mind. Here are brilliance, depth, originality, as well as a variety and daring which would surprise anyone who takes the word 'classical' to imply marmoreal correctitude. Like all literatures at all times, classical literature also includes authors of lesser calibre, and they are part of the story too. However, I have supposed that readers are likely to want mainly two things: a reasonably full survey of the greatest authors, and a picture of the broad shape of literary history. I have tried to keep a balance between these two aims. 'Literature' for my purposes means writing that has an aesthetic intent or value. Accordingly, works on science, medicine, engineering, grammar, geography and so on do not appear; I have also left out most of the minor historians. Plato is a literary master of the first order, but otherwise I have considered philosophy only insofar as it had literary consequences.

'Begin at the beginning,' said the King of Hearts, 'and go on till you come to the end: then stop.' The first part of this command is easily obeyed, the second harder. To have included late antiquity, even were I qualified to do so, would have changed the balance of the book drastically. I have chosen to stop around AD 100, making an exception for the three great Latin writers active in the second century AD. Even so, a book covering two languages and a period of a thousand years must be selective. As it happens, a comprehensive and balanced account of classical literature is not possible, even in principle, because the bulk of it is lost, and we are dependent on the accidents of survival (a matter that I discuss more fully in the second chapter). But in any case, I have naturally chosen to give most space to those works and authors whom I find most inspiring. However, that has not been the only criterion: some writers are hard to discuss without a good deal of historical background, because what remains of them is fragmentary or problematic, or simply because they stand apart from the mainstream of literary history. For one or more of these reasons I have described some areas compactly; in particular, comedy and oratory. The subjects that I have judged to be most essential are Homer, Greek tragedy, the greatest historians, and Virgil and the Latin golden age.

Much in this book is probably not controversial, but some things are, and readers should be warned that it gives a personal view. Indeed, it could hardly be otherwise: literature, if it is any good, demands the reader's response, and literary history must make judgements, if it is to be more than a list of facts. This book is both a narrative and a survey of some individual authors. Much of what the ancients wrote was never meant to be more than useful, and among more ambitious works the quality varies greatly. My foremost aim, however, has been to present the best of what the Greeks and Romans wrote, and to show, as well as I can, what makes it the best.

Homer

Wrath! – European literature begins not with the whimper of infancy, but with a bang. For 'wrath' is the first word of Homer's *Iliad*. We do not in fact know that the *Iliad* is the earliest Greek poem that we have; the Greeks themselves debated whether Homer or Hesiod had the priority. But it was to be important to Greek life and culture for a thousand years and more that so commanding a masterpiece stood at the head of its literature. Naturally, such a work did not spring from nowhere; it is the summit of a submerged mountain, the culmination of a long poetic tradition about which we can know little.

The first civilization to arise on the mainland of Europe was the Mycenaean, named from Mycenae, its greatest city. It was at its peak in the middle of the second millennium BC, and the *Iliad* retains some memory of that time. The Mycenaeans spoke Greek and they knew the use of writing, although they may have employed it only for practical purposes, but with the decline of this culture writing disappeared, not to be introduced again until the eighth century. Until then, verse could only be composed in the poet's head, for singing or recitation. Such must have been Homer's ancestry – but was there a Homer at all, or were the *Iliad* and the other Homeric epic, the *Odyssey*, the products of many authors? That question has been debated since the end of the eighteenth century.

The issue was transformed by the discovery, some eighty years ago, that these poems belong to an oral tradition. Any reader of Homer soon becomes aware that there is much repetition. In particular, phrases linking noun and adjective recur: 'swift-footed Achilles', 'unharvested sea', 'cloud-gathering Zeus', and so on. Such phrases, known in modern scholarship as formulae, are not only frequent, they are systematic. If the poet says that Achilles is doing something and wants him to occupy five syllables at the end of a line, he calls him 'noble Achilles'. If he wants him to occupy seven syllables, he calls him 'swift-footed Achilles'. The system has no redundancy: each time the poet wants a person or thing to fill a given amount of metrical space, he has one such phrase and one only.

Moreover, these phrases have linguistic features which show that they must have been invented at different times; one or two of them are very ancient, centuries earlier than anyone whom we could call Homer. There are also some variations in dialect, which are metrically useful to the poet. Homeric language, therefore, could not have been spoken at any one time or place; it is a construction which must have been formed over generations and handed down orally.

If a piece of gossip circulates round a village, being continuously altered and embellished with each telling, we might not wish to attribute it to an author; the story is the product of the village collectively. An oral poem might be like that.

On the other hand, a poem in an oral tradition need not be fully oral itself; the poet might learn to write, or dictate his work. Although scholars continue to disagree, we can now say with fair confidence that the *Iliad* as we know it is essentially the creation of a single mind, using traditional material, and that it was composed at the point of contact with writing.

There are two principal reasons for this. The first is that no one has been able to give a convincing account of how a work of such immense length could be transmitted by purely oral means. The second is more particular: in the poem's ninth book an embassy is sent to Achilles, and there are sometimes two ambassadors and sometimes three. Clearly there were originally two and the third was then added. A purely oral transmission should have corrected the anomaly. The only plausible explanation is that the poet changed his plan, did not adjust what he had already composed (after all, an oral poet has no concept of erasure), and the anomaly remained because the fact of writing had fixed it. The date of these two works is very uncertain. A common estimate is that the *Iliad* was composed in the later eighth century, but a good case can be made for a dating in the seventh. The *Odyssey* probably came into being between twenty and fifty years after the *Iliad*.

The Greeks possessed an enormous store of mythology, and a curious characteristic of classical literature, throughout its history, is that so much of it is based on myth. One among a number of heroic legends was the Troy story; it told that Paris, son of the Trojan king Priam, abducted Helen, wife of Menelaus, king of Sparta, and that to recover her an alliance commanded by Agamemnon, king of Mycenae, besieged Troy and destroyed it. The *Iliad* ('Tale of Troy') tells of an incident within this Trojan War. The *Odyssey* looks back on the war, and relates the subsequent adventures of one of its heroes. Much later, in the first century BC, Virgil told in the *Aeneid* how one of the Trojans escaped his city's destruction and founded a new people in Italy; and this became the central classic of Latin literature. The tale of Troy has thus come to have a large and enduring place in the western imagination.

There are simple plots in literature and there are complex plots; the *Iliad* has one of the great simple plots. During the siege of Troy, Agamemnon quarrels with Achilles, the best warrior in the army, and takes away his concubine Briseis. Achilles withdraws from battle. The sea-nymph Thetis, Achilles' mother, appeals to Zeus, king of the gods, who agrees to give the Trojans the upper hand in the fighting. Facing defeat, Agamemnon sends an embassy to Achilles, offering an enormous recompense and the return of Briseis. Unexpectedly, Achilles refuses, but yields to his friend Patroclus' entreaty to allow him to re-enter the fray. The Trojans' leading warrior, Hector, son of King Priam, kills Patroclus. The grief-stricken Achilles now returns to battle himself, kills Hector, and refuses to return his corpse. The gods tell him that they are angry at this; Priam comes alone to collect the body; and Hector is buried with full honours.

Every schoolboy knows that the Trojan War was fought between the Greeks and Trojans, and as far as Homer is concerned, every schoolboy is wrong. The Greeks have always called themselves Hellenes; the Romans, for some reason, called them Graeci, and Greeks they have been to most of the world ever since. But Homer never calls the besieging side Hellenes: they are Achaeans, or alternatively Argives or Danaans. The Trojans have the same language, gods and customs as their attackers, and are treated with equal sympathy. The *Iliad* is a story without villains: even the Trojan prince Paris, whose abduction of Helen was the cause of the war, is quite attractive, disarming in accepting his brother Hector's rebukes, and a usually brave and effective, if inconstant, warrior. The formulae tell a similar tale, for they are not meaningless: they present a good world, in which men are godlike, women beautiful, the earth fertile and the sea full of fish. The sense of the world's goodness is a part of the poem's tragic character: there is so much to lose.

When Aristotle in the fourth century analysed the nature of literature in his *Poetics*, and thereby invented literary theory, he observed that the Homeric epics each handle a single action. So the *Iliad* is not in fact the story of the Trojan War, but of one short episode within its ten-year length. After Homer, the work was divided into twenty-four books. Books 2 to 23 of the *Iliad* cover a period of only three days; the first and last books extend the whole action to a few weeks. Such expansiveness might seem to make Wagner feel terse; yet Matthew Arnold, poet and critic, famously described Homer as 'pre-eminently rapid'. This is true in two senses. Although the grand narrative unfolds across an immense distance, the battle scenes are a multiplicity of small incidents; there is no lingering. The speeches too are fast and forceful; the longest of them, Achilles' explosion in Book 9, is furious in its pace.

The *Iliad* is also rapid in metre. English verse scans by stress. Thus 'The cúrfew tólls the knéll of párting dáy' is a five-foot iambic line, because an iambic foot is an unstressed syllable followed by a stressed syllable, and that pattern comes five times. Ancient Greek, unlike its modern descendant, seems not to have had a significant stress, and ancient Greek verse scans by quantity – that is, by the length of time that it takes to speak a syllable. So an iambic foot in Greek is a short syllable followed by a long one (di-dum). The *Iliad*'s metre is the dactylic hexameter. There are six feet to the line; each of the feet may be either a dactyl (dum-di-di) or a spondee (dum-dum), except for the last, which is always a spondee. The great majority of feet are dactyls. So the verse moves lightly: the combination of ease and speed with epic elevation is the essence of Homeric style. The hexameter is a very flexible and expressive form: it was to be used throughout antiquity for epic always, but for many other purposes as well.

The *Iliad* is strictly contained not only in time but in place. With one small exception in the first book, the human actors remain in the city of Troy or the plain outside it throughout. The gods are more mobile, but even they are usually seen gathered together on Mount Olympus, or present on the plain of Troy, or in transit between these places. The combination of breadth and concentration is again essential to the poem's character. It is a story about human beings that gives much space to the gods. Those gods caused surprise even to the Greeks. They can seem trivial, frivolous and careless. Plato in the fourth century would not allow Homer into his ideal republic, because his idea of the gods was unworthy and set a bad example; and the best literary critic of antiquity, an anonymous author usually known as Longinus, remarked that Homer seemed to him to have made his men gods and his gods men. Formulae such as 'equal to the gods' apparently confirm that impression. Men and gods may fight one another: the Achaean hero Diomedes actually manages to wound Ares and Aphrodite. Much that existed in Greek religion – pollution, oracles, hero cult, fertility cult, ecstatic cult – is kept out of the poem, although it indicates that it is aware of most of these things. Homer, or his tradition, has shaped a distinctive picture of the divine. In a few places he gives a mighty representation of the gods' numinous transcendence, but mostly he sucks the numen out of them. If a warrior meets a god in the field, his response is not to fall on his knees in worship, but to consider whether to stand or retreat.

This idea of the gods is, yet again, part of the poem's tragic vision. Gods differ from men in hardly more than two ways. First, gods are immortal, and men die. Elsewhere in Greek religion we find that great men, like Heracles, could be promoted and made gods after their death; other heroes, even if they did not become gods, were felt to have enduring power, and became the objects of cult, honoured with sacrifice or libations. In the *Iliad*, however, the division between mortals and immortals is absolute. So near and yet so far – that is the drama of the conception. Second, more loosely, gods are happy and men unhappy. Once more, the formulae tell the story: 'the blessed ones', gods 'living at ease', 'wretched mortals'. The Christian idea is that God loves us, and that is part of his greatness. To understand the

Iliad we must invert that notion: the gods do not need to care, and therefore are they gods.

When Achilles chases Hector round the walls of Troy, the poet compares the scene to a chariot race, 'and all the gods looked on'. The comparison is telling: when we go to the big match, we believe ourselves to be passionately involved, but we leave the stadium and our lives are unchanged. The gods too, of whom some support the Achaeans, others the Trojans, can seem passionately partisan, but in the end their emotions are superficial. One might compare the apocryphal Chinese curse: 'May you live in interesting times.' It is the gods' blessing to be flat and simple, and the curse of man to be interesting. The last book contains two reconciliations or comings together. That between the gods is fairly brief and straightforward. That between two men, Achilles and Priam, is far more difficult, complex and profound.

The *Iliad* uses little metaphor, with one huge exception: the formal simile. Most of the similes fall into one of a fairly small number of types. The commonest of these is the animal simile: a warrior is like a lion or wolf or (once) a stubborn donkey. Many similes are taken from the natural world, and while single combat is the form of fighting that predominates in the poem, similes of clouds and waves are a way of representing mass battle. Similes help to enliven and diversify the battle narrative, but collectively they have a larger effect: they show the place of warfare within a world that contains so much else. That idea is also expressed by the shield that the god Hephaestus makes for Achilles. It depicts the whole world, with Ocean around its edges. A city under siege is one of the scenes upon it, but there are also images of marriage, dancing, reaping and vintaging. We are reminded that battle, on which our attention is so fiercely concentrated, is only one part of human experience.

Homer uses leaves as a simile several times. In every place but one the likeness is that of multitude ('as many as the leaves . . .'). The exception is peculiar in another way too, for it is the only simile spoken by any character in the story other than Achilles, given to the colourless figure of Glaucus because the poet has an idea of his own that he wants to convey: 'As the generation of leaves, so is that of men also. The wind sheds the leaves to the ground, but the forest burgeons and grows others, and they come forth in the season of spring.' We expect a plangent inflection, a sigh over the brevity of life, but instead we find a gathering energy – new growth, the inexhaustible vitality of the world. Here is the ethos of the whole poem in miniature, not low-spirited and melancholy but high-spirited and tragic. The poem is also down to earth. It celebrates everyday acts and appetites. If someone cooks meat, the poet describes the process. The description of fighting is in many ways stylized, but the actual killing is faced head on: bones smashed, guts spilled. The poem is not gruesome – death is always immediate – but it is direct and unflinching.

The *Iliad* is unusual in that its theme is not simply a hero but a hero's particular behaviour: the *Odyssey*'s first word declares its subject to be a man, but the *Iliad* announces its subject not as Achilles but as Achilles' wrath. In most heroic story the protagonist needs courage and endurance to win through, but essentially he responds to the challenges that external circumstances lay upon him. Achilles, however, shapes his own story. It is made clear, for example, that any other hero would have accepted the fabulous recompense offered by the embassy. In much heroic story the leading man is a kind of splendid brute (Siegfried, for example, in German saga), but Achilles is intelligent. He was brought up by his father to be both a speaker of words and a doer of deeds. He says himself that he is the best of the Achaeans in battle, but others are superior in debate. For pure eloquence, though, he surpasses everyone in the poem. Even more unexpectedly, he is also an aesthete: when the ambassadors approach, they find him singing about the famous deeds of men, accompanying himself on the lyre. That makes him the *Iliad*'s only poet and only musician.

In the *Odyssey* poets are honoured but subordinate people who perform in the halls of chieftains, a picture which surely reflects a historical reality. It was a remarkable idea to give the greatest warrior imagination and sensitivity. The poetry of his mind comes out in two strange similes that he uses. In his most furious speech he likens himself to a bird collecting morsels for her young and going hungry herself – an odd image, and for all his passion almost a humorous one. Later, talking to Patroclus, he compares him to a little girl running alongside her mother and tugging her dress until the mother picks her up; that simile is teasing and affectionate, but also self-aware, for Achilles recognizes that he is going to give in to his friend's request. And both times this supreme example of masculinity has the quirkiness to compare himself to a female. No one else in the poem talks like this.

There are two strange people in the *Iliad*. The other is the enigmatic figure of Helen, also self-reflective and also an artist, who is first seen in the poem embroidering a tapestry on which she is depicting the Trojan War itself. How shall we judge Achilles, this unusual hero? One reading sees the *Iliad* as a moral tragedy pivoting on the embassy. On this account Achilles has been essentially in the right in his quarrel with Agamemnon, but when he turns down the embassy's offer, pride and anger have led him into error, and he only recovers his moral dignity at the end of the poem, in showing magnanimity to Priam. This interpretation owes much to the idea, which we shall meet again, that tragedy depicts an essentially good person who falls as the result of a fault of character or some particular error. The moral breadth of the *Iliad* is such that perhaps it allows this as one way of understanding the story, but it suggests that this is not the best or deepest way. Why does Achilles so unexpectedly refuse? Ajax, the last of the delegation to speak, tells him that the gods have put an implacable spirit in him 'for the sake of a girl, just one girl', and this has been taken for the voice of stalwart common sense. But Ajax cannot be right: Agamemnon has offered to return Briseis, and if that is what Achilles principally wants, he is bound to accept the offer. The key lies elsewhere.

Odysseus, the first to speak, has been told what to say by Agamemnon, and he delivers the message more or less verbatim. But he wisely leaves out Agamemnon's last words: 'Let him be tamed . . . and submit to me, since I am the more kingly . . .' Achilles has not heard this, but it is as though he has, because in his great denunciation he refuses to marry Agamemnon's daughter, saying that he should find another Achaean for her, one who is 'more kingly'. Achilles differs from the other heroes not because he has seen less but because he has seen more deeply. Outwardly, Agamemnon has climbed down, but inwardly he is still asking his antagonist to yield. And the greatest of heroes must not yield. Achilles' father instructed him 'always to be the best and to excel over others'. That is a hero's imperative.

Homer shows the nature of heroism through a speech of Sarpedon to Glaucus; these two are Lycians fighting on the Trojans' side. Unlike the Trojans themselves, who are struggling for their survival, they fight as the Achaeans fight, because it is what heroes do. Sarpedon observes that they two are held in greatest honour among the Lycians, enjoying the best food and wine and possessing rich farmland, and therefore they should now stand in the front line, so that one of the Lycians may say, 'Not without fame do our kings rule over Lycia . . .' Sarpedon adds that if he could be ageless and immortal, 'neither would I myself fight among the first nor would I be urging you into battle glory-of-men'. This is not an idea of social contract or duty to others: if he were fighting on the Lycians' behalf, exemption from death would enable him to help them all the more. The hero's only duty is to himself: he has a certain position and he must act commensurately; he would be ashamed to do otherwise. Sarpedon does not want to fight: if he were immortal, he would not trouble to do so. The tragic paradox is that the fighting is worth while because it is useless, and because the greatest glory is only inches from the misery and humiliation of death.

Anthropologists distinguish between shame culture and guilt culture. The shame-culture ideal that Sarpedon expounds is not selfish in the ordinary sense of the word. It is the pursuit of virtue, of trying to be the most glorious human being that one can be, and the greatest glory is won in battle. Some people try to minimize the shame culture in the poem, feeling that it makes Homer look embarrassingly primitive; that is a great mistake. The shame culture is what makes the tragedy so stark. If Sarpedon could feel that he was giving his life for others, or for his country, there would be some consolation. But that softening thought is absent. Does Achilles, for his part, feel guilt or remorse after Patroclus' death? Some have thought that he does, but if we attend to the poem we shall see that it is not so. True, Agamemnon uses the language of fault, wriggling awkwardly around the question of whether he is to blame or not, but that is one of the ways in which he and Achilles differ. Of his friend, Achilles says merely, 'I have lost him', bare words of heartbreaking simplicity. He reflects that he 'was not to help' Patroclus or 'be a saving light' to him: 'If only strife would perish from among gods and men, and anger . . .' 'I am not to blame,' says Agamemnon; 'I am to blame,' Achilles might have said, but instead he neither condemns nor excuses himself. He looks inside himself from without and sees that there is anger in him. For Achilles that is a plain fact, not something that can be altered and repented. This stark objectivity is again part of the poem's tragic vision. Remorse can be comforting: it suggests that things could have been otherwise and better; it offers the hope of healing. Achilles does not have that consolation.

Before Hector faces Achilles, Homer gives us something rare in this poem, a soliloquy. We hear Hector talking to himself, and enter into his thoughts. Why does he go to meet his foe? His father and mother have told him, rightly, that Achilles will kill him, and that will be the end of Troy. And he is scared. The imperative is again shame: 'I feel shame before the Trojan men and Trojan women with their trailing robes, lest someone worse than I may say, "Hector trusting in his own might lost the people."' The terror and horror of the shame demand is that it compels him not only to his own humiliation but to the ruin of everyone he loves.

At the point of death Hector receives the momentary gift of second sight – an idea otherwise alien to the poem: he tells Achilles that Paris will kill him by Troy's Scaean Gate. This vision of a future event is ironic, for Hector has hitherto been the man who has not seen what lies ahead. In this he is contrasted with Achilles, who has known that if he continues to fight at Troy he will die there, and accepts that fate. What Achilles resists is the truth that he can do no more for Patroclus. He tries to do more to avenge him, attempting to mutilate Hector's body, killing prisoners at Patroclus' pyre, but it is all useless, and when Patroclus' ghost appears to him – ghosts too have hitherto seemed alien to the ethos of the *Iliad* – it can want only to be released into nothingness. Finally the gods show Achilles that he should put an end to his mourning and return Hector's body, for as the god Apollo says, 'the Destinies have put an enduring heart in men'. Or as Odysseus has earlier more dourly put it, one must bury whoever dies, hardening the heart, weeping for a day.

With Hector's death the story might seem more or less complete, but there are nearly two thousand more lines to come, and some astonishing surprises. Achilles holds funeral games in Patroclus' honour, and here the poet introduces a new tone: lively social comedy. A hitherto minor character becomes prominent, young Antilochus, high-spirited, shrewd, clever at manipulating his elders. He provokes Achilles to smile, for the first and only time in the poem – a great moment. Achilles himself is generous to Agamemnon, and gracious in soothing the bickering of others – ironic in a man whose quarrel with Agamemnon has made the story, but for once a warming irony. And here we bid goodbye to the Achaean chieftains, Achilles alone excepted. This buoyant episode is a vital part of the tale, for it shows the hero restored to his society, but once the games are over, it is as though they had never been. Achilles returns to his obsessive mourning, refusing to eat or, despite his mother's urging, to sleep with a woman. He turns away from those ordinary appetites that the poem celebrates.

What follows astonishes Achilles himself: he marvels as Priam appears before him, unannounced and alone, come to ask for the return of Hector's corpse. The encounter is difficult: Achilles is edgy, at one point threatening to kill the king if he provokes him further. The two men weep, and the sound of their weeping fills the house. They weep together, in a sense, but they also weep apart, for Priam weeps for Hector, and Achilles for his father, distant and bereft, and for Patroclus. An essential loneliness abides. But Achilles discovers in himself a new generosity: he returns part of the ransom that Priam has brought, himself laying it on Hector's body. He also speaks to Priam with a new pity, at the same time studying his own situation and seeing its futility, 'since far from my country I sit in Troy, distressing you and your children'. But he does not think only of himself, for his vision is now enlarged: he declares that Zeus gives a mixture of good and ill to some, nothing but ill to others, and he contemplates the life of a wretched fugitive without honour. He recognizes, that is, that there are people whose lot is worse than his own. Then he encourages Priam to eat. In the midst of this sublime scene the poem does not disdain a simple truth: that when people have food and drink inside them they feel better. Only now do the two men enjoy one another's company.

But the poet remains unsentimental. Priam marvels at Achilles, a man who looks like the gods; Achilles marvels at Priam's noble mien and speech. A distance remains. In his last words Priam asks for a truce: for nine days they shall mourn Hector, on the tenth bury him, on the eleventh raise a mound, 'and on the twelfth we shall fight, if it must be'. Achilles is last seen sleeping with Briseis. He can now be dismissed from the poem; and the final part of it describes the mourning for Hector. The last major speeches in this intensely masculine poem are given to women, as his wife, his mother and Helen lament over him in turn.

The *Iliad*'s conclusion shows natural appetites and rhythms restored: the man who had refused to eat has eaten and urged another to eat; the man who had refused sex is in bed with Briseis; Hector, once denied burial, receives the ritual honours, as the women keen over him and the body is burned. On the surface, we see rightness and goodness, and human nature has never seemed more splendid. Underneath, there is no change; Achilles has seen the uselessness and misery of his situation, but nothing can be done about it. The counterpoint between these things is profoundly tragic. The rituals for Hector conclude with a basic satisfaction, as at the end of a children's story: 'a glorious banquet in the halls of Priam'. Food and drink, those good, plain pleasures, are where we end. But beyond that immediate moment is war, with yet worse to come: Achilles will die, and Priam, and Troy be destroyed. It is the eleventh day, and on the morrow the fighting will resume, 'if it must be'. But Priam knew that the plea in those words was hopeless. The *Iliad* ends with feasting, and on the brink of hell.

The *Odyssey* is set ten years after the Trojan War. Odysseus has not returned home: the goddess Calypso has imprisoned him on a remote island, while his palace on his own island of Ithaca is occupied by local nobles, suitors for the hand of his wife Penelope. He has also incurred the enmity of Poseidon, god of the sea, for blinding his son, the cannibal giant Polyphemus. Zeus decrees that Calypso must let Odysseus go. Telemachus, Odysseus' son, leaves Ithaca in search of his father. Odysseus is shipwrecked, but makes landfall on the land of the Phaeacians, where he is found by the princess Nausicaa. In her parents' palace he tells his adventures, and how in stages he lost all his ships and companions. The adventures mostly involve monsters, like Polyphemus, but also the goddess Circe, with whom he had a dalliance, and an encounter with the spirits of the dead. Back in Ithaca, he is sheltered by the swineherd Eumaeus. Disguised as a beggar, Odysseus enters the palace and with his bow kills all the suitors. A coda ties up some loose ends.

Like the *Iliad*, the *Odyssey* can now be seen as essentially the creation of one great shaping mind, working upon traditional material. Like other works, it may of course have suffered later alteration or interpolation; in particular, there has been much debate about whether its strangely scrappy ending is authentic. Who was the author? Almost everyone in antiquity supposed that Homer wrote both epics, with only a very few 'separators' dissenting. The arguments for the poet of the *Odyssey* being a different man are of two kinds. The first kind is based on the linguistic details of the two poems; the second kind claims that the values and beliefs expressed in these works differ too much from one another to have come from the same mind. The linguistic evidence is ambiguous, and does not point entirely in one direction. The differences in ethos might be the consequence of a great imagination attempting a different kind of poem. The majority view today is that there were two poets, but the issue cannot be conclusively determined. We may, however, use 'Homer' as shorthand for the two poems taken together.

Clearly the *Odyssey* takes the *Iliad* as its pattern. Like the older poem it handles a single action: it is a tale of what the Greeks called *nostos*, 'homecoming' – how Odysseus returned and slew the suitors. The *Odyssey* is therefore not an odyssey, in the modern sense of the term: the hero relates his years of wandering in retrospect. We saw that the *Iliad* is as tightly controlled in space as in time, and here the *Odyssey* is in extreme contrast: Odysseus begins at the furthest distance imaginable, on an island in outer Ocean, and the narrative takes him into ever smaller spaces, first back into the Mediterranean world, then to his island, to his house, and lastly to the most narrow and intimate place, in bed with his wife. And this, as an ancient scholar observed, is the 'end' of the poem, the goal to which the whole story has been moving.

The *Odyssey* also contrasts with the *Iliad* in the breadth of its social range. The cast includes slaves and beggars and even a dog, and Odysseus apart, most of the more interesting characters are women. Recurrent in the poem are the themes of hospitality and test. People are tested by their treatment of strangers and the destitute. The suitors are bad hosts (they treat strangers with contumely); Polyphemus is a very bad host (he eats them). Alcinous, king of the Phaeacians, is a good host, but so is the slave Eumaeus. 'All strangers and beggars are from Zeus,' says Alcinous' daughter, Nausicaa, 'and giving is a small thing and welcome.' Much later Eumaeus speaks the very same words, with a humble addition, 'giving, such as mine'. Princess and pigman can alike be hospitable. But the *Odyssey* remains aristocratic in its values: slaves and subordinates are required to be loyal, and the disloyal are savagely punished.

Unlike the *Iliad*, this poem has a sub-plot. Indeed, Odysseus himself does not appear until the fifth book. Until then, the tale is of Telemachus, who moves outwards as his father moves inwards. He leaves Ithaca, visiting King Nestor, who had fought at Troy, and then the glamorous court of Menelaus and Helen at Sparta, which seems to his young eyes like the house of Zeus himself. When he returns home, the suitors notice in him an assurance that he had lacked before; and when his mother tells him off, he replies, 'I know and understand everything in my spirit, both the good and the bad; before I was still a baby.' Later, he will order her to her room, and she will obey in amazement, 'for she laid her son's shrewd words to her spirit'. He is now a man. His tale is the ultimate ancestor of the *Bildungsroman*, the story of a person's growth and formation.

Telemachus' adventure does not at all advance the main plot, but the poet likes to put different stories beside each other. We can see this with the hero himself. For there seem to be two kinds of Odysseus in the poem: there is the folk-tale trickster, cousin to Sinbad the Sailor and Jack the Giant-Killer, and there is the heroic warrior whom we met in the *Iliad*. Far from trying to disguise this doubleness, the poet enjoys it. The lying stories that Odysseus tells in the main narrative after his return to Ithaca, when he needs to conceal who he is, refer to real places, like Crete and Egypt; his 'real' adventures occur nowhere that we know at all. He begins his wanderings in the familiar world of the Aegean, but once he has been blown west of Greece in a great storm he enters fairyland. Its inhabitants are monsters or, if human, monstrous, like the cannibal Laestrygonians or the lethally entrancing Lotos-eaters. Some of these stories are likely to have been borrowed from other places, especially the saga of the Argonauts, as the poet seems cheekily to acknowledge when he has Odysseus describe the clashing rocks which, he says, had previously been passed only by the '*Argo* known to everybody'.

The poet also enjoys the transition between fairyland and our own familiar world, for he invents the land of the Phaeacians, delicately poised between the two. Their world is half magical: their ships steer themselves, King Alcinous' garden is fresh at every season, the gods visit them. But they are also reassuringly ordinary, and treated with delicate humour. Alcinous proposes some sporting contests 'so that the stranger may tell his friends when he returns home' how his people excel at these things. After Odysseus beats them all, Alcinous observes blandly that they are not outstanding sportsmen, but they like feasting, hot baths and changes of clothing, and (in the same language as before) that the stranger will be able to report that they excel in dancing and song. It takes no great skill, we may reflect, to enjoy good food and fresh linen. The Phaeacians are both everyday and elusive, and in the end they disappear from the story in the middle of a sentence: 'Thus the leaders and rulers of the people of the Phaeacians prayed to lord Poseidon, standing round the altar, while noble Odysseus awoke . . .' We never learn whether their prayer to Poseidon, who has threatened to punish them for helping the hero, is granted; indeed no one will see them again, for Alcinous has decided that they shall have no further dealings with other mortal men. It is curiously fitting that they should fade from the poem with this mysterious evanescence.

There are five principal women in Odysseus' life. Three of them he meets in the course of his wanderings, and each of these is seen in a landscape expressive of her character. The goddess Circe first tries to turn the hero into a pig, then has an affair with him, then freely helps him on his way. She is, as it were, a divinized *demi-mondaine*, easy come, easy go. Her palace of polished stone set amid forest and thicket conveys her mixture of wildness and sophistication. In a world of palaces, Calypso dwells in a cave, aromatic with burning cedar and juniper, with a vine rich in clusters running around its mouth. Outside is a wood of alder, poplar and sweet-smelling cypress. Dark, hidden, heavy with fruitage, this is the landscape of passion. Unlike these two, Nausicaa is a mortal woman, and yet she shares an aura of divinity, for the poet compares her to Artemis, and Odysseus tactfully asks her if she is a mortal or a goddess, Artemis perhaps. Odysseus first sees her by the stream of a clear-flowing river, the natural landscape for a young maiden, while he himself, naked and shaggy, is hiding in rough brushwood.

Like the Phaeacians as a whole, Nausicaa blends the charms of domesticity with the enchantments of distance. She has come with her maidens ostensibly to wash her menfolk's clothes. But she had another thought in mind when she asked her father's permission for the excursion, and he in turn realized this but said nothing about it. This gentle comedy has a moral element, in a poem much concerned with civility: reticence is a form of good manners. The scene of Nausicaa and her girls playing ball – a dance, not a competition – is the first depiction of ordinary, simple happiness. And nothing is to shatter it. She is clearly attracted to the stranger, and we seem to have here the beginning of a folk-tale pattern: the traveller who comes to a far land and marries the king's daughter. But Odysseus cannot marry Nausicaa, because he has a wife already. The poet could have contrived a tale of heartbreak, but he does something more subtle. She fades from the story, returning only when Odysseus is feasting with the Phaeacian nobles. Standing at a distance, she speaks two lines only: 'Farewell, stranger' – for she has not even learned his name – 'so that when you are in your homeland you may still remember me, since you owe me thanks for first saving you.' Odysseus briefly promises to remember her with honour, and that is all. The pathos is very light, the poet masterly in his restraint.

A fourth woman in Odysseus' life is his particular patron and protector, the goddess Athena. When he arrives on Ithaca, he encounters a herdsman, and prudently tells him a lying story about who he is. But the trickster has been tricked: the herdsman is Athena disguised, who grasps him and declares delightedly that even a god would have to be crafty to outwit him. There is something like friendship in this, such as one could not imagine between an Olympian and a mortal in the *Iliad*. The Olympian gods in general now have a more overtly moral function. Zeus delivers the first speech in the poem and there sets out the rules: mortals suffer also from their own follies, like Aegisthus, who committed crimes against which the gods had warned him. And the poem itself is more overtly moral, declaring that Odysseus' men likewise perished through their own folly, for they ate the cattle of the Sun. This sounds grim indeed, but adventure stories often depend on the suspension of ordinary sympathies; so in a western we do not mind if many subordinate characters are killed, provided that the hero and heroine survive. Similarly, although Odysseus loses every one of his companions, and there are many other killings, the poem is essentially a comedy: the hero triumphs and the transgressors die.

It would be wrong, however, to deduce from this that the *Odyssey* inhabits a different moral universe from the *Iliad*: the difference is rather a matter of the sort of story that each is. Both poems are, in a sense, experiments in feeling. In the country of the good king, Odysseus tells Penelope, the black earth bears wheat and barley, the trees are laden with fruit, the sea gives fish in abundance, and the people prosper. That was not something that anyone was likely to believe literally in the bleak circumstances of dark-age Greece. We might instead be guided by Miss Prism: 'The good ended happily and the bad unhappily. That is what fiction means.'

When Odysseus tells the Phaeacians his name, he also says that he comes from Ithaca and gives the names of the three islands near it, describing how they sit in relation to one another. He is fixing himself, giving his coordinates, as it were; Ithaca has its individuality, just as he has. He adds that his home is 'rough but a good nurse of young men', and explains how he rejected Calypso and Circe, because nothing is sweeter than home and parents, however splendid a foreign palace may be. Here literature begins the exploration of identity and belonging. Ithaca may not be the finest place, but it is where his affections are attached, 'a poor thing but mine own'. Likewise, he has rejected Calypso's beauty and offer of immortality in favour of the lesser beauty of mortal Penelope. Critics have sometimes asked whether it is Penelope or his possessions that Odysseus really wants back, but the man himself might find no need to make the distinction. The poem places a high value on the marriage relation. Odysseus tells Nausicaa that there is nothing better than when a man and woman live together in harmony; it brings pain to their enemies, joy to their friends – and then follows a phrase of puzzling Greek. It may mean only 'and they themselves are in high repute', but possibly it means 'and they know it best themselves'. If the latter is the case, the words are a tribute to the private depths of married love.

Penelope is the fifth, and ultimately the most important, woman in Odysseus' life. One of the *Odyssey*'s puzzles is why she is unable to recognize him, although his dog and his old nanny can readily do so. In naturalistic terms there can be no answer. Even before Odysseus reaches the palace she seems seized by a new hilarity. After he comes, in disguise, she is inspired to display herself to the suitors and make their hearts flutter, so that she may win more honour from her son and husband, and she laughs at her idle thought. It is as if she knew: somehow the mere fact of Odysseus' presence illuminates her, without her knowing how. Her trouble in finally recognizing him is inexplicable but mysteriously fitting: it is harder for her because there is so much more at stake. We can compare the ending of the *Iliad*: in both poems the hero is made whole through the sexual act; in both, a public restoration is followed by a private one; and in both, the private one is more complex and difficult because it goes deeper into the heart of the human condition.

But whereas the *Iliad* suggests the ultimate loneliness of the hero, the *Odyssey* is a social poem. Most of it takes place on islands. Islands can be places of isolation, like Calypso's Ogygia or Circe's Aiaia, but they can also be the units within which a whole society is contained, as is Ithaca. The *Odyssey* studies both man the individual and man as a social animal, and understands that these two elements of human experience are indivisible: at the end of it the hero has recovered his people, his property and his most private place.

Archaic Greece

Throughout antiquity the Homeric epics enjoyed a special prominence and authority. The Greeks had no sacred texts, in the sense of a body of canonical scripture demanding assent. That left a gap for another kind of text to assume a commanding cultural authority, and Homer filled that gap. These poems were the common possession of the Greeks. Aeschylus is alleged to have said that his plays were merely slices cut from the great banquet of Homer. The idea in this seems to be less that the plots for tragedies were drawn from Homer (in most cases they were not) than that he provided the pattern by which human experience might be nobly represented. As we shall see, the first true history-writing too was to be regarded, with reason, as Homeric in character. Homer's example may also have strengthened the Greeks' attachment to mythology as a source for imaginative literature. But from the start there was always a quite different strand of hexameter poetry. As with the *Iliad*, its first representative, Hesiod, is probably the inheritor of a long tradition of verse that only becomes visible to us at the point where it could first be written down.

Hesiod came from the rough mountains that formed the southern rim of the territory of Boeotia, north-west of Attica;

he was active around 700 BC. Two of his poems remain essentially complete: the *Theogony* ('Birth of the Gods') and *Works and Days*. To turn from Homer to *Works and Days* is to exchange the past for the present and heroism for hard scrabble. This is a didactic poem, and an aid to living. The 'days' at the end of the piece are a list of lucky and unlucky times: the thirteenth of the month is a bad day for sowing but good for setting plants out; geld pigs and cattle on the eighth and mules on the twelfth. This is useful information. The 'works' have much in common with the 'wisdom literature' found in various Near Eastern cultures, and most familiar to us from the Book of Proverbs in the Old Testament. There are adages conveying proverbial wisdom, often pungently expressed, and nuggets of gnomic instruction. Drink freely from the wine jar when it is full (the poet advises) and when it is running out, but be sparing with it in between. This is useful too, advising the hearer how best to make life tolerable in tough conditions.

Works and Days also contains aetiologies; that is, 'just so' stories which explain the origin of things. Thus the story of Prometheus (told in its full form only in the *Theogony*) explains where fire came from and why the gods get hardly any of the meat after a sacrifice. The story of the ages (the gods created and then destroyed first a golden race of men, then silver, then bronze, and we are now in the age of iron) is a 'soft primitivist' myth – a myth, that is, which supposes that mankind has lost an original paradise (like the story of the Garden of Eden). And Hesiod adds another element to the mix: himself. He gives us details about his family, his experiences and his way of life, and he is thus Europe's first individual. He reveals that his father migrated from Asia Minor to Boeotia and that he lives himself in Ascra, which he calls 'a miserable village, bad in winter, harsh in summer, never good'. He also says that he has never been to sea, except once, when he crossed from Aulis in Boeotia to Chalcis on the island of Euboea, where he won a poetry prize. This is wryly humorous: Chalcis is less than two hundred yards from the mainland. Some of his moral admonitions are addressed to the powerful generally, others to his brother Perses, with whom he has quarrelled over an inheritance. This is odd but vivid, and gives the poem a tang of individuality.

The dour peasant flavour of his work does not mean that he lacked the epic poet's high sense of his calling. He tells in the *Theogony* of how the Muses visited him as he was tending his lambs on Mount Helicon, gave him a staff and breathed into him a divine voice. This poem tells how Earth bore Sky, and Night bore Air and Day, how Sky lay with Earth and bore Ocean and other Titans, how Sky was castrated by Cronus his son. We naturally categorize the *Theogony* as poetry and as mythology, but there is another way of looking at the matter. The poem is an attempt to explain how the world came into being, by what laws it is governed, and why the human condition has come to be as it is. We can see here the prehistory of Greek science and Greek thought.

The early Greek thinkers have become known, with the wisdom of hindsight, as the Presocratics, the ones before Socrates (469–399). Thales, the first of them (in the early sixth century), said that all things are full of gods. Is this theology? He said that water is the beginning of all things. Is this physics? Later, in the fifth century, Empedocles said that the world is a balance or conflict between Love and Strife (and he mythologized these forces as the gods Aphrodite and Ares). Again, this does not easily fit our modern categories. Homer had been both poet and historian: he appeals to the Muses before, of all things, his dry catalogue of the Achaean fleet that sailed to Troy, because they have knowledge and we know nothing. But the achievement of Greek thought in the sixth and fifth centuries was to discover differences. They learned that fact was different from fiction, history from myth, natural science from philosophy. These are not the obvious truths that they seem to us. They also learned to separate the functions of verse and prose. Some of the Presocratics wrote in prose, but others used verse, Empedocles being the last of them. His surviving fragments convey strength and energy.

The *Iliad* and *Odyssey* always stood alone in scale and quality, but in the seventh and sixth centuries other epics appeared about heroes and heroic events; some of these were as much as half the length of the Homeric pair. We have only very meagre remnants of them. However, a number of 'Homeric hymns' have survived, so called because they were attributed to the supposed author of the *Iliad* and *Odyssey*. These are not hymns in the modern sense but poems in honour of gods and goddesses, usually narrating some event in which they were concerned; they vary in size from a handful of lines to more than five hundred. Most of the authors of archaic Greece – that is, the period from the eighth century to the early fifth century – whom we know at all exist today only in a few fragments, and that circumstance forces us to take account of how classical texts have survived.

Until late antiquity the usual form of a book was a papyrus roll. The amount of writing that could be fitted on to a roll without it becoming unmanageable was limited: in a verse text two thousand lines seems to have been an absolute maximum, and most verse books are half that or less. So longer works were divided into books, which were much shorter than the word 'book' suggests to us. The book as we think of it today, a sequence of sheets bound together – technically a codex – first appeared around the first century AD, and gradually became the dominant form. In a world without printing, texts endured only if they were repeatedly copied. Most of the classical literature that we have comes down to us in a manuscript tradition, that is to say from one or more manuscripts copied from an earlier manuscript at some time in the Middle Ages. All these manuscripts are copies of copies of copies; we have no autograph text of any classical author. For some texts the oldest manuscript remaining was written in the ninth century AD, but often it dates from some centuries later. In rare cases the manuscripts are earlier; thus we have a few manuscripts of Virgil, always the most widely read and admired of Latin poets, dating from the fifth or sixth centuries, none of which is complete. Some scribes make corrections; all scribes make mistakes. So the texts of all classical authors have suffered some degree of distortion. To describe a surviving text as complete, therefore, is to make an approximate statement, which does not mean that we have every single word; not only may the scribe have written the wrong word, but sentences may have been added or left out; in some cases fifty lines or more have gone missing.

Works survived only if people went on wanting to read them. Some very dull works of history survive because they were useful for teaching and learning. Greek lyric poetry perished because people lost interest. Even so, losses and survivals could be chancy. Homer and Virgil were pretty sure to endure because they were part of every schoolboy's education, but otherwise even the best authors were insecure. Among the Latin poets of the first century BC Lucretius and Catullus remain, while Gallus and Varius have perished, but it might have been different; these lost authors were much admired in their time. Our entire knowledge of Catullus, one poem apart, comes from a ninth-century manuscript found in the fourteenth century and copied before it was lost again. Our entire knowledge of Lucretius comes from two ninth-century manuscripts deriving from an earlier manuscript long lost. In the eighth century a scribe began to copy out the *Thyestes* of Varius and then changed his mind, thus destroying our chance of reading the most important drama of the Augustan age.

There are ways in which words which have not descended in a manuscript tradition can nevertheless survive, three in particular. They may be quoted by other authors. They may have been inscribed in bronze or stone. Or they may be found on papyrus. Papyri, mostly unearthed in upper Egypt from the late nineteenth century onward, have transformed our understanding of some areas of Greek literature, lyric poetry and comedy among them. Occasionally a papyrus gives us a text complete, but far more often these are literally tattered fragments, scraps ragged at the edges, or with holes in them. These accidents have an important consequence for the interpretation of classical literature, because they limit our ability to give a balanced history of it at any period. The Roman historian Velleius Paterculus, in the first half of the first century AD, thought that Rabirius, lost to us, was the best of the Augustan poets after Virgil. Would we agree? If Lucretius had perished, we would not have guessed his greatness or his influence. With Gallus and Varius we are left guessing. We should be guided by the spirit of Socrates, who allowed that he might after all be the wisest of men, because at least he knew that he knew nothing, whereas the rest knew not even that.

Besides the hexameter, another verse form was widely used throughout the whole length of classical antiquity: this was elegy. For the Greeks the genre of elegy was defined simply by its metre: it was verse composed in the elegiac couplet. This consists of an alternation between hexameter and pentameter. The hexameter is as in Homer; the pentameter is symmetrical: it takes the metre of the hexameter's first two and a half feet, and then repeats it. The last two feet are always dactyls. Tennyson provides an English example of this couplet, scanned in the Greek way by quantity, not stress:

> These lame hexameters the strong-winged music
> of Homer!
> No – but a most burlesque barbarous experiment.

The couplet structure encouraged poets to think and compose in blocks of two lines; it was admirably suited to epigram and to verse that aimed at neatness and concision, but given its comparative inflexibility its great popularity throughout antiquity is perhaps surprising.

The word 'elegy' would come to be associated in the western tradition with two subjects, love and lamentation, but from the start this metrical form was actually used for many purposes. Tyrtaeus and Callinus in the mid-seventh century BC wrote martial stuff, stiffening the sinews of the young, and the Athenian statesman Solon (died c.560) used it for his policy statements. The largest corpus of early elegy to survive is attributed to Theognis (mid-sixth century), but the greater part of it is not his, and so he has had the misfortune to become as much a problem as a poet. Another sixth-century elegist is the ironic Xenophanes. He observed that the Germans' gods have blond hair, like themselves, and added that if horses had gods they would look like horses. That was not scepticism; rather, a lively but serious attempt to probe the nature of the divine, to argue that the anthropomorphic idea of the gods was merely a local representation of a deeper reality. He is also classed among the Presocratics, and indeed he shows how indivisible poetry and philosophy might be at this time.

The most appealing fragments of early elegy come, in the late seventh century, from Mimnermus, in whom we first meet a note of voluptuous pessimism which has sounded in later European literature from time to time. He was also to give to the simile of leaves the plangent quality that seems so natural to us: we are like leaves that open out in the spring sunshine, and like them our time is brief. Death comes soon, or age, and once our prime is past it is better to die than live.

What is life, he asks in another poem, what is pleasurable, without golden Aphrodite? Once hidden love and gifts and bed, those flowers of youth, are over, may he die, for old age is wearisome and despised. Even nature can seem languid in his view: the Sun's lot is labour every day, and there is never rest for him. At the risk of anachronism, one may fancy a touch of Ecclesiastes in all this, and a touch of Oscar Wilde. Some of his verses seem to have been rather different from those that we can still read, but the Alexandrian scholar poet Callimachus in the third century was to reckon him more successful on the small scale than the large.

Archilochus (who died *c*.652) used elegiacs for an epigram declaring that he had abandoned his shield on the field of battle; never mind, he will soon get another as good. This deliberately flouted the code of honour. Archilochus is Europe's first pain in the neck: perhaps he was original in this, or perhaps he is the earliest survivor from an older tradition of cussedness. Mostly, however, he used metres based on the trochee (long short) and the iambus (short long); *iambi* was to become a term for invective verse. The most scabrous of invective poets was to be Hipponax (in the late sixth century), a bawdy thief and brawler who favoured the 'limping iambic', a line in which a spondee replaces the iambus in the last foot. His was the name most often invoked by later poets when they wanted to be abusive.

Archilochus was sometimes a purveyor of proverbial wisdom ('The fox knows many things, but the hedgehog one big thing'), and he had an eye: his description of the island of Thasos, 'like a donkey's back, crowned with wild woodland', is the first description, as far as we know, that conveys the individual character of a named landscape in the real world. He was notorious for his abuse of one Lycambes, supposedly because he had betrothed his daughter Neobule to Archilochus and then broken the agreement. His verses told about his and others' sexual activity with her in explicit terms; in one poem he rejects her contemptuously and seduces her sister instead. The longest surviving piece of archaic iambics is a mid-seventh-century exercise in misogyny by Semonides of Amorgos, in which different types of women are likened to different animals (all unpleasant, except for the woman like a bee). It is not much fun.

The term 'lyric' had a more precise meaning for the Greeks than it has for us: lyric verse was verse written in order to be sung. The lyric poets fell into two classes: the monodists, who wrote pieces for themselves or for some other single person to sing; and those who wrote for choral performance. These two classes were distinguished by metrical form. The monodists chose their stanzas from a repertoire of known stanza forms: the menu was large but not unlimited. Some of these forms are named from the poets who principally used them, and are likely to have invented them: the sapphic and alcaic stanzas, for example. The choral poet, on the other hand, devised a new stanza for each work. Typically he would write a 'strophe' (a stanza, literally a 'turn'), followed by an answering stanza (the 'antistrophe') in identical metre (and presumably using the same tune); there would then usually follow an 'epode', in a variant of the preceding metre. This pattern could then be repeated one or more times. The Greek dramatists were to compose their choral lyrics on the same principle.

The scholars of Alexandria, which became a centre of learning and research in the third century, collected the works of those whom they judged to be the nine best lyric poets, thus forming a canon. The earliest of these is Alcman, who lived and worked in the second half of the seventh century in Sparta, before it had fully developed the militarism for which it would become famous. He was especially known for 'maiden songs', composed for performance by choirs of young women. Typically these pieces seem to have had the maidens bantering among themselves, and they admit a good deal of homoerotic sentiment. One includes the words '. . . with desire that loosens the limbs, and she makes glances more melting than sleep and death'. This is the first time in European literature that sex is associated with death, an unexpectedly *Tristan*-like note in this archaic place. Elsewhere, in a context unknown, he was the first to expand the pathetic fallacy beyond a word or phrase: 'Now sleep the mountain peaks and gullies, the headlands and torrents' – and he adds beasts and bees, the 'monsters in the depths of the purple sea' and 'the tribes of long-winged birds'. Four hexameter lines also remain, in which he speaks in his own person, lamenting his old age and telling the honey-voiced maidens that his limbs can no longer carry him in the dance. If only he were that dark-blue seabird which flies with the halcyons over the flower of the wave, having a resolute heart. More than fifty lines of one maiden song survive, apparently simple in expression but remarkably difficult to interpret. But we hear a distinctive if elusive voice.

The earliest monodists of whom we have knowledge, Sappho and Alcaeus, both came from the island of Lesbos. She was born around 630, he perhaps a little later. Most monodists performed their pieces at the *sumposion* (in anglicized form, 'symposium'). The word means 'drinking party', and these all-male gatherings were an important social institution. Sappho could not be part of them; instead, she seems to have been at the centre of a changing circle of young women, in which homoerotic feelings could be openly expressed. Vulnerability is the spur to love poetry; it is when the beloved is able to say no that the poet has something to write about. Greek men typically had sexual relations with two types of woman: their wives, who obeyed, and prostitutes, whom they paid. So it is no accident that the best Greek love poetry is homosexual, for the boy must be courted, and he can refuse. The best love poet of all was doubly vulnerable, being both homosexual and a woman: not only can the girl say no, but she will in due course go off to get married. Indeed, several of Sappho's poems are concerned with parting or absence.

We are lucky to have one substantial poem of hers surviving complete; that this counts as luck shows how scant are the remains of lyric verse. It is a hymn or prayer to Aphrodite, but a prayer unlike any other. The goddess is addressed as dapple-throned, immortal, weaver-of-wiles: she is a fascinating mixture, remote, glittering, mischievous. In simple words, Sappho asks for her help, and recalls her previous visit, when she came from her father's house in her golden chariot, drawn by sparrows over the black earth. The poet recalls that epiphany: 'smiling with immortal face' (an exceptionally lovely line in the Greek), the goddess teased her: what is the matter with you Sappho, this time? Then, in phrases that rock gently like a lullaby, she consoled her votary: 'For even if she flees, soon shall she pursue, if she does not accept gifts, soon shall she give them, if she does not love, soon shall she love even against her will.' The poem ends with an unaffected and urgent plea for help again – for release from her troubles, and the fulfilment of her heart's desire.

The hymn makes Aphrodite into a character in Sappho's story, both distant and intimate. Through Aphrodite, Sappho can see herself through another's eyes, with a kind of detachment, as someone who does fall in love rather often. Yet that objectivity is combined with passion. The gentleness at the heart of the poem and its delicate humour do not lessen its intensity; the pain of love is vividly realized and exquisitely expressed, in language of simplicity, transparency and force. We have the poem entire because it was quoted by Dionysius of Halicarnassus, a critic of the first century BC; it was for beauty of sound and arrangement of words that he especially admired it.

In another poem Sappho summons Aphrodite to a sacred grove, where the altars are fuming with frankincense. She describes in lovely phrases the cold water trickling through the apple boughs, the whole place shadowed with roses, and enchanted sleep descending from the shimmering leaves; this is the place where she invites the goddess to pour gracefully into golden cups nectar mingled with the festivities. This is an exquisite depiction of the natural scene, but it is also mysterious. The evocation is both vivid and blurry. Actuality, mood and abstraction mingle together: water through trees, slumber from the flicker of foliage, flowers that seem to darken rather than brighten, a goddess who is divine but also a companion and even, it might seem, a hand-maid. Sight, sound, scent, sanctity, wine and wooziness are blended, and it is all done with simplicity and economy of means.

Longinus was to quote four stanzas from a poem that was probably complete in five to illustrate Sappho's ability to seize telling details and bind them into a whole. 'That man appears to me equal to the gods,' she tells an unnamed woman, 'who sits opposite you and listens close to your sweet speaking and lovely laughter' – and she describes the symptoms that assail her: her heart flutters, she cannot speak, a thin fire runs beneath her skin, she trembles and goes paler than grass. The language is controlled, but the experience is physically direct. There is no analysis – to ask if this is love or jealousy or both is beside the point – but pure unmediated sensation.

Sappho values the particular and private experience. Some, she declares, say that an array of horsemen, foot or ships is the fairest thing on the black earth, 'but I say that it is what someone loves'. Her example is Helen, who recked nothing of child or parents and left her husband, the best of men, for Paris. Likewise she too thinks of Anactoria, who is not here; she would rather see the lovable way she walks and the twinkle of her face than all the panoply of the Lydians. But there was a public side to Sappho too, for she was also famous for her wedding songs, in lyrics and hexameters.

Some of the former have a rough folk flavour. From her hexameters two similes remain. 'Like the hyacinth flower on the hills that the shepherds trample with their feet, and on the ground the purple flower . . .' – this was probably a metaphor for the bride's loss of her maidenhead. In another fragment the bride is 'as the sweetapple reddens on the topmost bough, the top at the topmost, and the apple-gatherers forgot it, no they did not quite forget it, but they could not reach it'. This is especially nice: the girl is exalted and inaccessible, but what does an apple do when it is ripe? It drops. Both similes suggest a tension – in play? in earnest? – between nuptial joy and lament for virginity lost.

There is something special about Sappho, not easily defined. Perhaps one might say that to an unusual degree her poems are purely poetry. Poetry of a really high order is usually something else as well: it is poetry and drama, or poetry and philosophy, or poetry and theology, or it advocates some idea of morality, society or the human lot. But Sappho's verses seem to be simply themselves. Literature of its nature cannot be an abstract art, but if all art aspires to the condition to music, Sappho's aspires with an unusual fullness.

Sappho and Alcaeus lived on the same island and wrote in the same dialect, and they seem to have admired each other. Accordingly, they are often discussed together. Yet from the evidence that we have, he seems no match for her: his surviving fragments show vigour and energy but few signs of greatness. Perhaps we have been unlucky in what the sands of Egypt have turned up. When Horace wrote his Latin lyrics in the first century BC, he used alcaics more than any other lyric metre, borrowed various themes and motifs from Alcaeus, and paid due tribute to him, but he may have liked the metre and the motifs less for their original value than for the new purposes to which he could bend them. Unless more papyri appear, Alcaeus' quality will remain uncertain.

Largest in scale of all the lyric poets was Stesichorus (first half of the sixth century), whose works brought epic narrative into choral metres: his *Tale of Geryon* was about thirteen hundred lines long, and his *Oresteia* ('Tale of Orestes') was in two books. Stesichorus ('Chorus-Master') may be a title rather than the name he was born with, but some have doubted whether such long pieces could have been sung and danced chorally. Perhaps some combination of solo and chorus was employed. We have more of *Geryon* than any other of Stesichorus' poems: the title character was a monster slain by Heracles, and the surviving fragments show a surprising sympathy for his unhappy fate. Geryon's mother is also given a speech of pathetic entreaty. Longinus called Stesichorus 'Homeric', and the Roman rhetorician Quintilian echoed that judgement, despite regarding him as too diffuse.

Anacreon (born *c.*570) was to be known for an easy hedonism, tinged with notes of humour and melancholy. At a drinking party he tells a servant to mix ten parts of water to five of wine 'so that I may be frenzied decorously'. Another time the slave is told to bring wine, water and garlands 'so that I may box with love'. He seems to have dealt a good deal in erotic disappointment. He asks a 'Thracian filly' why she gives him sideways glances and runs away from him. He tells a 'boy with a girlish glance' that he seeks him 'but you do not hearken, not knowing that you hold the reins of my soul'. He is bruised with sorrow that a youth has cut the hair that shadowed his tender neck. He can be gaily decorative: golden-haired Love hits him with a purple ball and summons him to play with a girl in pretty slippers. But she (coming as she does from Lesbos) disdains his hair, for it is white, and gapes after another. 'Hair' is feminine in Greek, and the surface meaning is that she admires younger and darker tresses, but we hear the double meaning: it is another girl that she is after. Anacreon knew the effect of crumpling into mildness: 'Cleubulus is the one I love, for Cleubulus I am crazed, on Cleubulus I gaze.'

Another piece, in the tripping rhythms that he favoured, speaks of age and death: his head is hoary, his teeth old, and little length of sweet life is left. He fears death, for the house of Hades is narrow, the way down is hard, and 'it is not simple for one who has gone down to come up again'. Here he uses the power of understatement; we shall not meet quite this note of grim levity again for another five hundred years, until Catullus. He exemplifies what might be called the Mimnermus streak in the Greek sensibility, an awareness of the brightness and brevity of life, handled with grace. Centuries later other poets were to imitate him in verses now known as the *Anacreontea*. Some of them are rather accomplished, but they tend to a mere prettiness, and their model always provided something more than that.

'Love like a smith has struck me again with a great axe,' Anacreon once wrote, 'and plunged me in a wintry torrent.' This metaphorical manner seems to have been more typical of Ibycus (also sixth century). In one piece Love gives him melting looks from beneath dark eyelids and drives him into

Aphrodite's net, but he trembles like an ageing racehorse yoked to the chariot once again. In his finest surviving fragment he is elaborately figurative. First he evokes 'the inviolate garden of the maidens', where in spring the quinces bloom, and the vine blossoms swell under shady leafage; 'but for me love sleeps at no season'. Instead, he is battered and shrivelled by a rushing north wind mixed with lightning. The untouched garden was to appear again as an image of virginity in Euripides' *Hippolytus*.

Three of the choral poets from the canonical nine were active in the first half of the fifth century. The oldest of them was Simonides, active in the late sixth to early fifth century. His is another great reputation that is now hard to assess. He was also known for his elegiac epigrams, but although we have examples of this genre surviving from his time, there is hardly anything that we can attribute to him securely. His most memorable lyric fragment contains the words spoken by Danaë to her baby son Perseus, half lament, half lullaby, as they drift at sea in a chest. 'Pretty face,' she calls him, 'lying in your purple robe'; 'Sleep, baby, sleep the sea, sleep immeasurable ill.' The verse of Simonides' nephew, Bacchylides (*c*.520–*c*.450), is fluent and pleasant. In one poem he gave a new twist to the simile of leaves: Heracles in the underworld sees 'the souls of wretched mortals by the streams of Cocytus, like the leaves which the wind sets quivering on the white-gleaming headlands of Ida where the flocks graze'. Before Bacchylides was found on papyrus, people supposed that it was Virgil's idea to apply the leaf simile to dead souls, but the Greek poet was first, and that quivering against a shining background imports a new visual vividness.

Pindar (c.518–c.445) resembles Hesiod in coming from Boeotia but in nothing else, for he was a late celebrant of the aristocratic values that infuse the Homeric poems; that is, the celebration of men with exceptional qualities of body, mind and daring. He composed many kinds of verse, but for us his fame rests on the only works by any of the lyric poets to have come down in a manuscript tradition: his victory songs, composed for choruses to sing in honour of winners at the principal sporting festivals of Greece. There are forty-five of them, gathered into four books: Olympian songs for events at the Olympic games, Pythian songs for those at Delphi (where Apollo had killed the snake-monster Python), Nemean for those at Nemea, and Isthmian for those at Corinth (the Isthmus). By far the longest of them is the fourth Pythian, the greater part of which tells the voyage of Jason and the Argonauts. It was surely in the mind of Gerard Manley Hopkins when he wrote *The Wreck of the Deutschland*, also centred upon the narrative of a sea journey; that poem, with its bold language, unique stanza form, and rhapsodic energy within a tightly disciplined form, is perhaps as near as one can find in English to Pindar's spirit (the 'Pindaric odes' of the seventeenth and eighteenth centuries are not much like).

These songs were occasional poems, commissioned by the victor or his city, and they had to include the victor's praise. Pindar combines this with the narration of myth and with moral reflection. His moves from one to another of these themes can be sudden and unpredictable. Hitherto the language of lyric had tended to be clear and fairly simple, but Pindar's style is dense and difficult, and his content much more thickly metaphorical. Later Greeks and Romans called him deep-voiced, mighty-voiced, immense; Horace compared him to a seething mountain torrent swollen with rain. Longinus classed Pindar and Sophocles together as men whose force sets everything on fire, although (he adds) they can also fizzle out for no reason. He was also taken as an example of the 'austere' or 'severe' style, a term which seems to indicate not austerity of outlook (for he revels in sumptuous things) but a mixture of boldness, ruggedness and exalted tone.

Pindar could be graceful: the romance of the young god Apollo and the tomboy Cyrene, told in the ninth Pythian, has great charm. But typically his imagination is grand and spectacular. The seventh Olympian was written for a boxer from Rhodes (the name in Greek means 'rose'). It tells how the island, destined to be bounteous to men and rich in flocks, once lay in the depths of the sea, but then grew from out of the moistness, and the Sun, parent of the piercing sunbeams, possesses it. For Sun lay with Rose (who is now a nymph), and fathered children who divided the land between them. Myth, land, sex and fertility are blended here. The first Pythian, written for Hiero, ruler of Syracuse in Sicily, begins with an invocation of the golden lyre; when Apollo plays, it can put even the eagle of Zeus to sleep, for the music has shed a dark cloud over his curved head and sealed his eyelids, but – a brilliant touch – his moist feathers ripple as he slumbers. The Olympian gods are enchanted, but their enemies are fearful, like the monster Typhos, imprisoned in Sicily under Etna, a mountain that is a 'nurse all year of biting snow', but that also belches fire and smoke sent up by the monster from below. Here myth and nature come together, but there is also an implicit allegory of the good ruler suppressing violence. With Zeus' help such a man can turn the people towards 'harmonious peace' (*sumphonos* is Pindar's word, from which our 'symphony'), and that recalls the power of music at the poem's opening. Such are the ways in which Pindar binds his disparate material together.

His language, so often sonorous or voluptuous, can also be plain. In the third Pythian, with eloquent simplicity, he says of a young woman in a myth that she 'yearned for things absent; many have suffered the same'. There through one girl's feeling is a timeless expression of romantic longing. In the eighth Pythian, probably the last of his songs, he turns for a moment flat and bleak. 'Creatures-of-a-day. And what is anyone? And what is he not? Man is the dream of a shadow.' In Greek the two questions are '*ti de tis? ti d'ou tis?*' *Tis* can mean 'who' (as in 'who did this?'), but also 'someone' or 'anyone'. *Ti* is the neuter form, 'what . . .?', or 'something' or 'anything'. *De* is a particle, one of the tiny words with which Greek adjusted meaning, sometimes 'and', sometimes 'but', sometimes lighter than either, barely translatable, a slight shift in the progress of thought. *Ou* is 'not'. From this material Pindar has made something gossamer light – like the dream of a shadow indeed. He needs no verbs: the English translation has used 'is' three times, but Greek can omit it, thinning the texture even more. The single word 'creatures-of-a-day' (*epameroi*) seems to have no syntax at all. And the thought – is it nihilist? The verse continues, 'But when the god-given gleam comes, bright light is on men, and gentle life.' Here and elsewhere he combines a sense of the brevity and fragility of human affairs with the possibility of glory. That idea of man's greatness and littleness may recall the tragic vision of the *Iliad*, but Pindar also holds out the hope of a serenity that in the epic belongs only to the gods.

The seventh and sixth centuries have been called the lyric age of Greece, and it is natural to think of that age coming to its climax and conclusion with Pindar in the first half of the fifth. But in fact the greater part of the Greek lyric verse that we can read today was yet to be written; it is embedded in tragedy and comedy. Among Pindar's contemporaries was the greatest lyric poet of all, who came from a city that had not hitherto done anything much to trouble the literary historian. His name was Aeschylus, and the city was Athens.

The Rise of Tragedy and History

We expect drama to exist in most societies at most times, and so it is surprising that the best Greek drama should have been so limited in place and period. But it seems always to have been agreed that by far the best tragedy came out of Athens and within a period of less than a century. It was agreed too that Aeschylus, Sophocles and Euripides outclassed all other tragedians: as early as Aristophanes' *Frogs* (405 BC) – in which the god Dionysus goes down to the underworld to find a dead poet to bring back to life – and perhaps much earlier, it is assumed that these are the big three. Aeschylus (c.525–c.455) belonged to the generation that defeated the Persian invasions; he fought at the Battle of Marathon in 490. Sophocles (c.495–406) and Euripides (480s–c.406) were each other's contemporaries.

The origins of Greek drama are obscure, but it seems to have grown out of choral performance. We have only the words of choral lyrics, but the Greek word *khoros* (chorus) itself refers to dancing, and the original experience was a combination of movement, words and music. Later Greeks believed that drama began with a single actor in dialogue with the chorus; Aeschylus was said to have introduced the second actor, and Sophocles to have been the first to use a third. Supposedly, there were never more than three speaking actors (other than the chorus and their leader), dividing all the roles between them, although one of Aeschylus' plays needs four (perhaps a special case).

These dramas were a mixture of spoken dialogue (usually in an iambic metre) and sung lyric. Normally only the chorus leader joins in the spoken parts, representing the chorus as a whole. The chorus sing a set-piece lyric (called a 'stasimon') at intervals through the play, but there are also more irregular lyrics, in which speaking characters may join. Aeschylus' *Suppliants*, although one of his late plays, is likely to reproduce the earliest form of tragedy. More than half of it is in lyrics (uniquely among extant plays), and the chorus, representing the daughters of Danaus, are in effect the principal character, the matter of the play being their search for sanctuary; for the greater part of it they interact with one character at a time, either their father or the king of Argos.

Dramas at Athens were performed at festivals. At the biggest of these, the Great Dionysia, the performances were spread over four days. The last part of it was devoted to comedy; for the festival's earlier part three playwrights were selected, and each produced four plays, which they directed themselves: three tragedies and a shorter 'satyr' play. Aeschylus in particular liked to link the subjects of his tragedies to form a trilogy, but this was not the general practice. The fourth play of each set featured satyrs, lustful mythological figures, part man, part goat, and was shorter and lighter in character. The dramatists were judged, and awarded first, second and third prizes. We do not know who did the judging, but presumably acting, music and dance were taken into account; so the information that a particular set of plays did or did not win first prize may not tell us much. These plays are compact: that is part of their force. Even the longest of them has fewer than two thousand lines, and the whole of Aeschylus' *Oresteia* trilogy is shorter than *Hamlet*.

Tragedians were prolific: Aeschylus is reported to have written between seventy and ninety plays, Sophocles more than 120, Euripides ninety. Seven plays traditionally attributed to Aeschylus remain, seven of Sophocles, and nineteen attributed to Euripides. So we have only a small proportion of what they wrote, and nothing, it appears, from the earlier part of each career. All the extant plays of the first two and ten of Euripides' descend from selections of their works made many centuries later in the Byzantine age, but the other nine of Euripides descend from one volume of a lost set of all his plays, and are thus a random sampling of his range.

It is natural to think of Greek tragedy as a formal genre, governed by a number of conventions, somewhat like traditional Japanese drama, but to its first audiences it was an almost new form, and one in rapid development. Its practices may have hardened into conventions in the fourth century, but by that time the great creative period of tragedy was already over. Some of what seem to us formal devices were techniques used by the playwrights, not because tradition demanded it, but to achieve particular effects. 'Stichomythia' – when two characters alternate rapidly, each speaking a single line at a time – is a case in point. At its best, this was a vivid way of dramatizing a tight argument, or a struggle of wills. Another example is the motif known by the Latin phrase *deus ex machina*, 'the god from the device'; it was a favourite resource of Euripides, and perhaps his invention; at all events, it was a development originating at some time in the fifth century, not a convention long established. The 'device' or 'machine' seems to have been a kind of crane supporting a platform which could be swung out into the view of the audience. Typically, a god or goddess appears aloft on the machine near the end of a play to resolve the action and dismiss the characters to doom or happiness. Perhaps Euripides used it too often, but we shall see what varied meanings he drew from it and how powerful it could be at its best.

When Aristotle produced the first theory of literature, in his *Poetics*, he made the nature of tragedy the heart of his enquiry. This work has so greatly influenced the understanding of tragedy that it is worth consideration before we turn to the plays themselves. Seeking to explain why the representation of suffering can give pleasure, Aristotle argued that tragedy shows disaster striking neither a wholly good man (which would be repellent) nor a bad man (which would be satisfactory) but a mostly good man who falls through some error. Like English 'error' Aristotle's word, *hamartia*, can mean either 'wrongdoing' or simple 'mistake'. It seems clear that he meant mistake, for his example is Oedipus, who killed his father and married his mother because he did not know what he was doing. Had he known, he would not have done so. Much later, a different theory was drawn out of Aristotle, according to which the tragic hero's fall has a moral cause. Either he has some flaw of character (say, jealousy, pride or indecisiveness) or he commits some particular moral wrong. This approach has been fruitfully applied to Shakespeare, and it may work for some Greek tragedies too, but in other cases we may find that the attempt to force these plays into the quasi-Aristotelian mould distorts them.

Aeschylus' *Persians* (472) is the earliest European play that we have. It is also his only extant play not to form part of a connected trilogy and the only extant Greek tragedy on a historical rather than mythological subject. All the characters are Persian; the theme is the news coming of defeat by the Greeks and the return of the beaten King Xerxes. In a sense this is a patriotic play – a messenger gives a vivid account of the Greek victory in the Battle of Salamis – but the tragedy is the Persians' and its breadth of sympathy looks forward to Herodotus' history (as we shall see later in this chapter). *Seven against Thebes* (467) is the last play of a trilogy. It is pervaded by a master image, of a ship at sea. The besieged city of Thebes is the ship and Eteocles, its king, is the helmsman, attempting to control and calm the frightened women who form the chorus; image and action convey a powerful sense of fear and constriction. In a series of speeches a messenger describes how one by one six enemy champions have advanced against Thebes. The seventh is Eteocles' own brother, Polynices: will he fight him? At this point the emotional balance of power pivots: Eteocles grows crazed with passion, and the women now become the calming force, as they try to dissuade him from so dreadful a deed. They fail, and in the combat the brothers kill each other. The play is constructed with a grand, block-like simplicity.

In this respect the *Oresteia* (458) is strikingly different. It is the unique survival of an entire trilogy. In the first play, *Agamemnon*, the king of the title returns home after his victory over Troy, and there his wife Clytemnestra murders him and his Trojan captive Cassandra. In *Libation Bearers* their son Orestes secretly returns from exile, is reunited with his sister Electra, and kills Clytemnestra and her lover Aegisthus. In the *Kindly Ones* (*Eumenides*) Orestes is pursued by the Furies – vengeful spirits, sometimes called by the appeasing name that gives the play its title – roused by his mother's ghost. It begins at Delphi, where Orestes seeks purification at the temple of Apollo; the scene then shifts to Athens, where he is tried in court, with the Furies prosecuting and Apollo defending him. The jury being tied, the goddess Athena casts her deciding vote in his favour. The Furies threaten vengeance on the city, but Athena persuades them to transform themselves into fertility goddesses, blessing the Athenian land.

Clytemnestra has by far the largest part in the first play, and Agamemnon appears alive in only one scene. But the early scenes are filled with the foreboding of his arrival, his murder (off stage, heard but not seen) is the climax of the action, and in the later scenes his corpse lies in full view. In their huge entry-song the chorus, elders of the city, look back to events ten years before. Contrary winds, sent by the goddess Artemis, prevent the ships from sailing for Troy; the army is hungry and distraught, and she can be appeased only if Agamemnon sacrifices his own daughter Iphigenia. In other versions of the myth Agamemnon had given some personal offence to Artemis. Here, though, her anger is due, presumably, to the Trojan War itself, a righteous expedition sanctioned by Zeus. We are denied the comfort of explaining away the king's dilemma by saying that he has in some way brought it on himself. Instead, the narration focuses intently on the actual decision. The chorus quote the king's own words: he faces his dilemma straight and without self-pity. It is hard to slay one's own child, to stain a father's hands with the streaming blood of his daughter, his delight. But how can he desert the fleet and fail his alliance? 'Which of these things is without evils?' In the end he puts on the 'yoke-strap of compulsion' and performs a deed which is, as the chorus say, impious, impure, unholy. It is also, we may reflect, what a goddess desires.

It is telling to compare this passage with the treatment of two sacrificial virgins in Euripides. Polyxena, in *Hecuba* (c.420s), dies calmly, taking care to place herself so that she falls where her wound will not be seen. Euripides' Iphigenia accepts her death for the sake of the cause, and it is not Agamemnon but a priest who shall do the deed (which in the event is miraculously prevented). By contrast, Aeschylus faces the full horror: Iphigenia's prayers and cries are unavailing, and in language of appalling beauty the chorus describe how the attendants hold her above the altar, gagged to prevent her uttering ill-omened words, lovely as a picture, her saffron robes flowing to the ground. We should be in no doubt what Agamemnon has to endure.

We shall not understand this passage unless we realize that in real life, especially in time of war, people do face such dilemmas, if not exactly in these terms. Shall the resistance fighter betray his comrades or allow his family to be tortured? The decision is unbearable, and yet a decision must be made; and whatever choice he makes, he will suffer the burden of guilt. It is both a moral choice and one without a determinate answer. Agamemnon kills the girl in a state of frenzy, but this is a keen psychological insight, for surely that is the only state in which anyone could perform so ghastly an act. Aeschylus is deeper than his critics. Some have said that Agamemnon is compelled by pure necessity and there is in effect no decision to be made; but the poet shows him making it. Others have blamed Agamemnon for deciding wrongly – as though anyone could slaughter his child except under extreme pressure. In such cases, for an outsider to tell the agent that he has chosen right or chosen wrong seems impertinent, maybe even hard-hearted. When we look upon such circumstance, surely sympathy is the morally mature response. Aeschylus here penetrates the abyss of human experience. He has sometimes been censured for having a primitive moral outlook. On the contrary, this is one of the profoundest things in literature.

Half way through the play Agamemnon enters, accompanied by a silent figure who proves to be his captive, the Trojan princess and prophetess Cassandra. How shall we assess him? Judgement has varied widely: according to one scholar, he is a great gentleman, thoughtful towards Cassandra, courteous to the queen; according to another, we see a corrupted tyrant, a braggart, flaunting his concubine before his wife. Clearly both views cannot be right (and both may be wrong), but the fact that such divergent opinions have been put forward at all is perhaps a clue. For this is an external scene, not one in which we are admitted into the minds of the characters: the king and queen are great people upon a public stage, and we observe them from without.

In the later part of the scene Aeschylus creates a magnificent spectacle: Clytemnestra orders purple cloths to be strewn on the ground, and urges Agamemnon to walk into the palace across them. He declines: to tread on these precious and delicate fabrics is to destroy them; only a god should have such things strewn in his path. An eastern king like Priam might behave like this, but he will not. Clytemnestra persists, and they lock horns in a short, dense passage of stichomythia. The language is of battle, victory and defeat: 'It befits the successful to be conquered', 'Does this victory mean so much to you?' He yields, and steps on the cloths, after taking his boots off in a gesture of humility. Clearly he is deeply uneasy about the act; so why does he do it? Not from arrogance – it is mere inattention to suppose so. But from what combination of weariness, chivalry, weakness of will? In life we do not have pat answers to such questions, and in this respect the scene is like life. The play invites us to ponder the question without resolving it. One thing is sure: king and queen have fought a mental battle, and the victory has gone to her.

Clytemnestra has a natural reason for this show: to turn the gods against her victim (it does not follow that she succeeds). And perhaps, as well, she simply enjoys exercising the power of her personality. However, the play throughout shows little interest in her motives; rather, we look upon this great figure and marvel. (We can contrast the Clytemnestras in the *Electra* plays of Sophocles and Euripides, who explain and defend themselves as Aeschylus' queen does not.) After the murders she declaims a magnificent speech of triumph, rich in imagery, into which suddenly comes a present tense and a few words of Shakespearian simplicity: 'And I strike him twice.' The language then grows even richer, as she exults in the shower of blood that bespattered her, adding that she rejoiced no less than the crop rejoices in the god-given rain, in the birth-pangs of the sheath. With resplendent perversity, metaphor is folded within metaphor, Agamemnon's death-blood likened to life-giving rain, herself to the ear of corn, the corn's breaking from the sheath to childbirth. These are wicked words, but there is something wonderful about them. Earlier, when the king had consented to walk on the purple, she proclaimed, 'The sea is there – and who shall drain it? – breeding ever new the gush of much purple precious as silver . . .' There is a lust here for the size and abundance of the world that captivates; after some fashion, you have to love this woman.

When Agamemnon enters the house, we expect his death to follow shortly, but Aeschylus springs a surprise. Cassandra, who had seemed to be one of those silent characters common in Greek tragedy, begins to utter – at first, sounds without syntax, almost without meaning: 'Otototoi, alas, ah, Apollo, Apollo.' It is the start of a vast psychodrama, a dialogue between Cassandra and the chorus which moves from song to speech, and from shattered fragments to a final wholeness. It is an interior drama, in contrast to the scene shared by the king and queen, whom we saw externally. In prophetic frenzy she sees the coming slaughter, but she also takes us further into the past than we have been before – to Agamemnon's father, Atreus, who killed the children of his brother Thyestes and tricked him into eating them in a cannibal banquet. The house breathes of dripping blood, she says, and there is an aroma as from a tomb. Bemused and literal, the chorus leader supposes that she has scented animal sacrifices and festal perfumes. At first helpless, she achieves a kind of defiance, foretelling the avenger who will requite the deaths of Agamemnon and herself. But her last words are more than what she calls 'a lamentation for myself', since she now has a larger vision: 'Alas for mortal affairs: when they fare well, a shadow may turn them, and if they fare ill, a damp sponge at a sweep blots out the picture.'

All prosperity is unstable – the idea that a shadow can knock it over is a superb imagining – but there are those who meet only with misfortune and oblivion. In her very last words it is to those others that she extends the greater part of her compassion: 'And I pity this much more than that.' There can hardly be a better example anywhere of how context can transform poetry. Out of its place, there could hardly be a duller line: apart from 'pity' every word is flat and drab. In its place, it is a marvel. She began the scene inarticulate, wholly imprisoned in herself. She has passed through the beauty of lyric horror into the calmer tones of dialogue, and now finally, like Achilles at the end of the *Iliad*, she has broadened her vision to encompass the whole of humanity: in the midst of her suffering she has the moral largeness to understand that there are others whose lives are worse than her own. At the end of her long emotional journey she is drained of everything but the plainest words. And now, clear-eyed and unillusioned, she walks into the house and to her death.

Agamemnon is so mighty a piece that one might wonder how the playwright could follow it, but Aeschylus has the answer. We might compare those symphonies in which the greatness of the first two movements might seem to allow no adequate continuation; yet the scherzo and the finale may be entirely satisfying, each in its own way. Whereas *Agamemnon* was noble and public, *Libation Bearers* is domestic. Orestes and Electra are very young: they are 'chicks of the eagle', Agamemnon, and they lean for support on the chorus, who are women slaves of the household. In the first part of the play there is a long invocation of the dead king (the title comes from the libation which the chorus bring to pour to his spirit), but events move so briskly in the later parts that this is in terms of the action perhaps the liveliest of Greek tragedies. A servant pops on and off. Aegisthus has a whole scene to himself, but it is less than twenty lines long. Another scene, touching and gently humorous, presents the single appearance of Cilissa, Orestes' old nanny, who feels genuinely the grief at the false news of his death that his mother only pretends to feel. This is the first sketch of a type who will become familiar: the comic servant. The treatment of this figure can easily be sentimental or patronizing, but not here. Clytemnestra herself now seems a more ordinary character, but she has not lost her resource: when she realizes that Orestes is alive after all and present, she first calls for an axe, and, when that fails, turns to words. The stichomythia in which she fights to persuade her son not to kill her is brilliantly done. This is a vivid and subtle play, and in the way that it continues and develops the imagery in *Agamemnon*, a deep one also.

At its end, having killed his mother and her lover, Orestes still needs to go to Delphi for ritual purification, but the action might seem to be almost complete. If the *Kindly Ones* had perished, we would never have guessed its content. Although the trial of Orestes at Athens occupies its middle part, the characters who dominate are divine: Apollo, who defends him; Athena, who presides over the trial; and the Furies, who form the chorus. At the play's start we hear of aboriginal goddesses: Earth, who is mother of Right, who is mother of Phoebe (in turn the mother of Apollo). The Furies, for their part, are children of Night. All these female chthonic powers are older than the Olympians themselves. Despite this immensity of temporal view, this play is also uniquely parochial, containing unmistakable allusions to current affairs in Athens. There is no parallel for this in any other tragedy.

Moreover, the Athens of this play is quasi-democratic. It has no king – this too is unique in tragedy – with Athena taking the place of one. As the play proceeds, the boundary between the theatre and the actual life of the spectators begins to blur. Orestes is tried before the court of the Areopagus, close to where the audience are sitting in the Theatre of Dionysus, this spring day in 458. When Athena calls on the 'Athenian people' to judge the case, she seems to address us as well as the jurymen on the stage. She herself seems half goddess, half embodiment of the city itself. When the Furies consent to forgo their wrath against Athens, they descend to become fertility goddesses, enriching the very soil of Attica on which we stand. In the final moments, when attendants escort them in a torch-lit procession, the celebration within the story and the celebration of the Great Dionysia outside it seem almost to be fused into one.

What are we to make of this extraordinary conception? The anthropologists' distinction between nature and culture is useful here. The play offers glimpses of a cosmic dislocation, a conflict between the Olympian gods and older, darker powers. The Furies are in part culture goddesses, concerned to punish murder, roused from subterranean slumber to action by the ghost of Clytemnestra, whose potency is such that she reappears – another dramatic surprise – in the third play also, even after her death. But under Athena's persuasion these Furies will become nature deities as well, both undergirding the state and fertilizing the soil. The drama moves towards a radiant revelation of unity, in which nature and culture blend, the Olympian goddess and the primeval earth powers are reconciled, past and present come together. The parish pump is part of the universe; we inhabit both locality and totality; and so the ephemeral controversies buzzing in the politics of Athens at the moment also find their place within the great cosmic vision.

The dramatic power of the *Oresteia* is inseparable from the overwhelming boldness, force and beauty of the language that clothes it. Aeschylus' style is usually rich, but it ranges from plainness to extreme strangeness; in the more complex passages, which are many, it is perhaps the densest and most daring in all literature. His imagery, too, is unique in the way that metaphors running through the work interrelate, joining in new combinations and producing new insights. The Greek words for 'house', as in English, can mean either a building or a family, and that doubleness is constantly exploited. 'Inside' is a key word: the interior of the house is woman's place, but it is also where the killings are done and the blood spilled. There are images of constriction: nets, fetters and enfolding cloths. There are images of vulnerable creatures: Orestes is a cowering hare, Cassandra like a nightingale; Agamemnon's children, as we saw, are chicks of the eagle. There is song, both beautiful and sinister: the song of Cassandra the bird and the revelling song of the Furies that her prophetic frenzy brings to her inner ear. Wealth is perilous; Agamemnon tramples the wealth of his house, both actually and symbolically, as he walks on the purple. Clytemnestra wraps him in cloth to murder him; she boasts that she has cast over him a measureless net, 'as for fishes, an evil wealth of raiment'. So it is his wealth, almost literally, that kills him. The ground is as vividly present as the house. Libation is poured on the ground for the dead Agamemnon. The earth is so saturated in blood that it can drink no more. Blood remains inside the house, purulent and festering. Clytemnestra is likened to snakes and other monsters – these too fester in the house – and in fear of the avenging Orestes she dreams that she suckles a snake at her breast. But a short account of the *Oresteia*, whether of its language or its action, can seem merely to scratch the surface. No work of literature is more richly freighted, and like the purple-bearing sea it is inexhaustible.

For the Romantics *Prometheus Bound* was the quintessence of Aeschylus: their taste for the egotistical sublime drew them to this drama on a cosmic scale, the story of a hero who defied god himself. But it is now clear that it cannot be by Aeschylus, because it is too different from his authentic works in too many ways, ranging from details of language and metre to larger matters of style and outlook. It was perhaps written in the 440s. Prometheus was the Titan who stole fire from the gods and gave it to mankind; in this play he is a more universal benefactor, who has also taught men mathematics, writing, ship-building and the domestication of animals. Zeus condemned him to be chained to a rock and to suffer for ever, since as an immortal being he could not die. *Prometheus Bound* was part of a trilogy, and probably the middle play of the three: in the first, he stole the fire; in the last, *Prometheus Unbound*, he was freed in exchange for a secret that he possessed.

In the first scene of the surviving play Prometheus is brought to a desolate wilderness by Power and Force and his chains are riveted to the rock. When they depart, Prometheus, hitherto silent, breaks out into a cry of anguish to the elements, sky, winds, waters and mother earth. The words in which he describes the sea, 'the countless laughter of the waves of the deep', is Aeschylus' most famous phrase, or would be if he had written it. The chorus then enter, graceful Daughters of Ocean, who contrast with the motionless Titan. Prometheus is visited first by the god Ocean himself, a cautious compromiser, and then by the play's only mortal character, Io. She is another of Zeus' victims, raped by him and then driven all over the world by a gadfly sent to persecute her by Zeus' jealous wife. Again, her frantic movements contrast with a hero who cannot move at all. The messenger god Hermes arrives to demand that Prometheus surrender the secret that Zeus needs, and when Prometheus refuses declares more punishment: the Titan will be buried under a crushing weight of rock and an eagle will daily devour his liver. The earth shakes, thunder and lightning break forth, and above the noise Prometheus calls his mother,

Earth, to witness, in the play's last words, that he suffers injustice.

That represents a discovery. Earlier in the play, he has allowed his virtue to be a fault: 'Willingly, willingly I erred, I shall not deny it.' He knows, he says, that Zeus is harsh and holds justice beside himself. Might is right: it is as though justice were an object kept by the person strong enough to seize it. By the play's end Prometheus has rejected this for the simple truth: his punishment is wrong. And indeed the work is extraordinary for the way in which it shows Zeus as plainly bad. He has recently come to power, 'the young chieftain of the blessed ones', as Prometheus calls him, and maybe he will change in the future, but for the present he is mankind's enemy. This goes far beyond showing the gods as harsh or inscrutable, as other authors do.

This playwright also has a taste for spectacular effects: Ocean, for example, enters in a chariot drawn by a bird, and his daughters likewise in a 'winged car'. Much of the 'spectacle' must have been represented by words alone: the heavenly scent of the daughters, the lightning and shattering rocks (only the thunder could be produced by a machine). By contrast, the language is simpler in style than Aeschylus', and with much less imagery. The play sags a bit in the middle, as though the author does not quite know what to do between the fierce conflicts at the beginning and end. Its dominant theme is stark, bold and a little crude, but the conception has an undeniable grandeur, and the thought that omnipotence itself can be defied, maybe even overcome, added a new idea to the repertoire of the human imagination.

*

Aeschylus' *Persians* was a rare experiment in putting recent events on to the stage. We might be surprised that his example was so seldom followed, but for whatever reason, mythology remained the staple of tragedy, and the field was free for authors of a quite different kind to describe and analyse in another form what real people had said and done. History-writing, as it has been practised in the west for two and a half thousand years, was invented with remarkable speed by two men, Herodotus and Thucydides. Little is known about Herodotus' life. He came from Halicarnassus on the eastern seaboard of the Aegean (modern Bodrum), within the Persian empire. Probably he was born in the 480s or a little later and died in the 420s. The second half of his history recounts the wars launched against the Greeks by the Persian kings Darius and Xerxes in the early fifth century; the first half charts the rise of Persia, mixing narrative with descriptions of most of the peoples of the known world, including a whole book devoted to Egypt.

Before Herodotus there were two kinds of writing on which he could build. One kind was the history of cities: these seem to have been uncritical compilations, beginning typically with a mythological founder and proceeding chronologically down to the writer's own time. The other kind was ethnography. Ethnographies seem to have been somewhat miscellaneous collections of everything that could be found out about a particular foreign people – a gathering of materials that might include some genuine intellectual curiosity, an interest in quaintness and anecdote, a penchant for weird customs, and a curiosity about marvels. We might think of the sort of mixture to be found in an article in *National*

Geographic Magazine. Herodotus' first insight was to see that these two kinds of enquiry could be brought together, and that each could be transformed.

Another insight was to realize that history could be art. This is the first work of art in Europe to be written in prose. It was also the longest work of any kind that had yet been created. In later centuries he was called the 'most Homeric' of writers. We can understand that description in various ways. Like the poet of the *Iliad*, he shapes a baggy mass of material into a unity: despite the disparate nature of his ethnographies, he does not lose sight of the goal towards which his story is moving. As in the *Iliad*, there is an epic grandeur: the crossing of the Hellespont by Xerxes' colossal army (Herodotus' numbers must indeed be hugely exaggerated) may recall the spectacular deployment of the Achaean host in the *Iliad*'s second book. Like the *Iliad*, he tells a tragic story; and as in Aeschylus' play, the tragedy is that of the Persians. Breadth of sympathy is among Herodotus' merits as a historian.

In one respect he is closer to the historians of our own time than any of his successors in antiquity. The Greek word *historia* originally meant simply 'enquiry'; that is what Herodotus means by it. Modern theory distinguishes between 'diachronic' and 'synchronic' history. Diachronic history is the narration of events over time. Synchronic history is the study of things that change slowly or not at all: social and economic structures, patterns of belief and behaviour, and so on. Ever since Thucydides, 'history' has meant diachronic narrative, at least until very recent times. Modern historians who explore collective mentalities and the *longue durée* are in fact going back to the origins of their craft. Herodotus was there first.

In his opening sentence he declares himself to have not one purpose but several: that the happenings of mankind should not be forgotten through the passage of time; that great and marvellous deeds, whether of Greeks or barbarians, should not lose their fame; and to set out the cause why they went to war with one another. One aim is to maintain the factual record; another is, like the poets, to celebrate great and wondrous things; the last is to look for explanation. Here is another momentous innovation: the idea that history should combine description with analysis. 'Cause' is the word that Thucydides was to pick up and investigate.

At the same time, Herodotus began the discovery of historical method. Thus he distinguished three kinds of evidence: there is what you have seen, what you have read, and what you have been told. He was readier too than later Greek and Roman historians to acknowledge uncertainty. Perhaps he does not quite make a firm distinction between myth (the stories of Europa and Helen, for example) and history, but he comes close to it. 'My own duty,' he wrote, 'is to say what is said, but not to believe the entirety of it. Let this principle hold for the whole work.' He exercises judgement, but he also gives us the evidence.

Herodotus was also a powerful storyteller on the large scale and a lively anecdotalist on the small. Yet, with all these merits, he has often been regarded with suspicion in antiquity and after, at worst as a liar, at best as an amiable gossip. In the earlier part of the history, especially, many of his stories bear what to us is an obviously folk-tale character. In his first book he narrates the rise and fall of Croesus' Lydian empire. It is brilliantly told, with little details slipped in early which will prove significant much later. One twist is especially fine. Near the start of the tale the wise Solon advises Croesus to count no man happy until he is dead. Much later, when Croesus is about to be burned to death by the Persian king Cyrus, he exclaims that Solon was right. Cyrus is curious, and when Croesus explains, he spares his life. And thus the words that seemed to portend Croesus' fall become the source of his salvation.

The story of Croesus has an artistic purpose: it foreshadows on a smaller scale the tale of rise and fall which is to become the subject of the work as a whole. It also has a historical purpose: it illustrates how empire overreaches itself. But the story is almost entirely fictional. Perhaps it does not greatly matter: throughout antiquity it was difficult to write serious history except about periods close to one's own time, and older story always tended towards the legendary. But many of Herodotus' anecdotes of the Persian Wars itself feel like folk tale too. This is so much part of his essential flavour that one would be sorry to lose it, but undoubtedly he was too credulous.

'The divine is altogether jealous and trouble-making,' Solon tells Croesus. A bodeful sense of the gods' presence hangs over the work. This in itself need not compromise its character as history – it was to be the sceptical Latin historian Tacitus who invoked 'the gods' anger against the Roman state' – for the idea of divine providence or envy can be combined with an explanation of events in purely natural terms. When Xerxes is pondering whether to invade Greece,

Herodotus gives speeches to two of his counsellors, Mardonius arguing in favour, Artabanus against. Of course, these speeches are invented, but such invention is an effective way of setting out a political issue – one that later historians were to imitate throughout antiquity. Xerxes decides on invasion, changes his mind, and then two days later changes it back again. All of this makes sense on a practical and human level. But Xerxes' final decision is provoked by two dream visions of a young man, who then appears to Artabanus, prompting him too to reverse his judgement. Herodotus does not actually say that these visions were sent by a god, and it remains just about possible to understand them naturalistically as the unconscious experience of a ditherer. But such stories seem to look back towards Homer; certainly not forward to Thucydides. None the less, Herodotus' achievement was huge: one has only to compare the historical books of the Old Testament to see that he is the foundation from which history as we know it has developed, and that they are not. It is not anachronism, or merely the glibness of hindsight, to assess him by the criteria of a modern historian, for that essentially is the aim towards which he was striving, although he could not of course have seen it that way himself. His was a great leap forward; another was soon to follow.

Herodotus seems to have played no personal part in the great events of his lifetime; by contrast the Athenian Thucydides (c.460–c.400) had been a man of action. During the Peloponnesian War (431–404), fought between Athens and Sparta, with their respective allies, for dominance in the Greek world, he served as a general. Defeated by the Spartan commander Brasidas in 424 – an episode which he narrates with apparent dispassion – he spent the next twenty years in exile. By his own account, he had begun writing about the Peloponnesian War on its outbreak. He is likely to have out-lived its end, but his history is incomplete: not only does it break off abruptly in 409, but the text as a whole is in varying states of finish.

Thucydides took the bold step of removing the gods entirely from history. To be sure, he acknowledged that people might be influenced by supernatural belief – as when the Athenian general Nicias disastrously refused to let his men abandon the siege of Syracuse and sail from Sicily because of soothsayers and a lunar eclipse – but even this kind of motive he mentions rarely, and he never uses the gods themselves to explain any event. He does not even admit Herodotus' sense that there is a divine jealousy some-where at the back of things. This should surprise us more than it usually does, for if the gods exist and act, they ought to be one of the causative forces influencing human affairs. Thucydides' move has been so decisive and so permanent in its effect that we may easily miss how radical it was. It does not follow necessarily that he was an atheist (on that we can only speculate): rather, his idea is that the historian has a particular job to do, and god talk belongs elsewhere.

That job was analytic. This war, he says, was the greatest 'movement' (*kinesis*) among the Greeks and beyond – a cool word for an immense effect. His attention is fiercely concen-trated upon process and change; that is why he shuts out the synchronous enquiries that Herodotus had enjoyed. His pur-pose is scientific and he looks for pattern: he pronounces that if the reader who wants a clear picture of what happened and of what is likely to happen in the future in the nature of human affairs judges his work to be useful, he will be satisfied. And he notes dourly that the lack of fabling in his work may make it less attractive – a clear jibe at Herodotus. Like his predecessor, he is concerned with causes, but he adds a new development: the idea that there are two levels of causation. He sets out the immediate reasons why hostilities broke out, but there was also a deeper, underlying cause, and that was fear. Having built an empire, the Athenians could only feel safe by strengthening and extending it: any sign of weakness would be fatal. But the more powerful the Athenians became, the more the Spartans and other Greeks felt threatened. That was the long-term problem, and war was the inevitable outcome.

As a scientific historian, Thucydides includes a detailed account of the plague that devastated Athens in 430. Sickness, after all, is one of the things that befall human beings, and Thucydides also wants to show how the fear and desperation induced by the plague corrupted human behaviour. The moral effect of war is one of his abiding themes. His most direct analysis of this comes in his account of the horrors produced by revolution in Corcyra (modern Corfu). It changed the relation of words to realities, he says: unthinking recklessness was held to be comradely loyalty, caution was taken for cowardice, good sense was the disguise of unmanliness. The democrats argued for equality, the oligarchs for the wisdom of an aristocracy, but the real motive force on both sides, Thucydides holds, was avarice and ambition.

Here he speaks in his own person, but the greater part of his analysis is developed in the speeches which he gives to the actors in the great historical drama. In a world without shorthand or recording devices his readers were well aware that the speeches could not be verbatim reports, but nevertheless he made a point of explaining his method. He tells us that he has tried to keep as closely as he could to the general purport of what each speaker actually said, but he also states that he has made the speakers say 'the needed things', or 'what was necessary'. What he meant by this has been much discussed. Probably he contradicted himself. We can indeed see a tension between the speeches as historical events and as ideal explanations of the underlying issues.

There is another consideration: Thucydides narrates events in a fairly clear and straightforward prose (in fact his narrative can at times be a little dull, in a way that Herodotus hardly ever is), but the language of the speeches is extraordinarily difficult. It is difficult, in turn, to understand why it needs to be quite so knotty, and to estimate what effect it had on its first readers, but it is hard indeed to believe that men addressing popular assemblies or arguing for their lives talked like this. The content of the speeches points to a similar conclusion: there is a general absence of the kind of appeal to sentiment that we might expect from an orator.

The issue is sharply raised by the 'Mytilenean debate'. The people of Mytilene, on the island of Lesbos, had rebelled unsuccessfully, and the Athenians decided to kill all the adult males and to enslave the rest. But they immediately had doubts and debated the matter again. Thucydides presents

two speeches delivered on this second occasion. The demagogue Cleon insists that exemplary punishment is necessary
and any weakening would be dangerous. His argument is purely
on the grounds of expediency, but so is that of his opponent
Diodotus (otherwise unknown): the question is not one of
justice but of the Athenians' self-interest, and a mass slaughter would only make future enemies more desperate. But
Thucydides has already told us that the Athenians held the
second debate because their decision seemed to them 'great
and cruel'. A second ship, sent to Mytilene with the news that
the slaughter was rescinded, travelled with great speed,
whereas the first was dawdling on its unpleasant errand.
(The second ship arrives in the nick of time.) So Thucydides
allows the element of conscience in the Athenians' behaviour, but excludes it from the two speeches. It is possible that
as a matter of historical fact the speakers used only arguments from expediency, but more likely it was Thucydides
who pared away the emotional side, to focus on the stra-
tegic issue.

Most of the speeches are advocacy or debate, but the most
famous of all is different: the oration by Athens' great statesman Pericles, spoken at a mass funeral for the Athenians
killed in the first year of the war. As elegy, commemoration
of sacrifice and expression of patriotism it is incomparable,
but it is also Thucydides' opportunity to set out the ideology
of Athenian democracy. This Pericles recognizes the role of
emotion: contemplating the greatness of Athens, her citizens
should become her 'lovers', seized by a romantic passion for
their state. He also acknowledges the importance of such
relaxations as games and festivals. But Thucydides gives him

his own tough-mindedness. The cultural glories of Athens are tersely dealt with: 'We-love-beauty with economy, and we-love-wisdom without softness.' Of domestic and family satisfactions there is barely a word.

The modern reader, associating democracy with personal freedom and the right to be left alone, may be startled at how collectivist is Pericles' ideal. The Athenians are unique, he says, in regarding someone who takes no part in public life not as a man of leisure but as useless. For Pericles (or Thucydides) is concerned, once again, with the mainspring of power: we are called a democracy, he explains, because it is the majority not the few who run the state. (The Athenians would regard today's liberal democracies as oligarchies, modified only by occasional elections.) The idea is both egalitarian and elitist: everyone is equal before the law, but excellence is honoured; in politics poverty is no bar and the only criterion is merit. The special merit of the funeral oration itself is to combine hard-headedness and exaltation.

Readers have always been struck by how modern Thucydides seems, how vast the gulf between him and Herodotus, but there is one respect in which his method is less like that of the modern scholar. He gives only his own version of events, excluding the views of others. Some of his omissions are deliberately expressive. When he has Pericles say that it is best for women not to be spoken about at all, either for good or ill, he knows that his readers will be aware that Pericles was attached to Aspasia, whose intelligence and charm had made her the most famous woman in Greece. When he mentions the demagogue Hyperbolus once only, to say that the people of Samos killed him, 'a worthless fellow', he probably expects us to realize that Hyperbolus had played a considerable part in Athenian politics and that some people thought he had been important. It is Thucydides' considered judgement that Hyperbolus had not counted. But the omission of competing viewpoints does mean that we have to trust him. How fully impartial he was is a question that has been much debated. Clearly he admired Pericles and thought poorly of Cleon (who had been his personal enemy), but those assessments are open enough. He believed that the Athenian empire was hated by its subjects; whether he was right or wrong about that – still a matter of fierce disagreement – it is the judgement of a realist. Tacitus, the greatest of the Roman historians, believed that history should be written from an angle, with a controlled passion. That was not Thucydides' way. No historian seems so free of illusion, so liberated from the allure of sentiment, or to look with so clear and penetrating an eye.

It is a hard and unblinking eye, but not exactly a cold one. Dionysius of Halicarnassus, the critic active towards the end of the first century BC, whom we have met as an admirer of Sappho, cited Pindar and Thucydides as examples of the austere style, which allowed 'harsh and dissonant juxtapositions . . . as when stones are selected and laid together in buildings, with their sides not squared off or polished smooth, but remaining unworked and coarse-hewn'. Bold, unadorned, the beauty of this style lies 'in its quality of antiquity and its patina'. We may be surprised to find the poet linked to a historian who disowned charm, but there is poetry of a kind in Thucydides' very intensity, and rigour has its own romance.

The Later
Fifth Century

For at least the last two hundred years the fifth century BC in Athens has been regarded in the west as one of the culminating moments of civilization; for some of the Romantics it was the greatest time of all. This culture has also been admired as one that achieved an unmatched unity, poise and completeness, where beauty of mind and body were valued alike, where art attained a classic perfection, and where the great spirits, Phidias the sculptor, Pericles, Sophocles, Thucydides and Socrates, in some sense made common cause. There is an element of truth in this, but it conceals some important realities. One is the huge gap between the Greeks' visual and literary art at this time. Visually, they aimed at perfecting a small number of forms: the nude male and clothed female body in sculpture, in architecture the Doric and Ionic orders and the post-and-lintel method of construction. Their literature, however – whether verse, history or abstract thought – was daring and innovative, sometimes wild or experimental, and constantly searching for new ground.

This was also a time of uncertainty, of shifting ideas and values, a ferment associated especially with the men who became known as the sophists. These were itinerant teachers, many of whom made their way to Athens. They were a mixed bag: some taught rhetoric, some philosophy, geography or mathematics. A few were intellectual grandees, who attracted disciples, others were pretty humble. But collectively they began the story of higher education, and the buzz of their activity provided the background noise from which the great voices emerged.

The author who seems most independent of this milieu is Sophocles. He was known for his easy temper; he was popular, and held high public office. He was the middle of the big three tragedians (although not many years older than Euripides, whom he briefly outlived), and Aristotle was to take his *Oedipus the King* as the type of tragedy. For some or all of these reasons he has often been represented as the most classical of the tragedians, the one in whom that calm and balance supposed to be the mark of fifth-century Athens were most consummately achieved. In Matthew Arnold's words, he 'saw life steadily and saw it whole'. But we might rather think of him as strange, savage and extreme.

Among great poets perhaps only Dante gives more prominence to purely physical pain. Philoctetes howls from the agony of his festering wound; Heracles in the *Women of Trachis* dies in torment from the poisoned robe that he has put on; Oedipus puts his eyes out with the pins of his wife's brooch; Antigone escapes death by starvation only by hanging herself; Ajax tortures animals, having intended to torture his comrades in arms. Sophocles is also the most enigmatic of the three. Many people expect to get something at the end of the tragedy – some consolation, moral, or enlargement of understanding. Sophocles is more likely than any other great tragedian to frustrate that expectation.

His *Ajax* (which like most of his plays cannot be closely dated) is a case in point. It is set at the end of the Trojan War. Before the action begins, Ajax has been offended because the Greeks have awarded the armour of the dead Achilles to Odysseus rather than himself. In revenge he has intended to bind, torture and murder the Greek chieftains, but the goddess Athena has saved them by sending him mad, so that he has glutted his cruelty on sheep and cattle instead. Early in the play he returns to sanity, and realizes the depth of his humiliation. Despite the pleas of his concubine, Tecmessa, and his men, who form the chorus, he kills himself. But although the protagonist is dead, there is still more than a third of the play to come. Teucer, brother of Ajax, wrangles about the fate of his corpse with the Greek chieftains Agamemnon and Menelaus, who demand that it be left unburied, until the prudent and generous Odysseus, previously seen conversing with Athena at the start of the play, intervenes, insisting that Ajax was noble and the best of the Greek warriors after Achilles. So the work falls into two unequal parts: the first of these focuses upon a wild, grand and dreadful man; the second depicts the rather petty squabbling of lesser people. Athena, the only deity in the play, appears at the beginning rather than the end, as we might have expected, so that the divine seems to withdraw from the scene, instead of entering it to produce an authoritative resolution.

The heart and depth of the play lie in a short scene which consists only of a speech by Ajax. He is speaking to himself, although Tecmessa and the chorus hear him. With a new largeness of vision he declares that immeasurable time changes all things. Even he, who had once been so hard, has been softened by his woman: he now feels pity at leaving her a widow and his son an orphan. But he will go to cleanse himself and escape the wrath of the goddess, and he will bury his sword, digging a hole in the ground where none can see. Tecmessa and the chorus suppose that he has abandoned his plan of killing himself, but they are deceived. A little later Sophocles has the chorus leave the performing area – a great rarity in Greek tragedy – and another short scene presents Ajax majestic and solitary and speaking what the dramatic conventions hardly ever allowed, a pure soliloquy. He affirms his resolve to die, and falls on his sword – another powerful breach of the conventions, a killing on stage.

Ajax's great speeches are so magnificent, his presence so compelling, that the later part of the play seems an anticlimax, and it is hard to see how even the most skilful performance could overcome this problem. But we may still ask what was Sophocles' purpose. Ajax's insight seems so profound that in some sense we are bound to feel ourselves with him. A greatness has passed from the earth with his death, we may be tempted to think, and the little men are left behind; and yet we can hardly rest satisfied with this elegiac sentiment. Ajax was a monster, his intended act of vengeance unspeakable, his actual act disgusting; and it seems intolerable that we should put him above the decent, god-fearing Odysseus. The play gazes at these things and gives no answer: we are left not nursing a moral but in a state of appalled wonderment.

Another play that falls into two parts is *Antigone*. Oedipus' sons, Eteocles and Polynices, have been killed fighting one another for the kingship of Thebes. The new king, Creon, has decreed that Polynices, as a traitor who has attacked the city, should not be buried. Antigone, Polynices' sister, defies Creon and performs a symbolic burial. Haemon, Creon's son, betrothed to Antigone, tries to dissuade his father from condemning her to death, but their encounter becomes a bitter quarrel. Antigone is taken away to a cavern where she will be left to die. The seer Tiresias now enters to warn Creon to reverse his decision. After some resistance he gives way, but Antigone has already killed herself; so too has Haemon. Creon's queen appears briefly, and soon after we learn that she has become the third suicide. Creon is left wanting nothing but death.

A famous interpretation of this play, associated with Hegel but not originating with him, sees the essence of the tragedy in inevitability. Creon's duty as king is to maintain the order of the state, and therefore he must forbid the burial of Polynices; Antigone's moral duty is to her family and to the divine law which requires kin to bury their dead. Private morality and public morality each have a compulsive force, and here they are directly opposed. There can only be a disastrous collision, and that is what tragedy is: the inescapable smash of ineluctable forces.

This is an eloquent conception, but it does not describe the play that Sophocles wrote. At the start it may briefly look this way, but it soon becomes clear that Creon is a small man, prickly and defensive, with the harshness that comes from weakness. Antigone makes a powerful affirmation of her moral position: there are unwritten and eternal laws of the gods which trump the written laws of man. Creon has nothing similar in response. When he wrangles with his son Haemon, he loses the argument hands down; the contrast between the edgy father and the son who cannot quite hide the knowledge of his own superiority is finely observed (another place where stichomythia is used to telling effect). The sinister omens from the gods show that they hold him to have done wrong. His initial resistance to Tiresias' report of them is petulant and deluded. It is a cruel irony that his most sensible act, to take back his decision, is another sign of weakness: he crumples, appeals to the chorus for advice, and obeys it.

Creon has the largest part, but Antigone is the play's hero. She has the stubborn, difficult, uncompromising character typical of Sophocles' male protagonists. She is severe with her more cautious sister Ismene (from what motive we are left to guess) and in only one line does she express love for Haemon (some assign it to Ismene, but that is surely wrong). She stands starkly alone, without the sympathetic support that Euripides' Medea and Phaedra, for example, enjoy: this is rare among those Greek dramas that bear a woman's name as their title in having a male chorus. She is the first woman to be a figure of heroic virtue, the ancestress of Joan of Arc: Clytemnestra had power and daring, but Antigone has goodness. For all her iron resolve, she is human, and in her last lament she unburdens herself of loneliness and despair, as she goes to die 'unwept, unfriended, unwed'. Her suffering is in every way tragic: it is intense, it is chosen, and it has purpose. When the focus turns to Creon, instead of quality of suffering we have quantity of suffering, and at the end a mess almost bloody enough for Elizabethan drama. The later part of the play is better integrated than in *Ajax*, because Creon has been at the centre of the story throughout, but there is a similar descent from grandeur into a smaller, uglier scene. The audience is left not with a sense of resolution but troubled.

Oedipus the King is masterly in construction; its plot has always been admired as one of the best ever made. Oedipus' previous history emerges in the course of the play. He was brought up by the king and queen of Corinth and believed himself to be their son. Learning from an oracle that he was fated to kill his father, couple with his mother and have children by her, he fled from Corinth to Thebes. On the journey he met a stranger; they quarrelled, and in the altercation Oedipus killed him, along with most of his retinue. He rescued Thebes from the Sphinx by solving her riddle, married the queen, Jocasta, whose husband, Laius, had recently died in unknown circumstances, and became king. In the course of the play he learns that Laius and Jocasta are his true parents. Jocasta kills herself and Oedipus puts out his own eyes.

The play's traditional status as the purest type of tragic drama may conceal the fact that Oedipus' story has two elements more akin to folk tale than to tragedy's heroic naturalism. The first of these is the Sphinx's riddle, which only Oedipus is clever enough to solve. The second, and more important, is the idea that he is doomed to father-killing and incest, whatever he does. It is near impossible to imagine how a person would behave under such a persuasion; he might at least reflect before marrying a woman much older than himself, one might think. Sophocles' achievement is to take a very odd sort of story and transform it into heroic tragedy. Oedipus' history also resembles the 'appointment at

Samarra' (a man in Baghdad sees Death give him a threatening look, and flees as far as he can, to Samarra; Death later explains that his look was not of threat but surprise: 'I had not expected to see him in Baghdad, for I have an appointment with him tonight in Samarra'). The irony is that the very act of avoiding his doom is what accomplishes it; but again, that is more a folk-tale irony than the usual tragic kind.

This is, like *Agamemnon*, a public drama. At the beginning a cluster of suppliants is gathered before the palace. Oedipus speaks the very first words, 'Children, new offspring of old Cadmus'. He speaks as the father of his people. The chorus, who appear a little later, are elders of Thebes, representing the citizenry as a whole. At the same time this is the story of a unique catastrophe falling upon a single man. Aristotle has sometimes been criticized for analysing tragedy too much in terms of plot, but he was right at least with this play, for plot is the essence of it. Sophocles' especial ingenuity is to break Oedipus' discovery of the truth into two stages: he learns first that he is Laius' killer, and only later that Laius was his father and his mother is now his wife. He also skilfully arranges that Jocasta shall realize the truth earlier than Oedipus. Although the truth that he killed the previous king, and is himself the man whom his decree has cursed and banished, is bad enough, his courage rises again when a messenger arrives with the news that the king of Corinth is dead and was not, after all, his father. Oedipus, he reveals, is really of Theban birth. He asserts his determination to know the truth, however humble his birth may be, and the power of his personality carries his high spirit to the chorus, who abandon their usual grimness for a brief song of delight. From this high point the plunge to disaster is all the more precipitous.

The play's construction enables triangular scenes of great power: three characters pull in different directions. Oedipus wrangles with his brother-in-law Creon, and Jocasta tries to mediate. While the messenger from Corinth unfolds his story, she listens in silence, but at some point she realizes the whole truth, and pleads with Oedipus to enquire no further. The tension between her desperation, the messenger's eagerness to please and Oedipus' combination of determination and mild contempt for what he supposes to be her social snobbery is keenly dramatic. In the next scene Oedipus interrogates an old shepherd. The Corinthian messenger, who knows half the truth, encourages the shepherd to speak out; the shepherd, who knows it all, miserably tries to keep silent; Oedipus moves from anger to wretchedness.

Sophocles does not trouble to make Oedipus easily likeable. In the early part of the play he quarrels bitterly with both Creon and the seer Tiresias, unjustly accusing them of treachery. He threatens the shepherd with torture if he will not speak. Although he was provoked, a less angry man might not have killed the stranger whom he met on the road to Thebes. But his essential *hamartia* has nothing to do with his character: it was involuntary. And we see his pride and strength, for us to judge how we will. He chooses to blind himself. He is a man of extremity: he wishes he could destroy his other senses, hearing as well. With pride (is it?) or in bare recognition of reality that he declares, 'None among mortals is able to bear my woes but I.'

Aristotle famously said that tragedy works its effect through pity and terror. The second of those words might well surprise us: I pity the death of Agamemnon, but why should it frighten me? But *Oedipus* is indeed terrifying: it looks down into the abyss of horror and sees no bottom. Sophocles and Thucydides were political leaders of the Athenian state in the same generation. They have often been contrasted: Thucydides the modern rationalist, Sophocles representing an older order, an imagination haunted by gods, oracles and atavistic fears. But from another view they belong together, both from hope set free, recognizing that there is no ghastliness so great that we may be protected from it, no ultimate safety on which we can rely. It is one aspect of the Greek imagination, this stare at the emptiness.

Two plays survive from Sophocles' extreme old age, and they are very different. *Philoctetes* has the vigorous characterization and sharp presentation of moral conflict typical of Euripides. Stark and forceful, it is the only extant Greek tragedy without a woman in it. At the start of the Trojan War, the Greeks marooned Philoctetes on an island because he had a suppurating wound that would not heal; but he also has a magic bow which they need, following the death of Achilles, if they are to capture Troy. Odysseus and Neoptolemus, Achilles' son, come to get it, the former a machiavellian content to use deceit to obtain his ends, the other a young man with scruples. The tale ends happily, with Heracles appearing *ex machina* and bringing the news that Philoctetes will be cured and earn glory at Troy.

Whereas this play shows Sophocles learning a trick or two from his younger rival, *Oedipus at Colonus* has the flavour of a late work. And uniquely in extant Greek drama it has the character of a sequel: Sophocles seems to be looking back to his earlier play about the king and completing the story. Aged and fugitive, Oedipus comes to Colonus in Attica, where Theseus, king of Athens, gives him sanctuary. Ultimately, the blind man will have an inner vision of where he must go to die. The death itself, told by a messenger, is 'wondrous, if any man's was': the god thunders and calls to Oedipus – 'Why do we delay to go? You have tarried too long' – and the old man disappears. The play is filled with the spirit of place: Oedipus' body, sleeping in the earth, will give strength to the land of Attica in future time, and the chorus celebrate the beauties of Colonus, shady and melodious with birdsong but also haunted by the goddesses of the underworld. Yet this is not an easy play: Oedipus is still angry and difficult, and not long before the end he curses his son Polynices. Beautiful, mysterious and disturbing, it is a strange blend of bitterness and serenity. And it is perhaps the only work surviving from antiquity that reads like the summation and closing of a life's work.

An air of controversy hung about Euripides, the third of the great tragedians, in his own time. Some thought him subversive, or too radical, or too close to those dubious sophists. That does not mean that his importance was doubted, or even that he was unpopular. He won first prize for his plays only four times during his life, and once posthumously, but more significant is the fact that he was selected for the competition over and over again. Aristophanes sent him up in two of his comedies, but the fun depends on the audience knowing his works well. In the centuries after his death he became the most popular of the tragedians.

He was criticized by some contemporaries for introducing a hero in rags on to the stage. And it can indeed be said that he made tragedy more naturalistic. Although his leading characters are still kings and princesses, the actions of his dramas tend to have a more private and domestic character (although Aeschylus had anticipated this in *Libation Bearers*), with the chorus sometimes being not representatives of the city but confidantes of the leading character. More oddly, he was said to be a misogynist. Certainly, he showed women planning and carrying out bad deeds, but he looks sympathetically at the extremity that has driven them to these actions. He allows them to explain themselves and to reveal their inner thoughts; we see into their minds and motives as we did not with Aeschylus' Clytemnestra. *Medea* (431) may fairly be called a feminist play: she eloquently, and accurately, sets out the disadvantages that women suffer, and the female chorus support her.

Some modern critics have also seen Euripides as an anti-war author, especially in the *Trojan Women* (415), but that is not quite right. True, he shows that defeat and enslavement are misery for the defeated, but Homer and Aeschylus had known that well enough; he also makes the victors stupid and cruel, but that is not the inevitable consequence of war. In both the *Suppliants* and the *Children of Heracles* Athens launches aggressive war, and we are encouraged to approve. The distinctive quality of the *Trojan Women* is the passivity of its characters, helpless victims; it has some of the character of a documentary. It is also the only surviving Greek tragedy in which a character – the captive Trojan queen Hecuba – is on stage continuously from beginning to end.

A tragedy need not end in misery; no one would doubt that the *Oresteia* is a tragic work, although it ends in celebration. But in any case, by one definition any work performed on the first three days of the greatest dramatic festival of Athens, other than the satyr plays, was a tragedy simply by virtue of that fact, and some of Euripides' plays are not tragedies in our sense of the word. *Helen* (which follows the curious story that Helen never went to Troy but spent those ten years quietly in Egypt) has the flavour of what we might call the comedy of intrigue or adventure. The hero of *Ion* is a virtuous youth who has been brought up in the sanctified atmosphere of the shrine at Delphi; the heroine, Creusa, the victim of rape by the god Apollo many years before, is a touching figure. There are alarums and excursions as Ion narrowly escapes being poisoned and Creusa is condemned to death for murder, but the discovery that Ion is her son by Apollo brings about the happy ending. The recognition of a long lost child was to be a favourite motif in later Greek and Roman comedy. Plays such as these seem closer to the spirit of *As You Like It* or *The Winter's Tale* than to *Hamlet*.

Yet Aristotle, who thought that the best tragedies ended in affliction, called Euripides for that reason the most tragic of the poets, and indeed his most powerful works are dark. *Medea* is set some years after the voyage of the Argonauts in quest of the Golden Fleece, when Jason wooed and won her. Back in Greece, he has decided to dump her, so that he can marry the daughter of the local king; he will keep their children and she will go into exile. Medea, who has knowledge of magic, contrives the agonizing death of her innocent rival (this happens off stage, but is poignantly described), and after an internal struggle kills her children. She finally appears aloft, in a chariot borrowed from the Sun, with the infant corpses; Jason pleads to have the bodies for burial, but she refuses, and the play ends in angry altercation.

Medea is a bleak, clear, bitter play. Both its leading characters are bad, and essentially it is a play without gods. True, a figure appears *ex machina* at the end; however, Euripides' *coup de théâtre* is that this is no deity, but Medea herself. Here is a resolution that is no resolution: families are destroyed, and murder goes unpunished. Jason is acidly portrayed: a mean little man, smug, chauvinist, sententious and hypocritical. Medea's crime is self-destructive, but in a sense not irrational. It is not only that she wants to hurt Jason: she wants to keep the children for herself, and the only way that she can keep them is by killing them. That is why it is so telling that she hugs their corpses to herself. At the play's heart is a monologue in which Medea laments the forthcoming loss of her children, deplores the misery which her own self-will is bringing her, changes her mind, deciding to spare the children, and then changes it back again. This is a study of the divided mind, and it began a theme that was to have an enormous influence on later writers.

It also brings the theatre close to the sophists arguing in the market-place, by introducing a type whom we can call the 'acratic heroine'. To explain: Socrates' philosophical concerns were essentially ethical. One problem that preoccupied him was the puzzle of moral failure. How can it be that if I know a particular course of action to be right, I may none the less take the opposite course? Must not reason be compelling? How can it be overborne? His answer is summed up in the 'Socratic paradox': 'No one willingly does wrong.' In modern jargon this is an 'intellectualist' account of moral failure: every voluntary action is directed by a reasoning process and accordingly every act of moral wrongdoing must be the product of mistaken reasoning. Plato was dissatisfied with this answer, and in the *Republic* he reckoned to have solved the problem by dividing the mind into three, the reasoning, desiring and spirited parts. (It is an account which may have influenced Freud.) He took as an example the necrophiliac who deplores his disgusting behaviour at the very moment that he indulges it. The desiring part of the mind enjoys gazing at corpses, while the reasoning part of the mind censures it. Plato later thought of an objection to his own theory, which he set out in his *Parmenides*; it is unclear whether he believed that the objection could be overcome. Aristotle was also discontent, and devoted some of the most penetrating chapters of his *Nicomachean Ethics* to the issue, which he called *akrasia*, 'non-control'. We can usefully make the adjective 'acratic' from this.

The acratic heroine – for this divided figure is almost always female – is likely to have fascinated writers for several reasons. There was a literary interest in the creation of complex character, and a philosophical one in the nature of mental conflict. A growing liking for more tender and domestic themes turned authors' attention more towards women, who may in any case have been thought more liable to indecision than men. Later, in the Latin poets especially, there is also the frisson of the forbidden – we meet heroines who have fallen in love with their enemy, or another woman, or their own father – and sometimes we detect the lubriciousness of the male gaze, lingering over a damsel in attractive distress. But this is to look forward: meanwhile, Euripides was to create the most subtle and profound of such heroines in his *Hippolytus* (428).

The hero of this play is that rare thing in Greek mythology, a male virgin, dedicated to the worship of the virgin goddess Artemis. Aphrodite, goddess of love, resolves to destroy him for slighting her, and makes his stepmother Phaedra fall in love with him – a passion that is both adulterous and incestuous. Phaedra starves herself and hides her secret, but her confidante, the Nurse, worms it out of her and reveals that she has a 'medicine' which will solve the problem. After some resistance, Phaedra agrees to its use. In reality the Nurse's only medicine is to tell the secret to Hippolytus, who is appalled and threatens to reveal the truth to his father, Theseus. To save her honour Phaedra kills herself, leaving the false message that Hippolytus has raped her. Hippolytus, who has been tricked into an oath of silence, cannot defend himself to Theseus, who curses him and calls on his own father, the sea god Poseidon, to destroy him. A 'bull from the sea' forces Hippolytus' chariot on to rocks, and he is fatally wounded. Artemis appears and reveals the truth; Hippolytus is carried in, forgives his agonized father, and dies.

In depicting the interplay of complex character this play perhaps comes closer to some concerns of modern drama and the modern novel than anything else in ancient literature. There are four principal characters; Theseus is movingly but straightforwardly drawn; the other three are exceptional creations. Hippolytus is the first representation of the religious temperament. He is dedicated to the hunt and the open air, and his evocation of the inviolate meadow where he communes with Artemis is beautiful. But we also become aware of a certain narrowness, exclusivity and intolerance, the other aspect of his otherwise charming youthfulness. The Nurse's relationship to her mistress is both devoted and domineering; she is unscrupulous and deceitful, but out of misguided loyalty, and when Phaedra at last bitterly rejects her, she becomes poignant. Phaedra herself is the deepest study of all. Her reflections on the nature of shame and honour are both humanly and philosophically enthralling. Seized by a passion that she cannot help, she clings to virtue, and it is the most pitiful of ironies that it is her very concern for her modesty and honour that finally drives her to a terrible crime: in effect, she murders the man she loves. And what of that medicine? Did the Nurse really deceive her? The play does not give a direct answer, but it seems likeliest that she has guessed the Nurse's real intention, while the ambiguity in her language gives her the excuse to yield. That is psychologically very fine.

This is a family drama, intensely human, but it is framed by two goddesses. Aphrodite, who speaks the prologue and then disappears, is ruthless: she will punish Hippolytus this very day; Phaedra too will die, collateral damage. At the play's end Hippolytus expires before our eyes, one of the very rare occasions in Greek drama where a person dies on stage. Artemis has appeared aloft, *ex machina*, and for the first time he beholds her; hitherto, as he has said early in the play, he has been with her and spoken with her, 'hearing your voice but not seeing your face'. It is, in a sense, an epiphany, and yet how far from the radiance which that word might suggest. The Greek word for 'farewell' is *khaire*, 'rejoice', and Hippolytus uses a form of this verb to say goodbye to the goddess: 'Go on your way rejoicing, blessed maiden; easily you leave our long companionship.' This is one of drama's supreme moments, and also one of its most religious. Hippolytus has, in effect, given his life for Artemis, and now he realizes that she does not care about him: she is indeed blessed, she will go her way happy, their parting is indeed easy for her. She will not even stay for his last moments, as it is not proper for a goddess to defile her eyes with the sight of the dead.

Yet this is not the fist-shaking at the deity beloved of the Romantics – the 'Don Juan in hell' or Promethean pose. That is what a lesser artist might have done here, but Euripides is wiser: his Hippolytus simply accepts. We meet here a sacralization of the Homeric idea that the gods are godlike for the very reason that they do not need us. Like Hector at the point of death, Hippolytus has a revelation in his final moments, but whereas Hector saw a future human event, he sees the nature of a deity. It is a vision, bleak, spare, utterly unillusioned, of the beauty of divine impassibility. Perhaps there is even in this, for Hippolytus or for us, a kind of austere consolation: he dies, to borrow the words of a later, atheistic poet, 'from hope and fear set free'. Later Greek and Roman thinkers were to insist that god can do no evil; the cruel gods of mythology cannot exist. For earlier Greeks it was different. The gods exist; the job is to come to terms with them.

A cruel and beautiful form of worship is the theme of one of Euripides' last plays, the *Bacchants* (*Bacchae, c.*406). It is the story of resistance by Pentheus, the king of Thebes – young and honourable but insecure and narrow-minded – to the cult of Dionysus, newly arrived in Greece from eastern lands. Dionysus has punished the women of Thebes who disbelieved in his power by sending them crazy; they are now out on the mountains in a maenad state. Pentheus is right to think that there is something amiss, wrong to suspect these women of licentiousness. From the lyrics of the chorus, a band of female devotees who have followed Dionysus from Asia to Greece, we may learn that his is a religion of instinct and ecstasy. Two elderly Thebans who misunderstand this are Cadmus, Pentheus' grandfather, and the seer Tiresias. Cadmus is pleased to have a god in the family (for Dionysus' mother was Semele, Cadmus' daughter); Tiresias offers an intellectual's account of the Bacchic cult's allegorical meaning. A humorous scene shows them dressed like the maenads in animal skins, shaking their wands and trying some aged dance steps. When Pentheus sees it, he is appalled – literature's first example of a young person finding his elders simply embarrassing.

Disguised as 'the Stranger', Dionysus confronts Pentheus in three successive scenes. In the first the Stranger is Pentheus' prisoner and apparently entirely in his power. In the second Pentheus rejects the Stranger's offer to settle the trouble peacefully, and then yields to the Stranger's proposal that he should go to spy on the maenads, falling under his spell. In the third scene the Stranger brings Pentheus on dressed as a woman and in a hallucinatory state. This is humiliation but much worse is to follow: we learn that Pentheus' mother, Agave, and the other maenads have torn him apart, in their crazed condition believing him to be a lion.

The whole play is saturated in Dionysus. Dionysus speaks the prologue, and we expect him to say his piece, like Aphrodite in *Hippolytus*, and be done. But he then enters the play's action, and he is also the god who appears *ex machina* at the end. The chorus present the paradox of Dionysus, the god who is most violent and most gentle. The Stranger is always calm, in contrast to Pentheus' agitation. Dionysus is the god of release – from anxieties but also from inhibition. He is the god of quietness, the god who takes away care, but he is also associated with wine and desire and the ritual in which a live wild animal is torn asunder. What is the meaning of it all? Cadmus tells Agave that Dionysus has destroyed them 'justly, but too much'. That seems the truth of it, and it is perhaps as much as we can say: to press too earnestly for the meaning is to make Tiresias' mistake. The play declares the limits of rationality; Euripides digs into the dark roots of the psyche and explores the wilder shores of religious experience, fusing human and divine into one terrifying and entrancing vision.

Greek comedy, like tragedy, was dominated by Athens. Ancient critics divided its history into three: Old, Middle and New Comedy. The only examples of Old Comedy surviving complete are eleven plays of Aristophanes (450s–*c*.386). In later centuries comedies might be elegant and well constructed; the spirit of Old Comedy was to get away from all that. Those who see the comic impulse as essentially carnivalesque, the release of repression, the bubbling up of the id, rude and anarchic, from the depths of the psychic mire, will find that Aristophanes meets the criteria as well as anybody. The actors in Old Comedy playing male roles wore outsize leather phalli; Aristophanes describes the object in *Clouds*, 'dangling and red at the tip, thick, so that the children laugh'. His choruses are often fantastical, representing animals or things: clouds, birds, jurymen dressed as wasps. Some of his jokes are extraordinarily cheap. (*Frogs* cunningly begins with a set of cheap jokes about not making cheap jokes.) It can seem that any reference to farts or the effeminacy of one Cleisthenes or Euripides' mother selling herbs (the point of this last jibe is lost to us) is enough to raise a laugh. At least this spares us from believing that the Athenians spent all their time discussing ideal beauty and moral truth.

Most of these plays were written while Athens was at war, its land ravaged by the Spartans. This could easily have had a dispiriting effect on them, but Aristophanes usually manages to convert war-weariness into exuberance. His central figure is most often a man, an Athenian citizen, who may be middle-aged or older, although in three of the extant plays the principal role goes instead to a spirited woman. In *Peace* (421) the farmer Trygaeus ('Vintager') flies up to Olympus on a dung-beetle to ask Zeus to bring the war to an end. In the *Acharnians* (425) Dicaeopolis ('What's-Right-for-the-City') makes a private truce in order to live peaceably in the backwoods village of Acharnae; the play ends with him returning to the stage drunk, stuffed with food, his arms round a couple of dancing girls – the earthy, Falstaffian idea of human fulfilment. Some of these comedies show the world turned upside down. The heroine of *Lysistrata* plans to stop the war by getting the women of Greece to go on a sex strike. Despite her strong leadership, however, this is not a feminist play, for it represents fantasy, the picture of an impossibility. A later play, *Assemblywomen* (c.392), begins with the women of Athens taking over the government, but that theme is abandoned half way through, and turns to farce: the women have decreed equal sexual opportunities for all, and we are entertained by the sight of a luckless fellow fending off the amorous advances of several old hags. Aristophanes' most inventive and sympathetic treatment of women comes in *Thesmophoria Ladies* – the Thesmophoria being an all-female festival.

Aristophanes mocks Athens's leaders, notably the demagogue Cleon, and the question arises of how political these plays really are. In *Wasps* the principal characters are Philocleon and Bdelycleon, 'Love-Cleon' and 'Loathe-Cleon'. In *Knights* the central character is Demos ('The-People'), for whose favour the slave Paphlagon (representing Cleon) and a sausage-seller compete. The stage is set for a satirical allegory, but that is not quite what we get. Much of the play is devoted to mutual abuse between Demos' two suitors; these exchanges provide plenty of verbal invention (although they go on too long), but we miss the sharpness of genuine satirical intent. Extravagance rather than accuracy is the aim.

Much the same can be said about the mockery of Socrates in *Clouds*. We have three portraits of Socrates from men who knew him, the other two being Xenophon and Plato. Xenophon's Socrates is a sensible and worthy moralist; the difficulty with believing in this portrait is that he is not interesting enough for anyone to have bothered putting him to death. What everyone wants to believe is that the Socrates of Plato's earlier dialogues is the closest to the historical reality, and happily this is the probable truth. At all events, Aristophanes' Socrates, a cross between a teacher of sophistical rhetoric and a batty boffin, must be wildly unlike the real thing. The playwright's aim, well achieved, is simply hilarity, and if there is satire, it strikes less at Socrates than at the sophistic movement in general.

Aristophanes' blithest comedy is *Birds* (414), in which Peisetaerus ('Friend-Persuader'), accompanied by his comrade Euelpides ('High-Hopeful'), leaves Athens, joins the birds, is made their king and establishes a city in the sky, Cloud-cuckooland. Prometheus, carrying a parasol to hide himself from Zeus, arrives to say that the city is blocking the scent of sacrifice from reaching the gods, who are getting desperate. Poseidon and Heracles then come to negotiate, Peisetaerus marries Sovereignty, whom Zeus has given him for his bride, and becomes king of everything. The comedy of escape is here at its most extreme and fantastical, but escape from what? A charm of the piece is that it is never said: 'Don't mention the war' might be the motto.

In *Frogs* the principal role goes to the god Dionysus, who is made to be occasionally absurd. Perhaps we are startled by such disrespectful treatment of the gods; or perhaps we should be more startled than we usually are. We are familiar with a light or humorous treatment of classical mythology: we owe that to Ovid and to the Renaissance. But those are gods who have lost their numinousness: they have become decorative and literary. Here, however, we have mockery of real gods with formidable power. It was only a year or two since the audience at the *Bacchants* saw Dionysus arranging for the man who disrespected him to be torn to pieces on the Theban hills.

The Dionysus of *Frogs* goes down to the underworld to bring back a poet who can be useful to the city. That is in part a plot device to motivate a competition between Aeschylus and Euripides, but there does seem to be a more serious element to this work. A convention of Old Comedy allowed for a point in the middle at which the playwright, through the chorus, could address the audience directly, and here Aristophanes uses it to make a specific proposal: the participants in a recent oligarchic *coup d'état* should have their citizenship restored. In addition, the chorus of this play are initiates into the mysteries of Eleusis (the frogs that give the play its name appear only for the croaking chorus that accompanies Dionysus on his journey across the underworld River Styx). But the contest which takes up almost half the play is essentially an entertainment.

It is, fortuitously, the earliest piece of literary criticism in existence, but we need not suppose that Aristophanes himself saw it in those terms. In any case, he was bound to treat the two tragedians unequally: the spectators would be familiar with Euripides' plays in performance, whereas Aeschylus was a figure from the past, about whom few would know much. Accordingly, the treatment of Aeschylus is broadly comic: basically, the idea is that he was grandiose and ponderous. Euripides is much more subtly handled: especially delightful is a parody of his lyric manner, the lament of a market-woman who has lost her cockerel. Aristophanes also mocks a feature of his musical style, though the fun of this is sadly lost to us. Euripides is also nicely sent up in *Thesmophoria Ladies*. In *Frogs* the grounds on which Dionysus ultimately awards Aeschylus the victory are preposterous. Whatever Aristophanes himself may have believed about the moral function of poetry, the spirit of comic folly must prevail.

Aristophanes' last extant play, *Wealth* (388), is quieter than the others, and in part allegorical. The chorus are no longer part of the drama; the text merely indicates the places where they should provide an interlude, without supplying the words for it. This new manner seems to mark the beginning of Middle Comedy, about which we know little. New Comedy was to enjoy a long popularity and its most admired writer was another Athenian, Menander (*c*.342–*c*.292). A century ago any understanding of New Comedy had to rely on the second-century Latin adaptations by Plautus and Terence, and the problem was, as it remains, how much to attribute to the source, and how much to the adapter. Since then a complete play by Menander, the *Curmudgeon* (316), has been found on papyrus, and substantial chunks of several more of his works. New Comedy was broadly speaking naturalistic (no gods appearing, except perhaps to speak a prologue; no miracles), although the denouements often relied on unlikely coincidence (for example, a long lost daughter rediscovered). The plots usually involve a young man who is impeded from marrying the girl he loves. There are stock characters: cunning slave, sleazy pimp, comic cook, braggart soldier, cantankerous or amiable old gentleman. Lost in the original, but mediated through its Roman adapters, New Comedy was to have a great influence in the Renaissance and after; it is indeed closer to later European drama than anything else remaining from the ancient world.

The Fourth Century

By the end of the fifth century BC the great ages of lyric and tragedy were over, Pericles was dead, the Parthenon and the Erechtheum stood on the Athenian Acropolis and the sculptures of Phidias were already weathering. On one view this period, in Athens especially, was the zenith of Greek civilization and everything after was decline. Should we buy this story? Two exceptions are obvious: oratory and philosophy reached the greatest heights in the fourth century. On the other hand, there was a feeling even at the time that the vitality of poetry was ebbing. Choerilus of Samos, who wrote an epic about the Persian Wars towards the end of the fifth century, began by explaining that he had taken this recent subject because all other themes were exhausted. Perhaps for the first time the burden of the past was now becoming a theme for poetry. It is one that we shall hear again often enough, in Rome and in later Europe. Labelled 'the anxiety of influence' it can be admired as the height of sophistication, but it strikes an ominous note. Alexander the Great, king of Macedon from 336 to 323 and the first ruler with a concern to transmit to posterity not only the record of his deeds but a sense of his personality, would have wished, like other rulers, to be praised by good poets, but he had to make do instead with historians, who were added to his entourage. A story was told that when he crossed the Hellespont in 334 to make war on Asia, he made a point of visiting the tomb of Achilles, and there mourned not for Achilles but for himself, for the older hero had had the greatest of poets to sing his praise, whereas he had only Choerilus of Iasus, a byword for hack versification. For poetry, therefore, it seems right to regard the fourth century as a fallow period and the third as a time of revival.

Thucydides has also influenced the idea of Greek decline. When he said that the Peloponnesian War was the greatest *kinesis*, he did not mean that it was a turning-point, a fulcrum upon which the centuries moved – after all, he could not see into the future – but he could easily be interpreted that way. In reality this war made rather little difference in the long run. Athens was defeated but the Spartans did not choose to destroy it; the city revived, and democracy was actually more widespread among Greek states in the fourth century than before. It was the rise of Macedon and the extinction of the Greek city-states' independence by Philip II and his son Alexander the Great that changed everything and led on to the successor kingdoms into which the lands conquered by Alexander split after his death. We may ourselves prefer democracy to monarchy, but these kingdoms extended Greek power more widely than at any time before or since. The third and second centuries were also to be the period at which Greek science, mathematics and scholarship became most vigorous and creative.

History-writing also appears to have flourished, but all the historians of the fourth and third centuries have perished, with one exception. Xenophon (*c*.428–*c*.354) was the first jack of all trades among prose writers, one who was willing to take up almost any subject. In his *Hellenica* ('Greek Affairs') he became a historian, continuing the story of the Peloponnesian War from the point at which Thucydides had broken off, and then carrying the narrative on into the mid-fourth century – a workmanlike job. For a gentlemanly soldier of conservative disposition, he achieved a remarkable number of firsts: his *Resources* is the first work of economics; his *Education of Cyrus*, which tells the story of Persia's greatest king, is the first historical novel, indeed the first novel of any kind; his life of Agesilaus, king of Sparta, is the first biography; his works on estate management, horses and hunting are the first self-help manuals; his *Anabasis* is the first memoir. Like Plato, he wrote dialogues with Socrates as their central figure; in this case it is likeliest that Plato got there first, although we do not know for sure.

Education of Cyrus was a misnomer; the work covers the whole of its hero's life, and only the first of its eight books deals with his boyhood. This does, however, represent the first attempt to depict childhood as it really is, with the mixture of naivety and perceptiveness that we find in actual children. Truth to tell, the boy Cyrus is too purely virtuous for the depiction to get far, and the adult Cyrus is so perfect a pattern of kingship that he cannot interest us much. The same problem afflicts the life of Agesilaus, which is such pure encomium that little sense of the man's character can emerge. The *Anabasis*, Xenophon's most famous work, has another odd title, literally 'Journey Up-Country', although most of it concerns the journey down. It is the vividly told story of how a Greek mercenary army stranded in the heart of Anatolia, deep within the Persian empire, found its way home. The cry of the soldiers when they first sight open water – 'The sea, the sea!' – remains one of the most famous moments in classical literature. Xenophon refers to himself in the third person, but he gives himself a large number of speeches and takes the leading role. This established a pattern for the military or political memoir that lasted, as far as we can judge, throughout antiquity.

Rhetoric was the art of persuasion. As Cicero, writing with the authority that belonged to Rome's greatest orator, and others were to say, it had three purposes: to inform, to move and to delight. It should appeal to both reason and emotion. On this base two very different conceptions of rhetoric could be built. On one account, it was an ennobling art. The best orator is the man who can give his state the best advice. The Roman statesman Cato the Censor (234–149) defined the orator as a 'good man skilled at speaking'. Likewise Quintilian, who wrote his treatise on the education of an orator in the second half of the first century AD, declares that the orator must first of all be virtuous; the perfect orator must then combine the highest character with the most complete education; the nature of the perfect orator is wisdom. This exalted ideal had to compete with a more down-to-earth view. The aspirant orator learned to argue whatever case he was given (Roman education especially was based on this method of learning), and so the art of rhetoric could easily be represented as the ability to make the worse cause appear the better. And there is also a third idea of rhetoric, one that stresses the aesthetic element. Rhetoric is the study of using words as effectively as possible. In this view, literature as a whole can be analysed in rhetorical terms. And indeed, much classical poetry can be better appreciated once we see the element of advocacy in it.

These three ideas were not tidily separated in anyone's mind. Indeed, for all the attention that the ancients gave to the subject, arguably they never resolved the conflict between oratory as wisdom and oratory as deceit. That conflict was brilliantly exposed by Plato in his *Gorgias* (ironically, we must admire the forensic skill with which he has Socrates puncture oratory's pretensions). We may be no better today: at least, modern lawyers seem able to combine the belief that they deliver justice with the confidence that they deserve enormous fees because of their power to alter the outcome. Cicero had a lofty idea of his calling, but he was also ready to boast that he had thrown dust in a jury's eyes.

Classical oratory can be divided into two classes: speeches written for the law courts or political assemblies; and display or 'epideictic' oratory, written not to win a case or debate in the real world but to exhibit the speaker's skill. The Gorgias who gave his name to Plato's dialogue was an epideictic orator, a sophist from Sicily who came to Athens in the later fifth century BC and set himself up as a teacher of rhetoric. Two short specimens of his art survive, one of them being an exercise in paradox which praises Helen for her adultery. For law court or assembly there are extant speeches written in Athens in the late fifth and the fourth centuries by more than a dozen different hands. Ten of these orators are known by name; the other speeches have survived because they were wrongly attributed to one of them. The most attractive of the earlier orators is Lysias (450s or 440s–c.380). Not being an Athenian citizen (his father had migrated from Sicily), he wrote words for litigants and defendants to speak in court. The aim was to sound guileless and sincere; so he needed the art that conceals art and the gift of ventriloquism. Of especial interest today is the speech he wrote for a man who had killed his wife's lover, for the vivid if dispiriting picture it gives of an Athenian home and a woman's place in it. But his finest oration is one that he wrote, untypically, to speak himself. An attack on the oligarch who had killed his brother, it is eloquently plain and powerful. It ends tersely, with five successive verbs: 'Enough prosecution. You-have-heard, you-have-seen, you-have-suffered, you-have-him. Judge.'

Isocrates (436–338) began as an advocate in the courts, but later turned himself into a teacher of rhetoric. His most important works are essays on political themes, cast in the form of speeches. The central political issue of the fourth century was what to do about the rise of Macedon, and the ambitions of its king, Philip II; while some struggled to preserve the freedom and independence of the Greek cities, Isocrates advocated a Panhellenic crusade against the Persians under Philip's leadership. His style is exceptionally self-conscious. He avoids hiatus, which occurs when a word ending in a vowel precedes a word beginning with a vowel, and he constructs complex sentences, with elaborate subordinations. The effect is like neoclassical marble, skilful and cold. The best orators of the fourth century, the Athenian politicians Aeschines (c.397–c.322) and Demosthenes (384–322), began as allies and turned into bitter enemies. Aeschines came to the view that Greece had to reach an

accommodation with Philip; Demosthenes remained uncompromising, and believed, probably unjustly, that Aeschines
had been suborned by bribery. Three substantial speeches of
Aeschines survive, but effective though they are, he is inevit-
ably overshadowed by his rival.

Some of Demosthenes' speeches were made on behalf of
private clients, and some of these disputes were petty indeed,
but it was part of the art of rhetoric to expend one's full skill
on even humdrum matters. His most memorable works,
however, are political. He was as careful of euphony as
Isocrates (he too usually avoids hiatus), while managing to
remain passionate and natural. His three *Olynthiacs* address
the crisis caused when the city of Olynthus defied Philip and
was destroyed by him. His three *Philippics* have added a word
to the languages of Europe. *On the Crown*, formally a law-
court speech in defence of an ally (Aeschines' prosecution
also survives), but in a reality a political apologia and credo,
is his greatest achievement. (The 'crown' of the title was an
honour which the ally had proposed should be awarded to
Demosthenes at a public festival.)

Modern readers of this speech may be surprised at the
amount of space that Demosthenes gives to personal attack
on Aeschines, and the number of blows below the belt – his
opponent's humble origins and his lousy performances in his
earlier career as an actor. Part of the explanation is that the
audiences for speeches were connoisseurs of rhetoric, and
that even when grave matters were at stake they looked for a
kind of entertainment, or at least enlivenment. But the sin-
cerity of Demosthenes' loathing also comes through. This
apart, the oration is predominantly noble and energetic. It

ranges widely, including narrative (the evening when the news reached Athens that Philip had seized the city of Elatea), historical retrospect and, above all, a passionate fusion of patriotism and proud self-worth. Demosthenes does not deign to make himself likeable, for he had a bolder aim: to compel us to admire his intransigence.

Socrates separated philosophy entirely from natural science, and in this he was followed by Plato (c.429–347). Aristotle (384–320) too, although a scientist, kept his science apart from his abstract thinking. Plato was a well-born Athenian; Aristotle came from Stagira, an obscure town in Macedonia, but made his way to Athens to study as Plato's pupil. These are the two men from whom western philosophy as we know it descends, but the high praise bestowed on one of them has sometimes been accompanied by belittlement of the other. Here are two extreme views:

> The history of western philosophy can be described as a series of footnotes to Plato (A. N. Whitehead). He is the man who set the agenda. He is 'profoundly capacious in all his views' and embraces the small system of Aristotle as the solar system does the earth (Ruskin). His theory of forms is a hugely bold and creative attempt to make a single theory from which theories of mind, knowledge and ethics can be derived. Moreover, he goes beyond understanding: he provides passion and inspiration and reaches to the deepest parts of human experience. By comparison Aristotle appears earthbound, a worthy systematizer.

*

Aristotle was the greatest intellect of the ancient world, and perhaps of any age. His boundless curiosity embraced every area of philosophy and natural science, making contributions to the theory of knowledge, metaphysics, logic, politics, aesthetics and much more that remain lastingly important to this day. He combined the highest powers of mind with admirable judgement and the deepest kind of good sense: he is 'the master of them that know' (Dante) and in many fields 'to think correctly is to think like Aristotle' (Newman). If Plato was a genius, he was a crazy genius. None of his major ideas is even faintly plausible, and his political theory, if taken seriously, is repellent (especially, but not only, in his last and longest work, the *Laws*) and seems completely divorced from any understanding of human nature as it actually is.

All these claims have been made by intelligent and well-informed people. But most philosophers today would rank Plato and Aristotle among the very greatest of their number in the history of the west; some would consider them to be the two greatest of all. The speed and force with which philosophy as we know it got under way in the fourth century is even more remarkable than the birth of history in the fifth. We might reflect ourselves on the fact that philosophers have not yet agreed on any of the matters which these Greek thinkers brought to the table. Philosophy got off to a dazzling start; sometimes it can seem that only the last 2,300 years have been a little disappointing.

There is a notion that the world is divided into Platonists and Aristotelians: that, in Coleridge's words, 'they are the two classes of men next to which it is almost impossible to conceive a third'. This conception pits a Platonist tradition, lofty, transcendent, ideal, against an Aristotelian tradition which is practical and empirical. But we should not let it mislead us. For all their differences, Aristotle was Plato's pupil, as Plato had been Socrates', and they agreed on what the range of philosophy was, and the way in which it should be approached. Epicurus (341–270), in the generation after Aristotle, tried another tack. He began with physics. We can show, he argued, that nothing exists except atoms, infinite in number, and space, infinite in extent. These scientific truths then generate philosophical conclusions: that there is no supernatural order, no metaphysics; the only thing that a person can rationally pursue is his own pleasure; death is a matter of pure indifference; and so on. In a sense Epicurus was continuing the Presocratic tradition: natural science and philosophy working together. He was a powerful influence for several centuries, but in the long run it was the Socratic idea, developed by the two fourth-century giants, which would prevail. Without them, the story might have been quite different.

Although Aristotle's surviving works are voluminous, there was once even more. According to Cicero, his dialogues, which have perished, flowed like a river of gold – yet another aspect to this extraordinary man. No one would say that of the Aristotle that we know: the style of the extant works is flat and telegraphic. Yet we should not entirely write them off from the aesthetic point of view. Their very terseness has its own kind of force. It is hard to read the *Nicomachean Ethics*, for example, without being impressed by its density: no word is wasted, almost every sentence brings something pertinent and new.

Plato, for his part, was a literary artist of a high order. It is tempting to regard Plato as the patron saint of those for whom philosophy is an art, Aristotle of those for whom it is a science. Certainly, it was Plato's idea that understanding should come from the interplay of minds and personalities; his works are dialogues, and he never expresses any view in his own person. In most of them Socrates is the principal speaker, but in a few, probably late, he takes a lesser part, and in the *Laws* he does not appear at all, the chief role being taken by an 'Athenian stranger'. The *Apology* (*Apologia*) purports to be the speech that Socrates gave in his defence when on trial for his life in 399. That is an exceptional case, but in what are probably the earliest dialogues the individual character of Socrates is an important part of the whole. Typically a moral question is posed and the only conclusion is negative: thus *Laches* asks, 'What is courage?' and *Euthyphro* asks, 'What is piety?' Socrates' interlocutors put forward their views, which crumble under his interrogation, and the company is left in uncertainty. In the works which are likely to belong to Plato's 'middle period', the dialogue form becomes more perfunctory: Socrates expounds his views at length, and the others interject a few words of agreement from time to time. Some of the dialogues contain 'myths', allegories or supernatural stories, sometimes playful and fantastical, sometimes almost mystical.

The early works are usually lively, sometimes openly humorous, and Plato's mastery of the dialogue form enabled him to put across quite difficult ideas with remarkable clarity. In

Meno he presents the strange doctrine of 'anamnesis': that we existed before we were born, and that we retain knowledge from that previous existence. He does this by having Socrates question Meno's slave. Socrates shows that the slave has mathematical knowledge, and since he has not been taught it in this life, he must have acquired it before birth. It would be wrong to call the dialogue comic, perhaps wrong even to call it humorous, but it has a vivacity to it, a twinkle in the eye. And it does what every teacher should strive for: to set out an argument as lucidly and attractively as the nature of the subject allows. Some dialogues are especially generous in material that is not strictly philosophical: *Protagoras* gives an amusing picture of intellectuals and their coterie, and *Phaedrus* is set idyllically beside the River Ilissus. Most lavish of all in this respect is the *Symposium* (*sumposion*, 'drinking party' – not a symposium in the English sense). Towards the end the notorious Alcibiades reels in drunk and praises Socrates as his good angel; later the narrator who is recalling these events remembers falling asleep and waking towards daybreak; Socrates is still talking, telling Aristophanes that a good comic dramatist can write a tragedy and vice versa.

The *Symposium* is less a dialogue than a series of speeches on the nature of love; a prosaic physician gives one of them, a sentimental poet another. The most entertaining of these speeches is given to Aristophanes. He tells a fable. Originally human beings were spherical creatures each with two sets of genitals. Some of them had one male and one female set, while in others both sets were of the same sex. The gods then split each of these creatures into two, and ever since humans have been going round searching for their other half. Love is accordingly 'the desire and pursuit of the whole'. It is fitting that this tale should be put into the mouth of a comic playwright of exuberantly fantastic spirit, although we actually have nothing surviving from Aristophanes which is like this: we must suppose it to come wholly from Plato's own imagination.

Inside the comedy there are serious and original ideas. One of these is that people are inherently either homo- or heterosexual. That is a familiar notion to us, but it is rare to find it in antiquity. Another concept that Plato's Aristophanes presents is an ideal of romantic love: there is an ideal partner for each man and woman, a 'perfect fit', and sexual love offers a unique possibility of human wholeness. This shows us a good deal about the range and depth of Plato's thought. These are conceptions that have been developed and adopted many centuries after him. They are also conceptions that he himself rejects. But he has discovered them and presented them, and all within a context of high absurdity. He has, as it were, lured us into thinking deeply when we supposed we were only being entertained.

In this work Plato is not content with a negative outcome: he wants to assert positively what love is. The dialogue form does not give him the means to do this, and in any case he perhaps wants to go beyond reasoned argument to instinct and intuition; so he turns to a new device. When Socrates comes to speak, he does not set out his own argument; instead he proclaims the truth about love as it has been revealed to him by a priestess, Diotima. She does this partly through one of Plato's myths: Love is the child of Contrivance and

Poverty, conceived on the day that Aphrodite was born, not beautiful, but scruffy and resourceful. She then declares what the progress of love should be: one should proceed from the love of a beautiful individual to the love of all beautiful persons, then to the love of activities and institutions, and finally attain an initiation into the highest beauty, which is abstract and absolute. It is hard to square this with actual human experience, and yet there are extraordinary insights. Through Diotima, Plato describes love as 'procreation in the beautiful'; he has recognized the intimate connection of the creative and the sexual impulse in the human psyche.

The *Republic* combines the 'early' and the 'middle' Plato. The first two of its ten books could stand alone as a dialogue of the early type. The question posed is, 'What is justice?' Socrates refutes the proposals of his interlocutors, the chief of whom is a sophist, Thrasymachus, who advocates the theory that might is right. He is routed, but at this point, although we have learned some things that justice is not, we have learned nothing about what it is. That question is explored in the rest of the work in Plato's middle manner, with Socrates providing an essentially continuous exposition. The *Republic* covers a vast range of topics, but the unifying factor is Plato's theory of forms, which generates his moral theory, political theory and theory of knowledge.

Historians have been divided into 'lumpers' and 'splitters'. Lumpers believe that one principle (class struggle, say) explains all history, splitters hold that history is incorrigibly plural and complex. If philosophers can be divided along the same lines, Plato joins his polar opposite, Epicurus, among the lumpers: at this stage of his career at least, he has a single theory which unifies all aspects of philosophical enquiry. Like two works which we shall visit later in this book, Virgil's *Georgics* and Apuleius' *Golden Ass*, the *Republic* has a finale which is quite unlike the rest of the work and yet deeply satisfying. The subject is now the immortality of the soul, and Socrates abandons all pretence of dialogue to tell the Myth of Er, who died and came to life again, bringing with him the vision that he had received of the nature of the universe and the afterlife of the dead. And thus the long discourse at last breaks through, like no other philosophical work, into a final radiance.

The century after Plato and Aristotle saw the rise of rival schools of philosophy, of which the most prominent were Stoicism, founded by Zeno of Citium (335–263), and Epicureanism. A few minor works of Epicurus survive, and we can know a good deal about his physical theory from its later adaptation to Latin verse by Lucretius. Although the Stoics pursued virtue, and the Epicureans pleasure, both schools aimed at a negative ideal, *apatheia* ('not-feeling') and *ataraxia* ('not-being-disturbed') respectively. They are philosophies of salvation, maintaining that within the citadel of the soul the wise man, enlightened by their teachings, can be unassailably safe and happy. Adherence to these schools had some of the characteristics of religious commitment. Their importance to literary history lies in the way that they informed the lives and thoughts of educated people, especially in Rome.

The Hellenistic Age

'Hellenistic' is a handy label given by modern scholarship to the period between the death of Alexander in 323 BC and the victory of the future emperor Augustus over Mark Antony at the Battle of Actium in 31. With Alexander dead, his vast empire split into 'successor kingdoms', of which the most important, from a literary point of view, was Egypt, which was ruled by a Macedonian dynasty of kings all called Ptolemy until the last ruler, Cleopatra. On her death in 30, Egypt became part of the Roman empire, suffering the fate which the other successor kingdoms and the few surviving city-states had already met, and the last of Greek independence was extinguished.

Alexandria, the capital of the Ptolemys, became a centre of intellectual energy in the third century. The kings founded a library, the most famous in the ancient world, and the Museum ('place of the Muses') – not a museum in the modern sense but a kind of literary research institute. Eratosthenes, appointed head of the library in the later part of the century, was the greatest polymath of his time, a literary scholar, philosopher, geographer, poet and mathematician. He calculated the circumference of the earth, with remarkable accuracy. Although exceptional, his career illustrates the range of

Alexandrian 'scholarship' – if that somewhat cold word is understood to represent a wide-ranging intellectual curiosity. None of his works has survived, and we know about him only indirectly. Several hundred thousand words of Hellenistic prose are still extant, but most of them are translation of Hebrew scripture. Since little other prose of the early Hellenistic age remains, our impression of its literature is lopsided. But we do have at least some works by three poets active in Alexandria in the first half of the third century. They are Theocritus, Callimachus and Apollonius of Rhodes; none of them can be dated precisely.

Callimachus hailed from Cyrene, in what is now eastern Libya. He was a scholar and lexicographer, he catalogued the library of Alexandria, and he wrote on geography, ethnography and much more besides. Scholar poets have tended to keep the two aspects of their being apart (Hopkins and Housman, for example), but Callimachus' originality was to bring scholarship into his verse. In language and theme he cultivated quirkiness, the unexpected, the recherché. All that has come down in a manuscript tradition is about sixty elegiac epigrams and six hymns, revivals in a modern manner of the genre of the 'Homeric hymn', but papyrus finds have revealed a good deal more. His thirteen *Iambi* mingled invective in the manner of Hipponax with other material. *Hecale*, a short epic poem, about a thousand lines long, dealt with Theseus' heroic exploit of capturing the bull of Marathon, but its focus was on the humble old woman with whom he lodged and who gives her name to the work. This exemplifies a Hellenistic liking for modest and domestic themes, with a touch of sentimentality, as well as Callimachus' search for the unusual angle.

His largest work was *Origins* (*Aitia*, literally 'Causes'), in its final form four books long. This was a string of mythological just so stories explaining the origins of various customs and ceremonies; there were also two prominent passages in praise of Ptolemy III's queen Berenice, for Callimachus was, among other things, a court poet. The theme gave him ample opportunity for antiquarian scholarship, and he embraced it enthusiastically and (one may feel) disconcertingly. Thus the reader who turns to the love story of Acontius and Cydippe, the best preserved section of *Origins*, hoping to drop a happy tear or two, may be surprised to meet this:

> We heard of this your love from old Xenomedes, who set down the whole island in a mythological record, beginning with how it was inhabited by Corycian nymphs . . . and how those dwelt there whose rites Zeus Alalaxios always receives with the blare of trumpets, Carians along with Leleges, and how Ceos, son of Phoebus and Melia, caused it to take another name . . . and how of four cities Megacles walled Carthaea, and Eupylus, son of Chryso . . .

And so on, and on. The dryness is presumably intentional.

Homer had begun with wrath; Callimachus begins with a wrangle. It was certainly a new note. He opens with a counter-attack on his critics, whom he calls Telchines; these were spiteful, and perhaps rather obscure, mythological sorcerers. 'Often the Telchines grumble at my song,' he begins – on the grounds that he has not written one continuous poem in thousands of lines. He hits back: Mimnermus was better on the smaller scale; verse should be judged by its craft not by measurement. Apollo has told him that he should fatten up a sacrificial animal but keep his Muse slender; he should drive his chariot not on the wide tracks used by many others but along untrodden ways, even if they be narrow. At the end of his *Hymn to Apollo* he strikes a similar note: the god gave Envy a kick, and declared that the Euphrates was a big stream, but it carried a lot of dirt and garbage. This is contrasted with a slight stream from a sacred spring, pure and undefiled.

What then did Callimachus stand for? In the past it has been thought that he took up a strongly distinctive position, with a definite rejection of large-scale verse (although *Origins* was several thousand lines long) and the polemical assertion that art should be for art's sake alone. But it now seems likely that his claim was more general, and that he was appealing to all people of good sense. Clearly he prized originality: the paths where others have not been. He condemned turgidity, insisted that quality is what counts, and maintained that length is not valuable in itself. The tone may be combative, but the message is sweetly reasonable.

Callimachus also wrote elegiac epigrams. This genre had perhaps the longest continuous life of any literary form in western history, lasting more than a millennium and a half from the seventh century BC until deep into the Byzantine age. It can be hard to tell whether a particular epigram comes from the third century BC or the sixth century AD, but many of the best writers are of Hellenistic date; Asclepiades, Leonidas of Tarentum and Meleager of Gadara were three of the most accomplished. The form suited Callimachus too, bringing out a side of him that sought simplicity more than piquant effect. The polemical note is not absent ('I hate the cyclic poem,' one piece begins), but some pieces are erotic, and the funerary epigrams are especially notable. Six lines on one Heracleitus are his best-known work in the English-speaking world, thanks to the much anthologized nineteenth-century translation by William Cory ('They told me, Heraclitus, they told me you were dead'); readers who look back to the original will find it more economical. One epitaph is only a single couplet: 'Here Philippus a father laid his twelve-year-old son, his great hope, Nicoteles.' The Greek word order, in very literal word-for-word translation, is this:

Twelve-year-old the child father put-away Philippus
here, the much hope, Nicoteles.

The words conveying a general truth, 'child' and 'father', are put together, and then particularity is given by the two names, one at the end of each line. The sentence gives the bare facts; even the 'much hope' is factual, but it has more colour, and is reticently put into parenthesis before the dead boy's name makes the close. The restraint of this is the product of high sophistication.

Large claims have been made for Callimachus: he has been called the greatest Hellenistic poet, and even one of the great poets of the world. So far at least, such claims have been asserted not argued, and they are hard to credit. The overvaluing of Callimachus owes much to the idea that he vastly influenced the Roman poets of the first century BC, but this belief in turn is based on the assumption that, because they used him or alluded to him, they must have deeply admired him. Catullus translated a piece of his court poetry but, on his own account, because he wanted an exercise that would not engage his emotions. Virgil toyed wittily with the opening of Callimachus' *Origins* in his *Bucolics*, and dismissed him in his *Georgics*. Propertius announced that he was going to leave the theme of love to follow in the footsteps of Callimachus and Philitas, another Hellenistic poet, but this was a joke or a feint. In his last book, he called himself 'the Roman Callimachus', but this meant that he was now tackling Callimachus' subject matter, origins.

Ovid's judgement is especially interesting. The Romans liked to make a distinction between *ingenium* and *ars*. *Ingenium* can sometimes be translated 'genius', but commonly is not quite as strong: it covers the range suggested in English by 'talent', 'brilliance', 'flair'. *Ars* is not as wide-ranging as the English word 'art' derived from it; it means 'technique', or 'craftsmanship'. Callimachus will endure, Ovid said, because 'although he is not strong in *ingenium*, he is strong in *ars*'. That was faint praise. These Romans found Callimachus interesting, but there is no good evidence that they worshipped him.

Theocritus was born in Sicily but made his way to Alexandria at an unknown stage of his career. He called his poems *eidullia*, 'idylls'; the word means 'sketch' and does not carry the connotations of English 'idyll'. One of these pieces is a dialogue mostly between two bourgeois ladies of Alexandria who chatter together and then make their way through the packed streets, fussing and being jostled, to attend a sacred concert about the death of Adonis. This is one of the most appealing realizations of the Hellenistic taste for representing ordinary people and ordinary life; it is also perhaps the first literary work to enjoy the busyness of a great city. Although the women complain about the crowds and the discomfort, they are clearly having a good time, and so is the poet. Another poem with an implicitly urban setting begins, 'Where are my bay leaves? Bring them, Thestylis.' The whole poem is spoken by a woman who is performing magic rituals to bring back her faithless lover. Here is something else new: the dramatic monologue.

Theocritus' small oeuvre also includes a few good mythological pieces, but he is best known for his poems about the countryside, mostly in the form of dialogues between herdsmen. They do not exclude coarse raillery and sexual frankness, but the predominant flavour is one of elegance, and the figures in this landscape seem to inhabit a place of their own, undisturbed by the changes and chances of the world beyond. Theocritus could even give a pastoral colour to a monster from myth: in the eleventh Idyll, the song of the Cyclops, he turns Polyphemus, the cannibal of the *Odyssey*, into a lovelorn swain, wooing the sea-nymph Galatea with rustic gaucherie. The Cyclops' serenade is framed by the poet's address to his friend, the physician Nicias: there is no medicine to cure love, other than the Muses; thus Polyphemus 'shepherded' his love – better at least than paying a quack. This graceful banter sets the Cyclops at a distance: we sophisticates smile at his charming *naïveté*. It is a device that could easily be patronizing, but Theocritus has the tact and taste to bring it off.

The first Idyll is a dialogue between Thyrsis and an unnamed goatherd. The two men begin by setting the scene in sounds – the musical whisper of the pine tree by the waters, the piping of the goatherd, and Thyrsis' singing, sweeter than the plashing stream that tumbles over the rocks. The sound of the verses themselves is exquisitely melodious, with onomatopoeia, echo and half echo, pure beauty of surface enjoyed for its own sake. The poem's main subject is two works of art, one visual, one musical. The goatherd describes a carved wooden cup, which he will give Thyrsis in return for his singing the song of Daphnis. That song then occupies the poem's greater part.

Theocritus here explores the nature of art. The scenes on the cup include a fisherman straining as he gathers up his net for a cast, a fox stealing grapes, a boy plaiting rushes to make a cage for a grasshopper, a woman between two lovers, turning now to one, now to the other. These images represent either a moment in a rapid action, caught and frozen as by a snapshot, or action in time which sculpture cannot literally represent at all (the woman moving back and forth). There is an interplay between nature and artifice: the images struggle to escape from their static being and 'come alive', while at the same time we are shown that this liveliness is the product of the artist's virtuosity.

Thyrsis' song is likewise a concert performance, a showpiece. Like a concert aria it comes without context or explanation. Daphnis lies dying, while a maiden wanders searching every glade; the beasts lament him; shepherds, gods and nymphs visit him, with enigmatic or sorrowing questions; and, at last, 'Daphnis went to the stream, and the current closed over him.' It is all plangent and affecting, and yet it is a fiction, not reality, even within the fiction of Theocritus' poem. There is a subtle shift of register: Thyrsis' own world, however idyllic, is essentially naturalistic; Daphnis' world includes the goatherds and neatherds of Thyrsis' own experience, but has no solidity: it is riddling, evanescent and haunted by divinity. It is presented as poetry, not life, and yet is strangely beautiful. Theocritus has created a new aesthetic, one in which by some alchemy the poet's self-consciousness does not diminish the poignancy but enhances it. We are made aware of the artifice, and moved by the very virtuosity of the creator. It is an aesthetic which was to be recreated, as we shall see, in Roman poetry.

The seventh Idyll is Theocritus' most elusive work. It is set on the island of Cos; a narrator tells how he walked from town with a couple of friends and met a mysterious goatherd, Lycidas. Some hidden meaning seems to lie below the surface. After the goatherd has left them, the walkers arrive at a farm, lie down and drink wine. The poem now concludes by describing this place with unprecedented richness of effect, painting a picture, but also making music. The air is full of sounds: elms and poplars murmur, water plashes, cicadas chatter, frogs croak, finches sing, doves moan, bees hum. There is fruitage: pears and apples rolling at the visitors' feet, branches drooping under their load of sloes. And there are scents: the friends repose on sweet rushes and new-cut vine leaves, and 'all things smelt of the fatness of summer, smelt of fruit-time'. The senses unify in an evocation of juiciness, sappiness, heaviness, pleasant weariness. There is a slumberous blur and at the same time a searching for exactness: the summer – no, more precisely, the harvest time. And there is just a touch of the divine: a cave of the nymphs nearby, an altar of Demeter, nymphs mixing the wine that the companions enjoy. This is an extraordinary fusion, at once the portrait of a landscape, realized in exquisitely melodious language, and an exploration of human affect, of a mood of woozy enchantment. There had been nothing quite like this in literature before.

Theocritus is famous as the inventor of pastoral poetry, but to say this is a kind of anachronism. For pastoral literature, as it has developed since, is not simply writing about country life: it is writing about the country in a certain kind of way, a conscious latching on to a tradition, observing certain forms and conventions. Now, Theocritus could not follow pastoral traditions or conventions because before him they did not exist. Far from laying down the pattern for a new genre, he was discovering his own special sensibility. His verse shows the free flight of the imagination, not convention's chains. He is the one Hellenistic poet who significantly enlarged the range of poetic possibility; he discovered a particular kind of poise, in which engagement and detachment, distance and detail, charm of surface and warmth of feeling are combined.

Apollonius of Rhodes, despite his name, was a native of Alexandria itself; how he got his sobriquet is uncertain. He too was a scholar: he wrote studies of Homer and Hesiod, and became head of the Alexandrian library. His verse included *Foundations*, poems about cities, which presumably displayed an interest in origins and cultic practices shared with Callimachus. All his works are lost except for the *Argonautica*

('Story of the Argonauts'), an epic in four books. Jason voyages on the ship *Argo* with a band of heroes (the Argonauts) to Colchis, on the eastern side of the Black Sea, in search of the Golden Fleece. Medea, daughter of the king of Colchis, falls in love with him, and with her help he wins the prize. She flees with him and his men, and the last book recounts their circuitous return to Greece.

'Scholarship' in the broad sense is visible in this poem also. Apollonius gives an extensive description of the unique character of the River Thermodon (an obscure stream in what is now northern Turkey). The last book reworks the wanderings of Odysseus (rather too rapidly), but it takes the Argonauts even further, along the Danube, up the Po, down the Rhône and to North Africa. This improbable journey owes much to the Alexandrian spirit of enquiry and interest in geography and ethnography. It also gave Apollonius chances to use his considerable descriptive powers. Especially memorable is his picture of the treacherous Syrtis on the African coast, the shoals and seaweed, the dim expanse of sand, the mist merging into land like mist, the desolation – no beast, no bird – and everything held (phrase of sinister amiability) in an 'easy calm'.

But Apollonius is a puzzle: when the best parts are so good, it is odd that much of the poem should be so dull. His poker face is exemplified by the episode that takes up much of the first book. The Argonauts reach the isle of Lemnos, where the women have killed all their menfolk because they had preferred slave girls to themselves. Hypsipyle, their queen, welcomes Jason, and the pair become lovers. After a time, Heracles complains that the company are neglecting their adventure. Jason agrees to leave, Hypsipyle weeps for the loss of her man but speeds him graciously on his way, and he replies by saying that if she should find herself with a son by him, she should send him when he is grown to his grandparents in mainland Greece. The telling glides over both the bizarre aspect of the story (would you sleep with a mass murderess?) and its possibilities of pathos. The flatness must be a matter of deliberate choice – Homer's Odysseus tells much of his tale with a certain coolness, and Apollonius may have been seeking to emulate him – but it still seems a little disappointing. This episode was to have a spectacular afterlife, for it provided the story pattern for Virgil's tragedy of Dido in the *Aeneid*.

The finest moment in the first book comes when Hylas, the youth beloved of Heracles, goes to draw water and is taken by the nymph of the pool into its depths. It is night; the moon is full, the boy rosy with beauty, the enamoured nymph's spirit faint within her; she lays an arm on his neck, longing to kiss him, and pulls him down into her eddies. It is a wan, etiolated scene with just one sharp moment: the hard ring of the water as it splashes into Hylas' pot of bronze. This erotic episode anticipates the second half of the work. Medea enters the story, and at once the poem leaps into life. It becomes very largely a love story, as perhaps no epic had been before, and with the focus on the woman. Apollonius' Medea is another acratic heroine, torn between duty to her father and her passion for Jason, but she is also touchingly young, not the virago of Euripides. Her heart beats fast with love and anxiety for Jason, as a sunbeam quivers in a house, reflected from a bucket of water newly poured – the simile is just right for her innocence and agitation. In a rather ponderous speech of courtship Jason promises her future fame and glory at some length, but is cunning enough to end by telling her how pretty she is; that, the poet notes, is what worked. Her mixture of emotions is finely studied: shame, pride, even a hint that she hates Jason, a desire for selfless sacrifice, and despair. She wants to die, but then the fear of death hits her, and she abandons the thought. She delights in the 'heart-pleasing care of life', a nicely paradoxical phrase, and the light of the sun becomes sweeter to her than ever. We also see a youthful resilience as she forgets her cares and summons her maidens to her, almost as if she were Nausicaa.

We should perhaps see the *Argonautica* as an experimental poem, in some respects deliberately Homeric, in others modernist, with a hero who sometimes seems oddly passive, and who yields in interest to the heroine, once she has made her entrance. The story comes to no great climax, and the ending is strangely casual: no adventures on the last stage of the journey, but an easy run past Attica, up through the channel between Euboea and the mainland, and so home. This is the only Hellenistic epic that we have; there were plenty more, but Apollonius' seems always to have been regarded as by far the best.

A papyrus find has resurrected one more poet working in Alexandria in the mid-third century, Herondas, a writer of verse dialogues, who like Theocritus depicted ordinary urban life, but with a deliberately coarse grain: a pimp prosecutes one of his clients, a mother takes her son to a schoolmaster to be flogged, two ladies discuss the merits of a high-quality dildo. Roughly contemporary with the Alexandrian poets, but active elsewhere in the Greek world, principally in Macedon, was Aratus (c.315–c.245). His one surviving work is *Phaenomena* (the title refers to celestial objects), a didactic poem on astronomy and weather signs. It opens proudly: 'From Zeus let us begin . . .' This is one of those places where paganism adopts a tone that seems near to monotheism. Full of Zeus are all the streets and markets, the sea and harbours; we are also his offspring. He is kindly to men, guiding them in all their doings. There is a kinship with Psalm 139 in the Hebrew scriptures, with its assertion of the universal and all-encompassing presence of God. But there is a difference: the Psalmist declares that God knows his inmost thoughts, whereas the Greek philosophies maintained that the mind was wholly autonomous, guarded even from deity.

After this introduction the poet soon settles to his astronomical business. Its later part, on weather prognostications, allows him brief and attractive pictures of the natural world: oxen sniffing the air before the approach of rain, and ants hurriedly carrying their eggs out from their nests; mist wrapping the base of a mountain that shines clear at the peak. It was very widely read for centuries, and translated several times into Latin, by Cicero among others, and St Paul is made to quote from it in the Acts of the Apostles. This huge success has surprised some modern readers, but Aratus has had bad luck in being overshadowed by two later men from a barbarous land: Lucretius and Virgil were to lift the didactic poem to improbable heights. The former ignored him entirely; in the *Georgics* Virgil not only outdid him in charm and technique but his imitation occupies only part of one book, so that all of Aratus becomes only a minor part of a much greater scheme. But taken on its own terms his poem is an accomplished piece.

The verse surviving from the later part of the Hellenistic age makes a mixed bag. The only substantial piece of tragedy remaining is part of a play telling the Exodus story by a Jewish author named Ezechiel. From the early second century comes Lycophron's *Alexandra*, a dramatic monologue uttered by the prophetess Cassandra, a work of wilful and rebarbative obscurity, and at nearly fifteen hundred lines the longest non-narrative speech in classical literature. Two didactic poems by Nicander also remain, *Theriaca* ('Venomous Animals') and *Alexipharmaca* ('Remedial Drugs'). Both are about poisons and their antidotes – snakes arthropods in the first case, plants, minerals and some animals in the other – and they are not much more attractive than this description would suggest. Part also survives of his *Georgica* ('Farming'), which at least provided a title for Virgil. A few poets at this time picked up themes and motifs from Theocritus' idylls. One was Moschus, whose best poem is *Europa*, a brightly decorative piece of short mythological narrative. Another was Bion, who wrote a pastorally coloured lament for Adonis. A third, anonymous author in turn wrote a lament for Bion; this is historically important for English literature as the model for the pastoral laments for dead poets by Spenser, Milton, Shelley and Arnold. These writers are conventionally known as the 'Greek bucolic poets', but they are better classed as followers of Theocritus, imitators of a particular master rather than practitioners of an established genre.

The remains of Hellenistic prose are disparate in time and character. Probably from the first century BC is the anonymous *Wisdom of Solomon*, the most accomplished of Jewish writings in Greek, influenced by Greek rhetoric and handsomely adorned with metaphor. It also uses a technique that appealed to Lucretius: the wrong view is put with great eloquence, only to be calmly crushed by the truth. So the deluded are allowed to luxuriate in cultivated hedonism and pessimism, assured that life is a passing shadow with nothing beyond it, to be answered at last by the assertion that the souls of the righteous are in the hand of God, and that the godless shall be punished. Lucretius, of course, used this method in the opposite direction.

The only Hellenistic historian to survive in significant quantity is Polybius (200–118), and of him too the greater part is lost. His subject was Rome and the rise of its empire. A narrative historian, he was also keenly analytic. Rome's success, he concluded, owed much to its constitution being mixed, part monarchic, part aristocratic, part democratic. And he looked beyond the legalities to behaviour: brilliance of display and a kind of high theatricality were distinctive to Roman public life, he maintained. There is an anticipation here of Walter Bagehot's insight, in the nineteenth century, that a constitution benefits from having a dignified as well as an efficient part. As for religion, whereas fear of the divine was disapproved of in other states, in Rome it was encouraged as a matter of policy. The fickle and violent emotions of the mob were kept in check by invisible terrors, while grand public spectacles promoted social cohesion. His theory of the mixed constitution was to have a long afterlife, but equally interesting is his recognition that style and sentiment are also important within a society.

Any account of the later Hellenistic age is bound to be scrappy. Although that is partly due to the accidents of transmission, there is no escaping the fact of decline, in poetry especially. The seams had been richly mined and they were now exhausted. However, there is another way of looking at the matter, for it might be said that Hellenism was to enjoy a new literary flowering, but from another people and in another language: in the later third century Latin literature began. On one account, Rome triumphed: for some centuries its literature, and its poetry above all, became far superior to anything that the Greeks were doing at the time. On another account, the whole of Roman civilization was a subspecies of a greater Hellenism, the continuation of that great formative culture which the Greeks had created. Both accounts are in their way true.

The Roman Republic

'O Solon, Solon,' said the Egyptian priest, 'you Greeks are always children, and there is no Greek who is old . . . You are all young in your souls, and you have in them no ancient belief handed down by old tradition nor any knowledge that is hoary with age.' Plato tells this story in his dialogue *Timaeus*, and its significance is that it is a Greek story: the Greeks saw themselves as new, in contrast to the unchanging, immemorial depth of Egyptian civilization. They were right at least in this, that almost everything that matters most in Greek literature was radically innovative. Latin literature, however, was written beneath the looming presence of the Greek achievement, which like the upas tree threatened to blight everything in its shadow. From the start it was therefore haunted by a kind of self-consciousness that had hardly existed in Greece until the fourth century BC, and not greatly even then. For the first time an entire culture was modelled on another, and a whole literature imitated forms and themes that had been created in an alien tongue. An original achievement of the Romans was to invent imitation.

A peculiar success of the Greeks had been to make their culture so attractive that every people with whom they came into contact wanted to be part of it. No literature survives in Lydian or Lycian or other such languages of the eastern Mediterranean, and none seems ever to have existed. These peoples became Hellenized, and they began to write in Greek. A partial exception was the Jews, who had long possessed a great literature in Hebrew, but even they took up the new world language. In due course, probably by the end of the second century, the Hebrew scriptures had been turned into Greek, forming a collection which became known as the Septuagint, from the Latin for 'seventy', supposedly from the number of translators engaged on the work; and the books which became the Christian Apocrypha were written in Greek in the first place. The Romans never imposed their own language on the eastern half of their empire, where Greek remained the lingua franca. As late as the 50s BC Cicero could say that Latin had spread barely beyond its heartland, whereas a poem in Greek could be read wherever the Romans' weaponry had spread the Romans' power.

Should it then be a surprise that any Latin literature exists at all? The first Roman gentlemen to attempt literary work, such as Fabius Pictor and Cincius Alimentus, naturally wrote in Greek, and they wrote what was appropriate for a gentleman to write, that is, history. The first works of Latin verse, as later Romans saw it, were composed in the second half of the third century by a Greek, Livius Andronicus, who had been brought to Rome as a prisoner of war, a slave. He translated the *Odyssey*, and composed the first literary hymn in his adopted language. Ennius (239–169), whom the Romans would come to reckon their first great poet, came from Rudiae, in the heel of Italy. Southern Italy had been settled by Greek colonists; it was indeed known as Magna Graecia, 'greater Greece', and its principal towns were Greek-speaking.

Ennius himself said that he had three hearts, because he knew three languages, Latin, Greek and Oscan (a south Italian tongue). His origins placed him in the Hellenistic milieu, and had he written in Greek he could have had an audience all over that world. But he chose Latin. On one account that was a momentous decision, without which Latin literature might not have got going at all. Yet this story is not quite believable. A city that was conquering the world was bound to acquire aesthetic ambitions, and it would not for ever be content to express them in an alien tongue. Russian aristocrats spoke French in the eighteenth and nineteenth centuries, but in the end a vernacular Russian literature was bound to break through; and it was never the case that Roman ladies and gentlemen spoke a foreign language to one another as the Russians did.

'Captive Greece took her savage conqueror captive, and brought the arts to rustic Latium' – Horace's *bon mot* summed the matter up. Latin literature flourished, but in some ways remained a dependency. Its poetry is saturated in Greek mythology; most surprisingly, all classical Latin verse was to be written in Greek metres; not until late antiquity did that begin to change. This is the more remarkable in that Latin differs from Greek in two important respects. It has fewer short syllables; and it was spoken with a stress accent. Latin verse scans by quantity (longs and shorts), as Greek does, and so in each line the pattern of stressed and unstressed syllables may correspond to the feet or it may cut across them, as in music the stress may come on the strong beat of the bar or on a weak beat, in the effect that we call syncopation. Greek metres were, on the face of it, unsuitable to Latin, but the problem also opened up a new possibility: poets could introduce variety by mixing 'syncopated' and 'unsyncopated' feet. They could also create expressive effects: smoothness or drowsiness in unsyncopated lines, energy or effort where the syncopations were strong. Virgil was to become the supreme master of this metrical art.

From now on the history of classical literature becomes a history of two literatures, and one might expect to find a constant interplay between them henceforth. It is striking how little this was the case. Greek writers show small awareness that their Latin counterparts might have anything to teach them, and with few and minor exceptions Roman authors did not try to learn from their Greek contemporaries. The Augustan poets, for example, mined a very distant past: Horace went back to archaic Greece for his models, to Archilochus, Sappho and Alcaeus; Virgil to Homer and Hesiod. Even their interest in such Alexandrians as Theocritus and Callimachus took them back more than two centuries before their own time. The Romans were not, therefore, joining the Greeks in carrying forward a shared enterprise; rather Greek literature was for them already a classic object, essentially complete.

Latin literature was already self-conscious when Ennius described Homer appearing to him in a dream and declaring that his soul was now in Ennius' body. The poet Paul Valéry said that the nature of classicism is to come after; Proust suggested that nineteenth-century art had derived from self-contemplation a feeling of incompleteness that created its own novel beauty; both thoughts can be applied to the literature of Rome. And indeed Latin authors produced from their self-awareness some of their most fascinating effects. There is a charm in the sense of belatedness, the interplay of tradition and the original talent, an author's exploration of his relationship with the literature of the past. But this laid a trap into which some Roman writers, and rather more modern scholars, were to fall: there was a risk of literature becoming more about literature than about life, and even of being pleased when that occurred. We should perhaps be surprised that so many Latin writers succeeded in overcoming that danger.

Ennius tried many genres, and from his minor works one might suppose him to be a typical Hellenistic *littérateur*. He adapted the *Hedypatheia* of Archestratus, a versified good food guide, and translated Euhemerus, who had argued that the gods were really admired human beings who came to be regarded as gods after their deaths – a notion shocking to the pious mind. However, later Romans saw him as 'father Ennius', the rude ancestor from whose manly loins Latin poetry was engendered. Ovid declared him to be supreme in *ingenium*, rough in *ars*, the reverse of his judgement on Callimachus. An anecdote from very late antiquity tells that Virgil, asked why he was reading Ennius, replied that he was looking for the gold in the dung.

There does seem to have been a natural ruggedness to Ennius. Perhaps he was drawn to Latin because he felt suited to a language that was still raw as a literary medium. His masterpiece was the *Annals*, an epic poem on the history of

Rome. It begins magnificently. Dancing in the ancient world was typically a robust affair, and Ennius exploits that fact: 'Muses who with your feet thump great Olympus.' No other poem of antiquity opens with quite that note of rough energy. His fragments are mostly too short and disparate to allow us much sense of him; the most remarkable perhaps is a passage describing the dream of Ilia, the future mother of Romulus and Remus. Hitherto, dreams in literature had usually been stylized: thus Agamemnon's dream in the *Iliad* is a figure who stands by his bed and gives him a message. Here in the *Annals*, perhaps for the first time, is an attempt to represent a dream as it might actually be, surreal, inconsequential, disconnected.

The earliest Latin works surviving complete are comedies: the six of Terence (active 160s) and twenty by Plautus (active *c.*205–184). These were, overtly, adaptations from Greek New Comedy. Terence is frank about this in his prologues: the *Brothers*, he says, is based on an incident in a play by Diphilus (late fourth century) which Plautus had already turned into Latin. He explains that the *Girl from Andros* is made out of two plays by Menander, and defends himself against the critics who have objected to that. Their objection, we may notice, is not that he has been derivative, but that his adaptation has been too free. With these works we face the same problem as with New Comedy: how much belongs to the Greek original, how much to the Roman follower. There is only one place where a papyrus find allows direct comparison – between Menander and Plautus. We can at least say that the two Romans have rather different flavours. Terence offers the pleasures of clarity and elegance. These qualities are seen at their best in the *Brothers*: the contrast between the title roles – the indulgent and the severe father – is conventional, but gracefully done. Plautus is typically more exuberant, in language as in plot. The *Braggart Soldier* already conveys its flavour in its title and the name of the title role, Pyrgopolynices ('Fortress-Much-Victor').

Plautus' *Captives* is a comedy in more serious style. A brief epilogue observes that it is one of those rare comedies that make good men better: it contains no love story, no monkey-business with money or a suppositious child, no young fellow liberating a tart without his father's knowledge. That neatly shows the coin in which he typically dealt. A special charm attaches to the *Rope*, unusually set not in a Greek town but on a lonely seashore where some of the characters have been shipwrecked, which has a distinctive spirit of lyric fantasy.

The accidents of survival, which give such prominence to early comedy (there are no later Latin comedies extant), also tend to conceal that the second century was for the Romans their great age of tragedy; the two principal masters were Pacuvius (*c.*220–*c.*130) and Accius (170–*c.*86). The fragments are very few. The other important poet of the time was Lucilius (born 180). Well over a thousand lines of his have survived, but mostly in a multitude of very short excerpts, so that it remains difficult to assess him. The Romans came to regard him as essentially the founding figure of *satura*, a genre which they also considered to be uniquely Roman, without direct Greek precedent. Although this is the word from which our 'satire' derives, we should not assume that it necessarily carried the same meaning; the Romans themselves were unsure where the word came from, but their derivations suggest a melange or hotch-potch. The idea seems to have been of *satura* as an informal style of verse into which a mixture of topics could be flung. Horace was to discuss Lucilius in three of his own satires, and as we shall see, that view back from a later generation may perhaps give us the best insight into his literary character. Quite different were the 'Menippean satires' written by Varro. These were supposedly based on works by Menippus, a Greek Cynic philosopher of the third century about whom hardly anything is known, and were distinctive for mixing prose and verse. Varro's pieces seem to have been light essays on the vices and follies of his day.

The long-lived Varro (116–27) was an extraordinary polymath. He probably wrote more than any other Roman, and on a vast range of subjects: antiquarian matters, social, religious and literary history, law, philosophy, music, architecture and much more. Fragments apart, only two works remain: a treatise on agriculture (not very exciting) and parts of a long study of the Latin language. His range and energy made him unignorable; whether his was a genuinely powerful mind is more doubtful. But his was one of the two dominant intellectual voices in the last decades of the Republic; the other belonged to Cicero.

Cicero (106–43) too was a master of several trades. He early established himself as the leading orator in Rome. He was elected consul at the earliest legal age, in which office he crushed the conspiracy of Catiline. From then on, he was in one way or another on the losing side in the political battle, but he remained a significant force: the men who exercised real power wanted to have his support. Besides his published speeches, he was a prolific author of philosophy, poetry and rhetorical theory. However, his dominance of the age, in our eyes, is owed partly to two accidents. First, he is the only orator of the republican period whose speeches survive (we have all or part of fifty-eight); unlike Demosthenes, he stands in splendid isolation. Second, a large part of his correspondence is extant. We have more than nine hundred letters. About three hundred of these are from Cicero to his lifelong friend Atticus; the other side of this correspondence has perished. The remainder are mostly to friends, family and people of public importance; some are letters from others to him; a few are written to public bodies, or designed for a multiple readership, but the great majority are simply private. Apart from the letter of St Paul to Philemon, Cicero's correspondence includes perhaps the only genuinely private letters surviving which were written by any of the famous people of antiquity. (We do have letters from ordinary people, recovered from the sands of Egypt and even the bogs of Northumberland.) The consequence is that we know him better than any other person in antiquity.

We might expect posterity to have come to an agreed view of so visible a figure, but there is scarcely any aspect of his life and activity that has not been very diversely judged. Undoubtedly he was vain and petulant, but were these faults outweighed by courage (sometimes), charm (often) and energy (almost always)? Was he high-principled, or all too ready to lend his oratory to the defence of scoundrels? His poetry was sometimes mocked; a century and a half after his death the satirist Juvenal joked that if this author of the sublime *Philippics* had never risen above the level of his verse, he would not have needed to fear Mark Antony's vengeance. Actually it was, at the lowest estimate, thoroughly competent, as we can learn from the substantial fragments that remain. His philosophical works have been seen as merely derivative, and as a masterly sifting and synthesis of the various schools, skilfully adapting Greek ideas to Roman circumstances. His politics, expressed in his speeches, can be hailed as a lifelong championing of republican liberty against the autocrats, but they can also appear shallow. One of his ideals was peace with dignity; 'dignity' here means the respect that should be accorded to important people, and was not something to which the ordinary man could aspire. Another hope was for harmony between the classes, but these classes were the aristocracy and the gentry; he was uninterested in the lower classes, and never fully understood, as the winners in the struggle did, that command of the armies and the populace was the road to power.

One of his greatest assets was his style. He wrote the Latin that ever after others were taught to imitate; how far it was his personal creation is hard to judge. Flexible, various and lucid, his prose can be short and sharp or flower into elaborate periods. It can handle wit, emotion and calm rationality. It is the ideal style for almost every purpose, except perhaps the truly poetic or profound. His ambition was to master almost every kind of literature: indeed he represents his friends as urging him to write history too, so that in this field also the Romans might match the Greeks. Vanity apart, this does show the limits of his mind – as though it were enough to read a few books and convert their substance into an elegant narrative. That would not make a man the equal of Thucydides. But he took his philosophy seriously. Unable to accept the whole package offered by any of the main philosophical schools, he decided in the end that he was an Academic – the natural outcome for a man in this position, since the Academics maintained a moderate scepticism: their view was that in the absence of certainty, we must make do with probability.

The Nature of the Gods is among the philosophical dialogues that illustrate his clarity and fair-mindedness. In the first book an Epicurean argues his case, in the second a Stoic, while in the third and last book Cotta, representing Cicero's own position, holds that while the gods exist, we can say little about them with confidence. Each speaker is given a good run for his money. These dialogues also gave Cicero opportunities for colour. In the *Republic* Scipio Aemilianus relates a dream vision in which he was shown the universe and earth's place within it. Part of the *Laws* is set in a beautiful spot near Cicero's home town where two rivers meet; this leads him to reflect on the nature of social identity, rooted in ancestry, locality and state. Everyone from an Italian town, he suggests, has two fatherlands, Rome and his native patch. It is the beginning of a way of thinking that was to be deeply explored by Virgil. In *De Finibus* ('On the Bounds of Goods and Evils') Cicero represents his young self and his friends in Athens discussing historical memory and its instantiation in cities and places.

Some of Cicero's speeches were delivered in the law court, others to the Senate or to assemblies of the people. Orators first made their name by a prominent prosecution, and then built up a network of 'friendships' (this ingenuous word was given to political alliances) by acting for the defence. Accordingly, Cicero's only prosecution, in 70, early in his career, was of Verres, the monstrously corrupt governor of Sicily. Verres saw that the game was up and fled to Marseilles early in the proceedings; most of Cicero's vast indictment (the final speech is divided into five books) was never delivered but published as a showcase of its author's skills. It ends with a *tour de force*, an invocation of the gods in a single sentence more than eight hundred words long.

An advocate may pretend to a great deal that he does not actually feel, but we can usually tell when Cicero really means it. He cannot speak of the aristocratic populist Clodius without obviously genuine loathing. When he defended the consul Murena on charges of electoral bribery, he found himself on the opposite side from two 'friends', Cato and the great jurist Sulpicius Rufus. This required delicate handling, and Cicero used humour. (He was known for his wit: 'What a wag we have as consul,' Cato remarked sourly, and Julius Caesar flattered him by having a slave follow him around to write down his jokes.) Sulpicius is gently twitted as a dusty bookworm – what a contrast with Murena, man of action – while the mockery of Cato as a rigid unfeeling Stoic has a sharper edge. Sure enough, Cicero's correspondence confirms that he and Sulpicius were real friends, whereas although Cato was a political ally Cicero found him tiresome.

Cicero's sense of comedy was most inventive in his speech *For Caelius* (56); indeed his tactic is to laugh the case out of court. His problem was that Caelius was a louche young man, the former lover of Clodius' sister, the notoriously promiscuous Clodia. He needed to appeal both to the stern moralists on the jury and to those who could be persuaded that boys will be boys. He puts on various personae. He imagines that he is Clodius advising his sister. He wonders if he should talk to Caelius like one of those heavy fathers on the comic stage. Most ingeniously, he evokes one of Clodia's patrician ancestors, and has him utter a sombre rebuke. He then dismisses this 'hard and almost uncouth old gentleman' with a smile. He can thus have his cake and eat it: he can both utter the solemn denunciation and disown it.

He was often disingenuous and insincere. Some of the manufactured indignation may have been a kind of game, played before an audience which understood the rules. The abuse seems pretty unrestrained, but we may notice that certain things are not said: in a society as loose as the Roman aristocracy one would expect there to have been people who did not know who their fathers were, but the accusation of bastardy is never made. Cicero's invective *Against Vatinius* contains much that one might think unpardonable, yet a few years later we find Vatinius writing to Cicero in amiable terms. Was he unusually forgiving? The invective *Against Piso* includes much that seems false or frivolous: Piso's grandfather was a Gaul who wore trousers, he liked dancing and the company of Greeks, his Epicureanism was a licence for self-indulgence (Cicero the philosopher knew that to be a travesty). Perhaps we are meant to admire the very disingenuousness, as a mark of the orator's skill. At all events, Cicero's last speeches were sincere and indeed heroic: the *Philippics* against Mark Antony, the title of course invoking Demosthenes. This was Cicero's last throw of the dice, and he lost. Antony had him killed and his severed head and hands nailed on to the speakers' platform in the Roman Forum, where his sightless eyes gazed for the last time on the scene that he had commanded for so long.

Cicero's letters resist ordinary literary criticism. They contain a great deal that he surely would not have wished us to be reading – one reason why they give such a living sense of his complex personality. But he was in any case a brilliant correspondent, and his dash and vivacity, and even the liveliness of his hatreds, remain hugely enjoyable. He was matched for eloquence, however, by one of his friends: the letter of consolation that Sulpicius Rufus, the man whom he had teased in his speech *For Murena*, sent to him on the death of his daughter is an unaffected masterpiece.

Oratory apart, the future of literature must have looked bleak in the 70s BC. Epic, comedy, tragedy – the Romans had tried their hands at all these, and each had had its day, but these veins were all worked out, and there was no major writer alive anywhere in the Greek world either. No one could have guessed that the most brilliant half century in the history of Latin literature was soon to follow. But then no one can predict genius, and it was the explosion of two poets of genius upon the scene that began the transformation: Lucretius and Catullus.

This literary efflorescence occurred while the republican constitution which Rome had enjoyed for centuries was collapsing. In 49 BC civil war broke out between the two men whose careers in war and politics had made them the most powerful people in Rome, Pompey and Julius Caesar. Caesar won, had himself made dictator for life and was assassinated on the Ides of March 44. Civil war was renewed, between Caesar's former lieutenant, Mark Antony, and his great-nephew and adopted son, Octavian, ending only with the defeat of Antony and his lover Cleopatra, queen of Egypt, at the sea battle of Actium in 31 and their suicides in the following year. In 27 Octavian took the name Augustus ('Worshipful') and the centuries of rule by emperors began.

We know almost nothing about Lucretius (a few anecdotes from sources centuries later are fictional). All that we have is one poem, *The Nature of Things*. Even its date is unsure: the first half of the 50s is likely enough; it may have been the work of many years. Its subject is the philosophy of Epicurus, but by far the greater part of it is devoted to his physics – the theory that matter is made of atoms, which Epicurus had taken from the fifth-century thinker Democritus. Divided into six books and more than seven thousand lines long, it is vastly larger than any previous didactic poem. Its theme is natural science, and it has no people in it. Moreover, Epicurus' philosophy could appear especially earthbound: it holds that the only thing which a person may rationally pursue is his own pleasure, and with its absolute rejection of the supernatural it might seem to suck all the magic and mystery out of the world. This does not sound like a formula for success. The poem's greatness rests on three things: passion, intellectual energy and sheer poetic imagination. Unmistakably it is the product of a man who has undergone a conversion experience. It is, in turn, a work of evangelism, offering salvation: if we accept the truth of Epicurus' teaching, we can live a life worthy of the gods, and death will become a matter of indifference. The doctrine is not technically atheistic, as Epicurus allowed that the gods might exist, but it is purely materialist: nothing exists except atoms and empty space, and if the gods exist, they are made of atoms like everything else, and play no part in the creation or government of the world.

It is a surprise, therefore, that Lucretius begins with the most glorious act of worship in Latin literature, a great hymn to Venus. He celebrates her as mother of the Roman race, the Epicurean pleasure principle, the goddess of spring, the sex impulse, the source of public peace, the muse that inspires his own verse. Clearly she is a symbol, but she may seem to be symbolizing too many different things. That, however, is Lucretius' point. His is a vision of unity: everything – all processes, activities and experiences – is the product of atoms, moving, colliding or cohering. And we are to contemplate this atomic motion with adoration. His picture of Venus' effect has a startling vehemence: winds and clouds fleeing her presence, tearing rivers, birds and beasts struck by the force, even the violence of the sex instinct. Are these the words of a philosophy advocating impassibility? But it is possible to enjoy vigour in a spirit of detachment, and Lucretius' combination of energy and calm, while it may be surprising, is not illogical: we are to be rapt, it seems, by a kind of passionate serenity.

Lucretius' hymn culminates in the image of Mars and Venus united in love. He drew here on the Presocratic philosopher poet Empedocles, who, as we saw, mythologized the cosmic principles of Love and Strife as Aphrodite and Ares, of whom Venus and Mars are the Roman equivalents. But what does the image signify? Love is naturally taken to be harmony and union, and so it seems to be here. But Lucretius prays to Venus for an end to war, for the Romans to enjoy peace, and that implies that Venus should overcome Mars, the god of war. And indeed he is described as 'conquered by the eternal wound of love', looking up at the goddess with his rounded neck bent back, feeding avidly on the love of her as she pours her body around him. The paradox in the image is a profound symbol of the physical reality of things according to the atomic theory. The universe needs both love and strife and a balance between them: without the one there is chaos, without the other no change or new creation. But the universe as a whole coheres, and so the sum of things, presumably, is the prevailing of love over strife. Erotic love, with its language of wounds, conquest and surrender, gives him a sublime metaphor for this complexity. Epicurus' philosophy might seem to suck all the magic from the world; Lucretius' purpose is to find the romance in it. On the very largest and the very smallest scale there is immutability: the universe and the number of atoms in it are infinite; no atom is ever created or destroyed. In between, everything is mutable, for the atoms are in ceaseless motion. Lucretius delights in the interplay of change and changelessness.

Early on he tells us that human life formerly lay on the ground, crushed by religion; but Epicurus has defeated religion, trampling it beneath his feet. He adds that religion has often led to impious acts, recalling Agamemnon's sacrifice of Iphigenia, and summing up in a famous phrase: 'To such a pitch of evils could religion persuade.' So to call Lucretius 'religious' is a giant paradox; yet the poem is saturated in religious imagery, and it is fundamental to its character that it begins with worship. Epicurus' philosophy faced three especial difficulties. First, it could appear drab and unappealing, seeming to suck the romance out of the world. Second, there was the problem of altruism: on the face of it, no one has a rational ground to pursue anything other than his own pleasure, and yet the missionary project of seeking to convert people to the truth seems plainly altruistic. Third, Epicurus' claim about death is very strong – not merely that we should face it without fear but that it is a matter of pure indifference. Lucretius echoes one of the master's precepts in Book 3: 'Death therefore is nothing to us, nor does it matter a jot.' Rightly or wrongly, most people do not feel that.

Lucretius' project can be seen as an attempt to meet these difficulties. In the poem's first words Venus is presented as a mother. Later, father sky precipitates the rains into the womb of mother earth. This is language taken from fertility cult, with the sky as the male principle impregnating the female. Through this life-giving act plants grow, birds and beasts give birth, and, more surprisingly, 'we see fertile cities blooming with children' – nature and culture alike inspirited by the energizing force of atomic movement. In Book 2 he sounds almost scriptural: 'We are all sprung of heavenly seed; all of us have that same father', the father's moisture quickens mother earth, and in due course 'that which was sent from the regions of the sky is taken back again and the temples of heaven receive it'. In Book 5 he repeats with great emphasis that the earth is rightly called 'mother'. These metaphors of parenthood bind everything in the world, ourselves included, into a universal kinship.

In a very beautiful passage he explains that the ageing and dying of things is the creation of other things, 'And thus the sum of things is ever new, and mortals live in mutuality.' Immortal youth was traditionally the privilege of the gods; now our own world enjoys it. He also compares successive generations to relay runners in a race, passing on the torch from one to the next. The significance of this is that the runner wants to pass on the torch. Lucretius hints at an idea that he can perhaps express only through emotional colour rather than directly: we are members of a team, and can come to feel our deaths as fitting because they are the necessary condition for the everlasting freshness of the world. Although each person can rationally pursue only his own pleasure, the love of parents and children is a natural pleasure, and if we can feel a comparable sense of kinship with the world as a whole, we can come to accept, and even in a way desire, our own extinctions.

Now, one cannot instruct a person to fall in love. Only through persuasion of the emotions can Lucretius hope to make us seized of the romance of the universal kinship, and the only way that he can do that is by the power of poetry. That is why he must do his philosophy in verse and why the philosophy and the poetry in *The Nature of Things* are inseparable. It is likely that Lucretius followed Epicurus' principal treatise on physics, *On Nature*, fairly closely, but his work is intellectually as well as poetically original, because it infuses into Epicureanism a colour more characteristic of Stoicism. Thus, two centuries on, the Stoic emperor Marcus Aurelius

(AD 121–80) was to write, 'By the changes of the parts of universal nature the whole world continues ever young'; what benefits the whole is always lovely, and therefore the end of each person's life is no evil. If we find something hard to bear, we have forgotten 'the great kinship of man with all mankind'. Lucretius' insight was to realize that he could annex this style of feeling and knit poetic imagination into the roots of a philosophy that might seem especially unpoetic.

Lucretius' project was highly eccentric, the loneliest of Latin poems. The first eccentricity was the use of verse for philosophic argument. We saw that some of the Presocratic thinkers used verse, but by the end of the fifth century BC the Greeks had realized that prose was the right medium for philosophy, science and history. Second, this is a didactic poem that really means to do what it purports to do. Most didactic poems are pseudo-didactic; their real purpose is to give literary pleasure. You do not rush for Nicander's *Alexipharmaca* if a snake has bitten you, or to Virgil's *Georgics* for help with raising cattle. But Lucretius is genuinely doing philosophy, and he wants to convert us. His contemporaries did not notice; it is telling that Cicero, who admired him as a poet, entirely ignored him in his own philosophical works. Virgil is the only man to praise him for intellectual command.

Lucretius fused two streams of tradition in hexameter poetry, and that fusion becomes part of his meaning. There was the tradition of heroic narrative, descending from Homer, and didactic tradition, descending from Hesiod. Lucretius names Homer and Ennius in prominent places, but he names no didactic poet other than Empedocles, whose vehemence surely appealed to him. In effect, he gives to a didactic subject some of the characteristics of heroic verse. There is the poem's sheer length, for one thing. Moreover, Lucretius' diction is grand, rugged and sometimes old-fashioned in the manner of Ennius, to evoke epic loftiness. Like his religious tone, this elevated manner is not merely decorative but part of the argument: it asserts that Epicurus' creed is not only true but majestic and inspiring. In this poem the medium really is the message. And Epicurus himself becomes an epic hero. Lucretius gives him an extended eulogy in three places: he is praised as a man early in Book 1, as a father at the start of Book 3, and as a god at the start of Book 5. In the first of the passages Lucretius turns him into the warrior who has confronted religion, won the victory and returned in triumph; he is also the one whose mind has travelled beyond the flaming walls of the cosmos – an Odysseus of the spirit, as it were. In Book 3 Lucretius says that at the voice of Epicurus 'a divine pleasure and shudder grips me'; that mixture of delight and fear, as in the presence of a god, evokes a sense of the numinous. Once again, Lucretius brings a religious temper to his master's anti-religious doctrine.

He also extended the scope of didactic verse in the opposite direction: he can be satirical and occasionally colloquial. In Book 1 he sees off a succession of Presocratic thinkers; some of this is quite broadly comic. He ends Books 3 and 4 with long 'diatribes' – not diatribes in the modern sense, but rough, vigorous arguments, with touches of knockabout. Parts of the diatribe on love in Book 4 may not be wholly serious, but the diatribe on death in Book 3 is at the centre of his entire project. Here he blends satiric edge and declamatory grandeur to create a new tone; there is nothing like it in Latin literature, except a century and a half later in a few of the satires of Juvenal. The figure of Nature appears and rebukes the man who fears death, telling him not to be an ingrate and a blockhead. At the end Lucretius gives the reader a kind of spiritual exercise: here is what you can say to yourself from time to time. We should reflect on the great men who have died, like Xerxes and Scipio; the list culminates in Homer, the greatest poet, Democritus, the second best of all thinkers – and finally Lucretius says, very plainly, 'Epicurus himself died . . .' It is the only time that he names him in the entire poem, and a moment of simple but surpassing eloquence.

Lucretius can write with delicacy and grace when it suits him, but his commonest tone is dense, energetic and even a little cumbrous. Sometimes he is ostentatiously prosaic. He complains about the lumpish Greek word *homoeomeria*, a technical term which he does not need to use at all, let alone repeat. He mutters about the poverty of the Latin language. He uses ponderous connections, like 'wherefore again and again . . .' He takes the prosy word *ratio* ('reason'), again using it more often than he need, and forces it to become poetry. He repeats flat adjectives like *omnis* ('all') and *certus* ('fixed' or 'sure'), and makes them serve his vision of the universality of physical law and the inviolable security that the philosopher enjoys. But he also revels in the robust alliterations that had marked Ennius' epic style; Virgil alliterates like that when he wants to sound Lucretian. Lucretius dramatizes the fascination of what's difficult: where he is craggy or awkward, it is to express the recalcitrance of his material. He takes dull language and transforms it. And that too is part of his message, which glorifies the factual and the ordinary. After all, the Venus whom we worship at the poem's start is not something transcendent, that we find beyond or behind nature: she is the ordinary operation of nature itself, the atoms and their movement which constitute everything that is.

Lucretius is willing to give himself a hard time, testing his conviction by presenting the charm of false beliefs, only to override them. It is the technique that we met in the *Wisdom of Solomon*. When we look up at the stars (he says), it is hard not to think that there are divine intelligences in them – but no, that is false. In the diatribe on death the unphilosophic are allowed to lament poignantly that death will deprive a man of his dear wife and children; the detail of the children running ahead to snatch the first kiss is especially affecting. This is authentically eloquent, but the Epicurean faith can overcome it. Coolly, Lucretius crushes the beauty that he has made, and then a note of coarser grained satire is allowed to return.

We shall find in Catullus, Virgil and some other Roman poets a feeling for the detail of the physical world and a concern to apprehend it in words that had hardly existed in the literature of earlier centuries. It is already in Lucretius. Epicureanism did have this advantage as a poetic subject, that it held that philosophical truth was to be found through physics, and physical truth through an accurate examination of what we perceive. Lucretius records the effects of attrition: the ring on a finger thin underneath through wearing, the stone hollowed by dripping water, the hands of bronze statues rubbed smooth by the touch of passers-by. 'Do you not see . . . ?', 'Do you see *now* . . . ?' are favourite questions of his. He looks at children deliberately making themselves dizzy, and remembers how it felt. He captures the split second between the starting gates being thrown open and the horses bursting out. He studies the iridescence of a dove's neck, trying out colour adjectives and the names of jewels in a search for the truth of hue and sheen. He watches colour changing as a dyed cloth is pulled to shreds. He notices how an awning flapping over a theatre on a sunny day creates a submarine light rippling across the audience. He evokes the mixture of hoariness and glossiness in a stormy sea; he describes optical illusions.

This sense of particularity is attractive in itself but it also has a moral dimension. Looking at a puddle between the paving stones he sees that the reflections in it appear as deep as the sky is high above. A familiar sight becomes strange and wonderful. What could be more astonishing than sun, moon and stars, Lucretius asks, if we were seeing them for the first time; as it is, people are so jaded that they do not look up at the shining heaven. The blight of modern life, he says elsewhere, is a restless boredom, dissatisfied alike in town and country, at home and away. By contrast, early mankind used to smile and laugh, because everything was new and wondrous. Lucretius tells us that the world is eternally new; but he also wants to revivify the eye and freshen our own experience.

He combines this feeling for detail with a relish for the infinity of atoms and space; when he talks about limitlessness he likes to alliterate the letters *m* and *n*, resonating immensely. Much of his power comes from his ability to combine disparate and even opposite elements: lofty and everyday language, poetry and philosophy, the smallest particles of matter and the whole universe, epic and didactic verse, materialism and the numinous. And for all his vehemence, there is a reserve within Lucretius; he is proud and secret. The reason why we know less about him than the other poets of his century is that he tells us nothing. Virgil will tell us something of himself in the *Georgics*, as Hesiod had, and Nicander, but Lucretius is impenetrably private. His voice is very distinctive, but like a voice on the radio, we do not know where it is coming from. That passionate reticence has its own compelling force.

Solitary though he stands, Lucretius' indirect influence has been great. Didactic verse is the only genre in which the Romans clearly outclassed the Greeks. Moreover, there are only two didactic poems which rank among the greatest masterpieces, and they were written only a generation apart. That is no accident. Virgil began as a miniaturist, but *The Nature of Things* showed him a new world of imaginative possibility: here was a genre in which it was still possible to write with originality, and on the largest scale. More important still, Lucretius showed Virgil how a moral and spiritual vision might infuse the didactic form. That realization produced the *Georgics*, and the amplitude of the *Georgics* prepared Virgil for the *Aeneid*. With the *Aeneid* an epic becomes, for the first time, a poem about salvation: it argues an idea of how mankind may be secure. That too is a legacy of Lucretius; without him, the history of western literature would have been rather different.

Catullus (*c*.84–*c*.54 BC) came from Verona, north of the River Po, in the region which was officially Cisalpine Gaul until it was incorporated into Italy in the later 40s. It was a prosperous area, distant from Rome but richer than most of peninsular Italy, and it was to produce some of the leading figures of his and the next generation, among them the poets Virgil and Cinna and the historian Livy, as well as a number of lesser men. The assertive sophistication of the educated provincial can be detected in some of Catullus' verse. His poems can be classed into three groups. There are epigrams, in elegiacs; shorter poems in a variety of metres, mostly light in character; and a small number of longer pieces. Many of the shorter poems are the effusions of a young man about town: there is much talk of elegance and *savoir faire*, and mockery of those who lack these qualities; there is banter with his friends, and rough, sometimes gross, obscenity. Some of these pieces are finely turned, others surprisingly weak. But his most recurrent theme is love, especially love for the woman whom he disguises under the Greek name Lesbia.

Before Catullus, the little love poetry that existed in Latin paraphrased or imitated Greek epigram. He began something dramatically new, and he drew the next generations after him: for half a century and more Latin poetry was to be saturated in the theme of love. It dominated the verse of Catullus, Gallus, Tibullus, Propertius and much of Ovid. It is a large part of Horace's *Songs*. Virgil explored it in the *Bucolics*;

Propertius was right to hail him as one of the love poets. And Virgil ended the *Georgics*, a didactic poem, with something fairly rare in literature at any time, a story of passion burning within marriage, and indeed beyond death. His *Aeneid* put Dido's tragedy at its heart and celebrated the faithful love of the Trojan warriors Nisus and Euryalus. And then abruptly the theme vanished from Latin verse, as suddenly as it had appeared. It is natural to ask why.

As with Greek love poetry, it was crucial that the beloved could say no. In theory a Roman woman was entirely in the power of the head of her family; but whatever the law said, in the early first century there emerged an aristocratic milieu within which women could in effect do as they liked. Catullus' Lesbia was such a person. We have good evidence that she was a sister of Cicero's enemy Clodius – the very Clodia whom he attacked in his speech *For Caelius*, or possibly one of her sisters. It really does seem to be true: a young provincial aristocrat came to Rome, fell in love with the wrong woman, was driven to put his passion into verse, and changed the literature of Europe. Gallus' beloved was different: a glamorous Greek courtesan, whose favours Mark Antony enjoyed, and who impressed even Cicero by the charm of her company. The women in the later elegists – Tibullus, Propertius and Ovid – are different again: typically they are educated, of good family, but ambiguous in status; they may be in need of a protector but they can choose among the suitors for that role. They are likely to reflect the consequences of years of civil war, when prosperous families were ruined and women lost their menfolk. Many of these will have drifted to Rome and entered that demi-monde which the elegists evoke. As the civil wars receded into the past, that world will have diminished, and with it the material that it provided for verse.

So there were social reasons for the rise and fall of Latin love poetry, but there were literary reasons too. Like Lucretius, Catullus discovered a wide new realm of possibility that the Greeks had not colonized. There had been nothing like Roman love elegy in Hellenistic literature. Of course poets had written in personal terms about their loves before – Sappho alone shows that – but new was the representation of one obsessing passion, of a sense of hidden narrative, its different moods, the ups and downs in a developing story, found not in one poem alone but fragmentarily in many. The elegists found variations on the theme, some indeed borrowed from epigram or comedy: the rival lover, the pimp, the lament outside the beloved's closed door, quarrel and reconciliation, love as warfare, and as slavery. As we find these topics turning up in one poet and then another, we come to realize that they are not limitless. In the end the material was used up, and once Ovid had made fun of it, anguish was over.

The best of Catullus' epigrams are like those of no one else. They might be described as meditations on a point: they present a kind of bafflement, rather than the crispness that we might expect from the epigram form. 'I hate and love,' famously begins one of the shortest, two lines only; and he adds that if you ask why, he does not know. Another poem concludes that Lesbia's infidelity makes him love her more and feel affection less. The longest of all, at twenty-six lines, may seem too large to be classed as an epigram, and yet it is an epigram, albeit one vastly expanded, for there is no narrative, no progress, as there would be in the later elegiac poets: Catullus goes back and forth through his condition, frustrated, like a tiger pacing its cage. But he also speaks with a sublime simplicity: 'It is difficult soon to put aside a long love.' The other shattering event in his life was the death of his brother in distant Asia Minor, and one epigram marks his visit to the tomb, having crossed 'many seas and many peoples' to bid hail and farewell for ever. Resisting critical description, these lines display a quality uniquely important in this poet: authenticity. The later love poets were to write 'first-person fictions', but with Catullus we have to trust in the immediate relation of his verse to actual experience. Without that conviction, the poems would not work.

After the elegiac couplet, his favourite metre was the hendecasyllable, a light, buoyant, eleven-syllable line. For an English example of it we can turn again to Tennyson:

> Look, I come to the test, a tiny poem
> All composed in a metre of Catullus . . .

Twice Catullus mentions the metre while writing it: a friend who has pinched a napkin is warned to expect hundreds of hendecasyllables if it is not returned; and he summons his hendecasyllables to help him recover some documents from a 'dirty whore'. This is a fitting metre, in other words, for attack, for scurrility and abuse. It is surprising, therefore, that he should use it to speak to Lesbia. Another surprise: absent from the Lesbia poems are those descriptions of the beloved that have been the staple of so much love poetry – eyes, hair, complexion, figure. The only description of any part of her body anywhere is unflattering: her eyes red and swollen with weeping for the death of her pet sparrow.

That poem is addressed successively to Venuses and Cupids, to men of good taste, to the darkness of the underworld and to the dead bird itself – to everything but the person to whom it is truly spoken: Lesbia herself. A couple of lines trip by, rhyming by repetition:

The sparrow is dead that was my girl's,
The sparrow, the pet that was my girl's.

Then he imagines the bird on the road down to the underworld, a picture both sombre and ludicrous. He reproaches those dark regions 'which devour all pretty things', a collocation of the dark and the sentimental. Then the bird itself is rebuked: naughty little sparrow – it is your doing that my girl's eyes are pink and puffy. All this, we feel, is for her, to cheer her up with a blend of joke and sympathy. Colloquial, part grave, part humorous, tender and affectionate, it is a lover's consolation that we happen to overhear. No one had written with quite this combination of ordinariness and intimacy before, and it will be a very long time before we hear it again – more than a millennium and a half, maybe.

Here is the key to these poems: almost all love poetry, however passionate, and even when the beloved is the addressee, is at a distance; Catullus makes us present. Another poem begins, 'You ask, Lesbia, how many of your kissings are enough and more for me?' In what circumstances would she ask such a question? Only when her lover is pressing himself upon her. We are, as it were, in mid-kiss. Another time, 'Let us live, my Lesbia, and love,' and not care a penny for what muttering old gentlemen may say. Then, in the same tripping metre, he reflects that suns can set and rise again; when our brief light is gone, we must sleep through an eternal night. The thought is stark; the style is light; a brief shadow passes over the page, before the poem dissolves into kisses, kisses and more kisses.

Catullus also employed the 'limping iambic', the metre associated with Hipponax and the invective poem. In one place he uses it to argue himself roughly into sense. Here the drag in the metre conveys the doggedness to which he aspires. He tells himself to accept that the affair is over, and in the middle of the poem he declares that he is firm. Then he addresses Lesbia (this time clearly in his imagination only), and although he begins by affecting a lofty sympathy for her, gradually he recalls their past love with increasing intimacy, and by the poem's end he can only tell himself to be firm, no longer insisting that he is. This emotional journey, in only nineteen lines, ending in uncertainty, foreshadows the psychological exploration that Virgil would develop in his *Bucolics* and pass on to the later elegists. But in spite of Catullus' immense influence on love poetry, the business of writing about love in light metres was a thing that no one imitated. This is surely because other poets recognized that spontaneity and immediacy, the closeness to raw experience, were the essence of these pieces. You cannot imitate spontaneity; this was something that could only be done once.

Catullus' longer poems reveal a side to his literary character strikingly different from the shorter pieces. Each is, in one way or another, experimental. Four of them can be described as a poem within a poem – that is, a poem held inside an outer framework, or provided with an introduction in a different key. His *Attis* (Poem 63) was a technical challenge to himself: its rare metre, wild and rapid, is difficult to write in Latin because of the great number of short syllables. Its content is as bizarre as its form: Attis, who speaks much of the poem in his or her own person, has castrated himself out of devotion to the goddess Cybele, the Great Mother, and seems unsure whether to call himself man or woman. It is a *tour de force* of sexual weirdness and self-obsession.

Poem 66 is a translation of a typically dry piece of court poetry by Callimachus, incorporated into his *Origins*. Why has Catullus given himself this exercise? He explains in a prefatory address to a friend (Poem 65): he is too grieved by his brother's death to give voice to what the Muses bring to birth, and so he sends this exercise instead. That is a simple enough sentiment, but the way in which Catullus expresses it is extraordinary. The whole twenty-line poem is one enormous sentence, into which the death intrudes in parenthesis. It is strangely prettified: the water of Lethe, says the poet, is washing over his brother's pale little foot. Then in lines of elaborately patterned and melodious plangency he compares his enduring love with 'the Daulian . . . in the deep shadow of the branches lamenting the fate of lost Itylus' – by which he means the song of the nightingale, wrapped up in mythological fancy dress. It might have been frigid, but it is acutely poignant. For Catullus is finding a new kind of aesthetic, and exploring the effect of distancing. He persuades us that he has decorated and beautified the brother's fate not because he feels too little but because he feels too much: the pain would be too raw otherwise.

He wrote two wedding poems, the second of which contains a beautiful simile comparing the bride's childhood to a flower growing in an enclosed garden. There is very little imagery in his shorter poems; an exception comes at the end of one of his two experiments at writing the sapphic stanza, where after a ferociously obscene denunciation of Lesbia he ends by tenderly comparing his love for her to a flower at the edge of a field, which has perished, shorn by the plough which has just touched it in passing. Both similes seem to have been inspired by the imagery of Sappho herself. Catullus immersed himself in the sensuous most fully in what is by far his longest work, Poem 64. At a little over four hundred lines, this is a mythological narrative of moderate length, an example of what modern scholarship has called 'epyllion'. If the term is taken to mean 'little epic', it is misleading: such poems were not compressed or miniaturized versions of something naturally larger, but simply poems of the extent that their authors found suitable, and indeed Poem 64 feels generously expansive. This reservation apart, 'epyllion' is a useful label for a genre that lacks another name. If Catullus gave the work a title, it has been lost, and we perhaps do best to stick to the drab 'Poem 64', since the piece curiously refuses to be about any one thing.

At first it seems that it will be about the Argonauts, then it tells how one of them, Peleus, encountered the sea-nymph Thetis, and it begins to describe their wedding. But it then digresses to the story of Ariadne and Theseus, and after rather briefly returning to the wedding, digresses again to the career of Achilles, the son of the bridal couple, before concluding with a denunciation of human wickedness ever since the age of heroes came to an end. Like Theocritus' first Idyll, it has two inner sections, one a visual and the other an auditory work of art. The first of these is an embroidery on a bridal bed, depicting Ariadne waking on a seashore to find that Theseus has deserted her; the other is a wedding song performed by the Fates. But the proportions are very peculiar: the description of the embroidery begins after only fifty lines, and continues for more than two hundred, amounting to a little over half the entire work. Catullus thus set himself another challenge to his technique; for would not Ariadne so dominate the poem that the last quarter of the piece might seem an anti-climax? It is not a problem that he fully overcame, but the first three hundred lines are almost continuously inspired. The poem revels in visible beauty: the naked sea-nymphs emerging from the gleam and foam of the waters; Peleus' palace glittering with gold and silver and pink-stained ivory; above all the tapestry on which Ariadne is displayed.

Like Theocritus again, the poem explores art and illusion. Ariadne is only a picture, and the male gaze enjoys the beauty of her distress, her breasts revealed as the clothes slip from her body and the waves play with them at her feet. How can something so artificial, so enjoyable, be genuinely moving? And yet, somehow, it is. Ariadne seems to want to break out of her frame. The poet gives her a long, plangent lament, looks back to her earlier life, forward to Theseus' return to Athens, before reminding us again that a picture is all that this is. And then he springs another of his surprises. The image is not quite what we had thought, for it also shows the god Bacchus coming to her rescue with the privilege of his love. He is accompanied by followers with musical instruments, horns, drums and cymbals, their noise brilliantly realized with a battery of onomatopoeic effects. And then abruptly he shuts it off: 'Such were the *shapes*' with which the coverlet was adorned – and we are back in Peleus' palace again.

The oddest of Catullus' experiments is Poem 68. It falls into three unequal parts, which we can label A, B and C. Part A is addressed from Verona to a friend in Rome, who has asked for some love poetry. Catullus answers that he has no appetite for it any more, for grief at his brother's death. The friend has reproached him for his absence: while he has been away, he has been disgraced, as everybody of the better sort has slept in the bed that he has left. Catullus replies that this is not disgrace, merely a sadness. He adds that he is prevented from writing verse because he does not have his books with him; later perhaps things may be different. And there Part A ends, in uncertainty. Part B takes a different tone. It is again addressed to a friend – probably the same man as in Part A, although this is far from sure – and thanks him for providing a house for the poet's assignation with his beloved. Part C briefly looks back on Part B: here is the poem, he says, the best that he could manage. The piece is diffusive and weirdly digressive, but into each of its two principal parts two sharp lumps of reality passingly intrude: the brother's death; and Lesbia. The brother's appearances are brief: as with Poem 65, we may feel that anything more would be too painful. In Part B Catullus recalls Lesbia's arrival for an assignation: she put her gleaming foot on the worn threshold, and the sole of her sandal tapped on it.

It is not only Lesbia who stands on a threshold but western literature itself, for two things begin here. What has fixed itself in the poet's mind is something oddly ordinary, a contrast of textures, shining shoe on stone, the moment marked by the sharp sound. Here is a new feeling for the particularity of small, ordinary experiences, realized through visible and audible detail; we shall meet it again in Virgil. Second, we have here a fragment of narrative: Catullus is beginning to tell a story. And this in turn is the beginning of what we shall come to recognize as Latin love elegy: the protoplasm seems to be evolving before our eyes.

CHAPTER 8

Virgil

Cicero gave the young poets of his day the Greek name *neoteroi*, the 'newer men'. Catullus apart, these 'neoterics' have perished, but at least two of them, Cinna (died 44 BC) and Calvus (82–before 47), were his friends. Cinna's chief work was *Zmyrna*, which Catullus says was nine years in the making, probably a humorous exaggeration. It was notoriously obscure, and so it must have been very unlike Poem 64 in character. Its subject was another acratic heroine: Zmyrna (or Myrrha) was a woman who fell in love with her own father. The protagonist of Calvus' *Io* was a different kind of damsel in distress, ravished by Jupiter (the king of the gods, identified with the Greeks' Zeus) and then turned into a cow. An allusion in Virgil's *Bucolics* suggests that it aimed for a lyrical plangency. Calvus also wrote an elegy on the death of his wife or mistress. Cinna, Calvus and Catullus each composed a short mythological epic, but otherwise it is not clear that they had much in common; they formed a social group, but not necessarily a literary school.

These were gentlemen of means: they wrote verses because it pleased them to. In a world without printing, no one could earn a living from his pen except from commissions or patronage. Maecenas, one of the chief lieutenants of the man who would become Augustus, made himself into the most successful literary patron in history. He acquired Virgil and Varius early in the 30s BC, Horace not long after and Propertius some years later. Horace's friendship with him was especially close (and complicated), and an important subject in his verse. Maecenas patronized poets because he liked poetry; that must have been one of the reasons why they liked him. But was there a more self-interested motive? These authors were not expected to produce propaganda in any ordinary sense, nor were they intended to organize the opinions of their contemporaries: the elite who made up their readership were too well informed for that. Maecenas showed immense patience: a decade after he had begun his career as a patron, his poets had produced hardly anything that could be described as useful to the regime. The self-interest was of grander scope: it was to buy immortality by winning the admiration of posterity. Maecenas had one stroke of luck: he had Virgil. No one could have predicted genius of that order. But Maecenas' skill was to use his luck to create a brilliant school of poets through a blend of the shaping hand and the light touch; provided that they praised Augustus somewhere in their works, they could essentially be left to do as they pleased. The plan worked: the reason that Augustus has given his name to an age which the world has regarded as one of the culminating periods of civilization is not because of his political mastery, extraordinary though that was; it is because of the poets. Virgil and Horace were cheap at the price.

'Something greater than the *Iliad* is coming to birth,' wrote Propertius, at a time when Virgil (70–19 BC) had scarcely begun his *Aeneid*. His genius was recognized in his lifetime; within a generation of his death he was already a classic and a school text. Considering the enormous interest that the Romans took in him from the beginning, we know surprisingly little about his origins, other than that he came from Mantua, in what was then Cisalpine Gaul. In his first published work he honoured his patrons, but Maecenas was not yet among them. The young poet took a surprising decision: he would be directly and openly derivative. He even advertises the fact: in one poem he calls upon the Muses of Sicily and in another he declares that his Muse has been the first to sport in Syracusan verse – in each case a reference to Theocritus. He called the book *Bucolics* ('Herdsman Matters') and the individual poems *eclogae* ('select pieces'); hence the *Eclogues* as a common name for the collection as a whole. It consists of ten poems, which unlike the Idylls of Theocritus do not vary greatly in length. They are arranged with careful symmetry: Eclogues 4 and 6 are the two non-pastoral poems; 3 and 7 are singing competitions; 2 and 8 are about blighted or unrequited love; 1 and 9 treat the land confiscations that were taking place in Italy at the time. The odd-numbered eclogues are in dialogue form and the even ones are not. This unprecedented tightness of organization may make us wonder whether to regard the *Bucolics* as ten poems gathered into one volume or as a single work. Yet within this framework there are different worlds: some poems seem to be in a place of mythological fantasy, some in a Theocritean timeless present, while others refer to events of the present day in the real world.

In the past the *Bucolics* were sometimes seen as simple pieces of pastoral; in modern times they have been described as exceptionally difficult. But we should not mistake elusiveness for difficulty. There are a few allusions which we can no longer pick up, but that accident of time apart, these are not on the whole problematic poems. But they do resist attempts to pin them down. Where are we? One shepherd meets two others, 'both Arcadians', and yet a few lines later they are by the banks of the River Mincius, on the north Italian plain. There is no naturalistic explanation of this. Sometimes reality seems to be inside out: the satyr Silenus sings about Virgil's contemporary Gallus; surely, we think, it should be the other way round.

At the heart of the eighth Eclogue is a tiny vignette: 'I saw you when little in our enclosure picking apples with your mother (I was your guide), when I had now reached one year beyond my eleventh, and could now touch the fragile branches from the ground. When I saw, how I perished, how wretched delusion carried me away!' Everything here is delicate and exact: the elements are small, contained, fragile, precise, childlike. The scene is vivid, and yet also remote, for we are four stages from immediacy: Virgil has introduced the poem in his own voice; he has presented Damon, who sings a song in the persona of a suicidal lover, who recalls a moment many years in the past. The scene is like an image seen through the wrong end of a telescope, very far and very clear.

In the ninth Eclogue the land confiscations are introduced with similar indirectness. Two shepherds refer to the absent Menalcas, a poet who seems very like Virgil, and they quote four times from his compositions. Two of the quotations paraphrase Theocritus, with elaborate elegance; one speaks of the misfortunes of Mantua, Virgil's home town, and nearby Cremona. As with Catullus lamenting his brother, there is a distance, or several distances, between the verse and an actuality which might otherwise be too painful. Many things in these poems are at the edge of our field of vision. No woman speaks in them (in one a shepherd takes on a woman's role). A herdsman laments that he will be thrown off his land; but that will happen tomorrow, and no soldier comes on to the scene. We hear of winter, rain, towns, even Rome itself, but these things are noises off stage, hints of other times and other places.

The poems mostly present themselves as Grecian fantasy, but little lumps of reality appear, not all unpleasant. In the second Eclogue Corydon describes the gifts that he will bring his beloved: peaches hoary with a tender down, chestnuts, waxy plums. Here is a still life in words (and more than a still life, for these things are good to eat), textures of ordinary objects set against one another, enjoyed merely for themselves. This was a new sensibility, although its origins can be felt in the moment when Lesbia's golden sandal hit the threshold. This eclogue had another effect on Virgil's contemporaries. Corydon loves the boy Alexis, who does not love him back; the poem is his soliloquy, in which he berates the absent object of his passion. Now he is proud, now humble, now hopeful, now petulant or defiant, and at the end he declares that he will find another Alexis if this one spurns him. But there are sufficient hints that this is self-deception, and only Alexis will do. This psychological monodrama, with its lurches of mood back and forth, was to have an important influence on the Augustan elegists. As a whole, the *Bucolics* may well be the most influential group of short poems ever written, for they were to be the principal model on which a huge pastoral literature was to be based, in the Renaissance and for centuries after. And thus ten poems that were meant to be unusual and idiosyncratic became normative; it is one of literary history's great ironies.

With the *Georgics*, as we might expect from an author of his calibre, Virgil turned in a decisively new direction. Whereas the *Bucolics* had been compressed, fugitive, carefully enclosed and limited, the spirit of the *Georgics* is easy, open and expansive. It is a didactic poem about farming; the four books deal successively with arable farming; vines, trees and olives; stock-breeding; and bee-keeping. Varying very little in length, these books are symmetrically planned. In broad terms, the first and third are predominantly sombre in tone, the second and fourth airy. The first and third have long introductions, and end grimly and abruptly; the other two have short introductions and are rounded off with brief conclusions. Within this strong framework the poem is free and varied.

Through an allusion right at the start, Virgil indicates that his model will be Hesiod – but only for the first book. Part of the buoyancy of the *Georgics* comes from the way in which it breaks out of the Greek chrysalis and expands gloriously into fresh invention. The poet also shows more of himself as the work proceeds. In the first book he is almost as impersonal as *The Nature of Things*, but in the second he talks about his creative character, setting it against that of Lucretius. In the third he speaks of his plan for a future poem, and mentions his native Mantua, giving a description of the landscape, enlarged from a few words in the *Bucolics*: there are green fields by the waterside, where broad Mincius wanders with slow meanders and fringes its banks with tender reed. Most Italian rivers are rapid, stony and irregular, and this is an unusual scene; Virgil brings out the distinctive quality of his native patch. The poet sets himself in a landscape, making its individuality into his own seal-stone. Other poets were impressed, and followed him: Horace on his local spring of Bandusia, which he says that he will make as famous as the celebrated springs of Greece; Propertius on his native Assisi climbing the flank of the hillside, the shallow lake in the Umbrian plain which grows warm in summer, the hollow in the hills at Mevania where the mists linger.

This poem is not fiction, Virgil insists. 'Earths are on my hands' (in other words, his subject is the variety of soil types): almost we see the dirt under his fingernails. He had played with Callimachus in the *Bucolics*; now he bats him aside. Those mythological stories, he remarks, are all hackneyed now: 'Who has not written about the boy Hylas?' Now Virgil had given Hylas a memorable cameo in the sixth Eclogue; so he was also turning away from his earlier self. The poem loves nature but its realism recognizes that nature can be harsh or cruel. Much of the *Georgics* is severe or sombre, yet the overall impression is of luminosity and radiance; this is a poem that seems to be lit from within. In the first book Virgil's tone is strenuous, but he is not, like Hesiod, a grumbler. Two words recur, *laetus* and *durus*. The root meaning of *laetus* was 'fertile': 'What makes the crops fertile' are the opening words of the poem. But more often it meant 'joyful'; so that idea is present from the very first line. Joy springs from the solid earth. *Durus* means 'hard'; like its English equivalent it can be favourable or unfavourable, and Virgil exploits that ambivalence. The toughness of the farmer and his life is both arduous and admirable. The theme turns, however, to the destruction brought by storm and flood, and modulates from this into the devastation wrought by the present civil war. The ending of the first book is violent and despairing. Yet the frame holds; this is only part of the poem, and by its end the Roman state will be firm and secure.

Allegory takes ideas and dresses them in physical form. Virgil's idea is the reverse of this: he takes the solid actuality of the countryside and shows how moral and imaginative truth grows out of this earth. Crops, animals, the landscape, the farmer himself – these things do not symbolize, they signify. The poet talks about everyday farmyard nuisances – pests and weeds. Then he mentions, casually as it might seem, that the father, Jupiter, has not wanted things to be easy for mankind. The verse soars into a broad declaration of the divine purpose, which has sharpened human energy and inventiveness through the pressure of toil and need, before dropping down to those everyday nuisances again, finally leaving the topic with a wry joke. He moves between ordinariness and exaltation, most seamlessly in the praise of Italy in the second book. He is discussing, in standard didactic tone, the different terrains required by particular vines and trees. He notes that only India produces ebony, only the Sabaeans of Arabia frankincense – and at some point we realize that he has drifted into an excursus on the wonders of exotic lands. After some twenty lines of this he plants the mightiest conjunction in Latin literature. 'But,' he says, and that little word is transformative, for it reveals that everything that has gone before was only the first part of a colossal paragraph. *But* all these marvels are surpassed by the glory of Italy – and Virgil moves into the finest panegyric of a land ever written.

He explores the variety of Italy, taking us up to the Alpine lakes, inland to Umbria, down to the Bay of Naples. There is little direct description, however, until he encapsulates his country in two vignettes: 'So many towns piled up by men's hands on precipitous rocks, and rivers gliding beneath ancient walls.' Here are two characteristic Italian landscapes: the hill-towns of the Apennines and the river scenery of the plain; but here also is a blend of man and land, nature and culture, history, time and timelessness. It is one of the greatest moments of crystallization in all poetry. It appears to be the climax of Virgil's huge declamation, and yet the poetic outpouring continues to flood onward, culminating in the great men of Rome and finally one individual, Caesar (the future Augustus) himself. Surely this must be the climax, and yet there is a further crescendo to come as Virgil invokes Italy herself: 'Hail, great mother of crops, Saturn's land, great mother of men . . .' And there is even now one more figure to appear: himself. With a gesture of splendid pride, he ends the panegyric by asserting that he is the man who sings Ascraean (that is, Hesiod's) song through Roman towns. As rhetoric this is incomparable, combining immensity with compactness, superlative technique with emotional richness. But it is even more than this, a profound meditation on how mankind may flourish, through unity in diversity, through being rooted in land, city, history and nation. This was a theme that he would take up again in the *Aeneid*.

There is nothing in poetry quite like this second book, in its sustained happiness and endless melodious invention. It is the heart of the poem, its epitome. One might think of Nietzsche's phrase, 'joy yet deeper than the heart's distress': a kind of deep delight sustains the whole work, and wells up from the depths even in the more sombre books. It is in the first book that he speaks happily of the 'glory of the divine countryside', a phrase which loses force in English translation: but glory belonged to the public and military sphere, and 'divine' means 'god-filled'. Even pests like ants and moles are given a pleased attention, touched with humour, or the raven stalking solitary along the seashore (a couple of lines which delectably mimic the bird's strutting gait). In the third book, predominantly severe, he breaks out into an idyllic rhapsody about the shepherd's life, longer than anything of the kind in the *Bucolics*. The poem loves nature, but like all the most enduring kinds of love, this one is informed by understanding and without illusion.

The second book ends with another panegyric, on the blessings of country life. Virgil weaves into it a further theme. For the first time he begins to speak about himself – his ambitions, hopes and limits. He would like to write about the physical working of nature, he says, but if he lacks the mental power for this, may he at least love the woods and rivers of the countryside, though he be 'inglorious'. And he pays tribute to Lucretius, without naming him (he never names directly any of the poets whom he imitates): happy the man who could understand the causes of things and trample the fear of death beneath his feet. But fortunate too is he who has known the rustic gods, who may lead a rural life free from the storms of war. Among other things, this is a shrewd piece of literary criticism: Virgil, the poet, is the one man to praise Lucretius for his intellectual strength, recognizing that his philosophical force and moral energy are the essence of his poetic effect. But in assimilating himself to the country-man, Virgil is, by design, a little elusive. He ducks the direct challenge to his predecessor ('Happy the man . . . but fortunate too . . .'). Lucretius has inspired him, but he is himself a poet of a different stripe.

Near its beginning and end the praise of country life is tinged, very lightly, with melancholy. His rapturous account of the peace, beauty and virtue of this existence culminates in the declaration that Justice left her last footprints among country folk when she left the earth. Now, Justice departed at the end of the golden age, and so this colours rural being with an aureate glow: we are nearer to that fabled paradise in the country than anywhere else. But we are also shown that this paradise is lost. As he draws to a close, Virgil asserts that this was the life that made Rome and Italy, this was the life that golden Saturn lived on earth, before Jupiter, and before there were wars. With great subtlety he proclaims the continuity of country life with the golden age, but at the same time reminds us, once more, how vastly distant is that happy time. And so the great rhapsody ends with a long diminuendo, and Virgil shuts the door with the quiet remark, 'We have traversed a vast expanse across the plain, and it is now time to unyoke the horses' steaming necks.'

With the bees, in the fourth book, Virgil's touch is at its lightest. As he observes, his subject is (literally) small, but he hopes that no small glory will come from it. Again, this expresses his sense of the value lying in the intimate detail of the physical world. He is both grave and humorous as he instructs us to admire the valour, customs, community and battles of these tiny creatures. He enjoys looking at things from a bee's eye view. The bee-keeper is to hurl rocks into an ocean for his swarm to settle on – pebbles, we realize, in a pond. He even compares their busy work in the hive to the labours of the Cyclopes, the giants who toil below Mount Etna. The bees are real bees, but reflections on human society glance off them from time to time. So at one moment he refers to them – a passing phrase – as 'little Quirites' (that is, Roman citizens); at another that they surpass even such oriental people as the Medes and Egyptians in the deference that they show to their king. In a splendid set-piece he depicts a battle between two swarms of bees – their stings are weaponry, their buzzing is like a trumpet's sound, their glitter like armour, and a noble spirit surges in their small breasts. But all this fierce conflict and passion, he adds, can be calmed by tossing a little dust. A lesser artist would have drawn a moral from this; Virgil has the restraint to leave it to the reader.

Skittishly, he pretends that he would go on to write about growing flowers and vegetables, were he not coming to the very end of his task, and immediately he explodes the claim by digressing, for the first time, into personal anecdote, with a charming account of an old market gardener whom he had known in the far south of Italy. Half a book, in fact, will be enough to instruct bee-keepers, and then the poet springs his biggest surprise. Didactic verse presents a particular formal problem: how do you bring the poem to an end? Unlike a story, it does not come naturally to a climax and resolution. Hesiod's *Works and Days* merely dribbles away; Lucretius' poem may be unfinished, but even he shows no sign of knowing how to conclude it satisfactorily (indeed his last book is the least strong of the six). Virgil's solution was radical and brilliant: he would simply soar aloft into a new air.

Accordingly, the rest of the poem is given over to mythological narrative. Virgil tells the story of how Aristaeus lost his bees and discovered how to get a new swarm. His mother, a sea-nymph, tells him how to capture the sea god Proteus, who under pressure will reveal the secret. Grinding his teeth and rolling his eyes, Proteus tells in exquisite language – a deliberate incongruity – the tale of Orpheus and Eurydice. Aristaeus, he explains, is paying a penalty: Eurydice was running away from him when she was fatally bitten by a snake. Orpheus went to the underworld to recover her, but at the last moment he looked back (which Proserpina, goddess of the dead, had forbidden him to do) and so lost her again.

This famous story makes its first known appearance here; we do not know if it was Virgil's invention. But clearly linking Orpheus and Eurydice to Aristaeus was Virgil's own doing: the connection between the two tales is visibly artificial. His model was Catullus' Poem 64: the story within a story, the flimsy link between the two, the emotional heart given to the inner section. But he did not imitate Catullus' disproportion: once Orpheus is dead, Aristaeus' story is quickly wrapped up. This was Virgil's farewell to the neoteric manner, achieving a melodious plangency of almost operatic character; the style seems conscious of its own beauty and yet is deeply affecting.

No other long poem aspires to the condition of music as much as the *Georgics*, in proportion, construction, and development over time. It ends with an eight-line coda. At the time that Caesar was thundering by the Euphrates and making his way to Olympus, I Virgil was living in Naples, flourishing in the pursuits of inglorious ease, the man who in the boldness of youth had written of Tityrus in the beech tree's shade. This is superbly poised. Four lines are given to Octavian, the great public man, four to the humble private poet. There is self-deprecation, and yet the sentence sweeps on to culminate in Virgil himself, as the praise of Italy had done. The balance between modesty and assertion is beautifully maintained. The introduction of the author's own presence at the very end of the work was a device that would influence other poets, as we shall see, but we shall not hear this note again from Virgil himself, for his next and final work was to be an epic, and the epic poet traditionally hid himself.

Virgil set the *Aeneid* in the aftermath of the Trojan War. The hero Aeneas has escaped from Troy with some followers but is pursued by the hatred of the goddess Juno, wife of the supreme god Jupiter. His destiny is to found a city and establish the future Roman race. The story begins by plunging *in medias res*: Aeneas is in a storm at sea. The Trojans make landfall in North Africa near Carthage, whose queen, Dido, receives them hospitably. Juno and Venus, Aeneas' goddess mother, conspire to make Dido fall in love with Aeneas. In Book 2, at Dido's prompting, Aeneas tells the story of the sack of Troy, during which he lost his wife, Creusa; her wraith appeared to him and told him of the future destined for him in Italy. In Book 3 Aeneas continues the story with his years of wandering. Dido tries to fight her love for Aeneas, because she has sworn an oath to be faithful to her dead husband. Dido and Aeneas go hunting, a rainstorm drives them to a cave, and their love is consummated. Jupiter commands Aeneas to fulfil his destiny in Italy. Dido, learning of Aeneas' intended departure before he has managed to tell her, attacks him bitterly, and after he has left kills herself. In Book 6 Aeneas reaches Italy. Guided by a priestess, the Sibyl, he visits the realm of the dead in the underworld, encountering figures from his past, including Dido, and reaching the blessed region of Elysium, where his father, Anchises, shows him the unborn spirits who will become the heroes of Rome.

Books 7 and 8 explore central Italy. In Book 7 the Trojans are welcomed by King Latinus, but conflict breaks out between his rustic subjects and the Trojans, and this becomes full-scale war, with Turnus, a neighbouring prince jealous of Aeneas, leading the Italian side. In Book 8 Aeneas travels up the River Tiber to seek help from King Evander, whose settlement is on the site which will become Rome. Evander sends his son Pallas to fight with the Trojans. The book ends with Venus bringing Aeneas a shield, made by her husband Vulcan, which depicts future events in Roman history, with Augustus at the Battle of Actium in the middle. The last four books are devoted to the war, in the course of which Turnus kills Pallas. Finally, Aeneas and Turnus end the war by single combat, and Aeneas has Turnus at his mercy. Briefly he considers sparing him, but then remembering Pallas, kills him.

We inherit the notion that epic is the most arduous and ambitious form of poetry: as Samuel Johnson put it, 'The first praise of genius is due to the writer of an epic poem, as it requires an assemblage of all the powers which are singly sufficient for other compositions.' That idea is the consequence of Virgil: before and after him plenty of poets wrote epics without the sense that the task was one of extremest difficulty. But the *Aeneid* is indeed immensely ambitious. For the first time the theme is one of world-historical importance (an idea that he passed on to Dante and Milton): it unfolds destiny's plan for the future governance of the world. At the end of Book 8 Aeneas picks up the shield depicting events from the future history of Rome, 'lifting on his shoulder the fame and fate of his descendants'. Here the moral burden of Aeneas' duty to posterity becomes literal. Most epics were mythological, some historical; Virgil's is both, knitting the present into a story set in the legendary past. He also took the decision to parallel the narratives of both Homeric epics. Broadly speaking, the first half of the poem imitates the *Odyssey* and the second half the *Iliad*, although in detail the pattern is more complex and flexible. This gives the *Aeneid* an intense compression: it adapts the stories of both Greek epics into a work less than the length of either.

In choosing to parallel these poems he was deciding, as with the *Bucolics*, to be imitative. To march so closely by Homer's side was to go far beyond the consciousness of Greek precedent shared by all Roman authors; no other epic poet did anything like it. There was a story that Virgil, accused of plagiarism, remarked that his critics should try it: they would find that it was easier to steal the club from Hercules than to filch a line from Homer. True or false, the anecdote suggests that Virgil's purpose was not clear to everybody, and also that it would be very hard to bring off. Nevertheless, he used his relationship to Homer (and other authors) to illuminating effect. It enabled him to look at characters and situations in different lights, some of which may be equivocal or deceptive.

Aeneas' enemies call him a Paris, but that is clearly unjust: he is not a selfish seducer. The Sibyl tells Aeneas that a second Achilles awaits him in Latium, but in the end Turnus plays Hector's role, and it is Aeneas himself who becomes the Achilles of the poem. Dido combines the roles of Nausicaa, Circe, Calypso and perhaps Penelope, and we feel the weight that this lays upon her. Circe and Calypso are goddesses, who cannot be deeply hurt or humiliated; Nausicaa's liking for Odysseus does not ruin her. Dido will not be so fortunate. The poem's dialogue with Homer – the interplay of likeness and difference – is deepest and most searching, as we shall see, at its very end. None the less, the closeness to Homer is sometimes problematic. As Aeneas plods through a version of Odysseus' wanderings in Book 3, we miss the élan of the Greek poem. By contrast, the depiction of the confusion, violence and panic in the sack of Troy is original and brilliant; it is perhaps the finest war narrative in ancient literature, revealing a side of Virgil that we might otherwise not have suspected. In Book 5 Virgil adapts the games from Book 23 of the *Iliad* (the chariot race becomes a boat race): it is a clever literary exercise, skilful but lifeless. The risk in stealing Hercules' club was real.

One of Virgil's problems was how to fit Augustus into the poem. His solution was to have him appear in only three places: in Book 1, foretold by Jupiter as the bringer of peace; in Book 6, shown to Aeneas by Anchises; and in Book 8, the central figure on the shield. Perhaps the difficulty of presenting the boss as the culmination of world history was one that all Virgil's genius could not entirely overcome, but he came close. In this poem Augustus is not a person but an effulgence. What matters is that he is brought into connection with a serious idea of leadership, government and society which the poem explores by other means. One of these is the figure of Aeneas himself. He is introduced in the first sentence as a man doomed to suffer much 'until he should found a city', and that sentence ends with the 'walls of lofty Rome'. The defiant Dido declares, 'I have established a noble city; I have seen my own walls . . .' The poem shows a search for rootedness, for the solidity of buildings, for security. It is also a search for land and soil; when the Trojans make their first landfall in the poem, after the tempest, they possess the shore 'with great love of the earth'. That is emblematic of the *Aeneid* as a whole. Like *The Nature of Things* this is a poem concerned with salvation; unlike Lucretius, Virgil finds it not through the individual but in city, society, tradition and institutions.

The quest for home and earth is bound up with the exploration of Italy in Books 7 and 8. As in the *Georgics*, Virgil brings out Italy's diversity. Latinus' city is ancient and mighty; his house is both palace and temple, 'shuddersome with woods and the awe of the ancestors', physical and abstract fusing. His rustic subjects, by contrast, inhabit a simple, pastoral world. Virgil makes the familiar become strange: the Trojans see the River Tiber breaking out into the sea from thick forest, after having sailed past the scented and mysterious island of the enchantress Circe by night, hearing her song and the howling of her animals. Tiber is miraculously stilled before Aeneas travels up it to Evander's town on the site of future Rome; the trees and waters marvel, as though they had come alive, and the boat cuts through the woodland as though penetrating a jungle. Evander himself is a Greek who has settled in Italy, whereas Latinus is primordially Italian. He is a mixture of the noble and the humble, with an aura of modest country-gentlemanliness about him.

Here Virgil looks upon the distant past of his nation with an affection in which touches of quaintness and humour are mingled; it was a new tone that was to be much imitated by the other Augustan poets. One touch especially tickled their fancy: the collision of past and present in the picture of 'cattle wandering all over the Roman Forum and mooing in the chic Carinae'. These scenes also serve Virgil's sense of process and his idea of history, an interplay of change and continuity. Book 8 ends with the shield, on which is shown Augustus at Actium with the very same gods that his ancestor Aeneas rescued from Troy. And yet so much has altered: Aeneas has come from the east and is about to go into battle against Italians; Augustus leads Italians against the forces of the east.

With the story of Dido, Virgil put a tragedy, with some of the characteristics of a stage drama, inside his epic. We have already encountered the place from which he took the story pattern: the episode of Jason and Hypsipyle in Apollonius' *Argonautica*. That shows that if a hero is travelling the Mediterranean, there is no harm in him having a fling with a willing queen (or, as in the *Odyssey*, a goddess or two). And there lies the tragedy: it should have been all right. Only because Dido has sworn her oath to her dead husband and Aeneas has a unique burden of destiny imposed on him does the affair become haunted by guilt. The Homeric rules no longer apply. Once Dido and Aeneas have become lovers, she does not care for public opinion: 'She calls it marriage; with this name she adorns her fault.' We cannot securely say that this is the poet's own judgement – typically he sees things through the eyes of his characters, and 'fault' may rather be Dido's own feeling – but it does prompt us to think about guilt and blame, and indeed much discussion of Dido and Aeneas is based on the quasi-Aristotelian idea, which we have met before, that the tragic hero falls through some fault. Whose fault was Dido's tragedy, critics ask; was it hers or Aeneas' or the gods'? But this approach may be too forensic and too censorious.

Let us return to the place where their love was first consummated. Virgil does not describe the cave and he says nothing of what happened in it – not a word. Instead he speaks of Juno and primal Earth, of lightning and the sentient air and the ululation of nymphs from the mountain top.

In this marvellous imagining the bounds between nature, the supernatural and human experience dissolve. The cave is both savage landscape and shelter; Dido and Aeneas' passion is both the wild weather and a human huddling from the wild. Of course we know what happened in the cave. But Virgil's silence is not euphemism (in Book 8 the coupling of Venus and Vulcan is lushly depicted). Supremely beautiful and uncanny, these lines also have a moral significance. Dido and Aeneas preserve their privacy. To ask who first reached out to touch the other would be both prurient and absurd. Probably they could not say themselves. That is how these things happen.

This love story is also a tragedy of incomprehension. Dido has not understood that Aeneas, being the man he is, will be bound to obey the demand of destiny. Aeneas has not understood that she, being the woman she is, will be unable to survive his departure. That shows human imperfection, but again it seems otiose to lecture them on how they might have done better. As another fine storyteller put it, 'Judge not, that ye be not judged.' The poem contrasts Dido with Creusa, whose farewell amid the destruction of Troy is one of its most profound and moving moments. Creusa's wraith speaks to Aeneas. Is this Creusa herself or is it not? The poet seems to say both things, and this gives the scene a poignant elusiveness. She consoles her husband: 'Banish your tears for your beloved Creusa.' The mastery in this is that she tells Aeneas not that she loves him but that he loves her. That is the voice of trust and understanding, and these are what Dido and Aeneas do not enjoy. Creusa ends not with herself but by asking Aeneas to maintain his love for the child whom they share. Dido's denunciation ends with the child who does not exist: if only he had left her with a 'dear little Aeneas' – a touching drop into colloquial, domestic language – whose face might recall his father after he has gone.

Aeneas tries three times to embrace Creusa's wraith but it escapes him, 'like to the light winds, most like to winged sleep'. The lines are repeated without change when Aeneas seeks to embrace his father, Anchises, in Elysium; even in the realm of the blessed that simple human comfort is denied him. Virgil drew on an exceptional range of sources to make his underworld: Homer, Plato, Stoicism, Orphism, Roman history and more. Even the lyric poet Bacchylides made his contribution, inspiring the simile in which the dead souls are likened to leaves falling at the first nip of autumn. Virgil, however, adds a second simile (or these souls are like birds when the chill drives them over ocean to sunny lands), so a distant warmth faintly colours the scene. Other elements of the underworld are entirely Virgil's own. Aeneas' first moments there have a dreamlike quality. 'They were going darkly beneath the lonely night' – and the poet likens this to a journey in the dark. Similes usually compare things that are mostly unlike (a warrior is very unlike a lion in most respects), and thus focus the attention on particular points of likeness, but this one fails to focus or clarify, for we are in a realm where the bounds between metaphor, symbol and actuality have become confused. Aeneas encounters Grief, Fear, Hunger, Need and – sinister phrase – 'Evil Joys of the Mind'. These are not picturesque mythological monsters – those will come later – but 'shapes terrible to behold', not further described. Are these self-subsistent entities, or is this a psychic nightmare? Not since Aeschylus' Cassandra have we plunged so far into the mental abyss.

Ultimately the journey leads to Anchises and the show of heroes. Anchises ends his speech by declaring that others – the Greeks, evidently – will be better at sculpture, oratory and astronomy; 'do you, Roman, remember to rule the peoples with authority (these will be your arts), to build civility upon peace, to spare the conquered and by war put down the proud'. 'Roman' is a dramatic word, because Anchises is no longer addressing Aeneas, who is not a Roman and never will be; he is speaking to every one of us, now, in the reign of Caesar Augustus. Like the praise of Italy in the *Georgics*, this admonition begins with the acknowledgement of an inferiority, but its stern realism makes the peculiar demand on the Roman people all the more strongly felt.

Some readers have felt that Aeneas is a failure. This could mean either that Virgil failed to make him sufficiently vivid or sympathetic, or that he intended to present a hero who in some sense fails – in humanity or in achieving happiness. Whatever judgement we pass on Virgil himself, we should recognize that within the story Aeneas' weakness, if it exists, is more likely to be feeling too much than feeling too little. In the poem's second half especially there was a danger that the hero would become uninteresting, and there are signs that the poet was aware of it. In Book 11, at the funeral for Pallas, Aeneas conducts human sacrifice, a shocking act that passes with strangely little emphasis; presumably Virgil wanted to show the violence of his hero's emotion. And the poem's very last act is an act of passion, as Aeneas, 'terrible in anger', kills Turnus. But the *Aeneid* is not, as it has sometimes been called, a Stoic poem, advocating impassibility; it shows that emotion makes life difficult and insecure, that it gives hostages to fortune, not that it is something to avoid. The austerity of Aeneas' lot is that we are shown the happiness that in other circumstances he might have enjoyed. The marriage with Creusa was good. Life with Dido would have been good, had not destiny forbidden it.

In the storm, in Book 1, Aeneas wishes that he had died long ago in Troy; in Book 5 he contemplates abandoning his mission; in Book 6 he wonders why the souls of the dead who are awaiting reincarnation should have this terrible desire for life; in Book 12 he tells his son to learn virtue and toil from his father, good fortune from others. This might tempt us to see the poem as low-spirited and melancholic, in contrast to the high-spirited, tragic *Iliad*. But that is not quite right, or at least not complete. Aeneas does not see the whole truth, even about himself; in the longer view, moreover, the poem has throughout a conception of human progress, and in a few places there is loud proclamation of future glory. None the less, few readers fail to be struck by Virgil's sense of loss, his grief for young lives cut short, and this has led to the idea that there are 'two voices' of the *Aeneid*.

The metaphor is not ideal: it might be better to think of a single voice that speaks in varying tones. It is not conflicted for Virgil to see betterment in history and yet be haunted by the sorrows of the world; rather, it is the mark of a mature and many-sided mind. Certainly, the view that a voice of doubt and sadness is the 'real' voice and that the paeans to Roman achievement should be discounted misses one of the poem's dimensions. In the underworld Aeneas wants to spend more time with a dead comrade, but the Sibyl tells him that night is hastening on and 'we squander the hours in weeping'. That is the *Aeneid* in a nutshell: the impulse to linger compassionately and lament, but also the stern pressing on towards a great purpose.

At the end of the poem Virgil faced a problem, but he was a man who seems to have found problems of literary craftsmanship a stimulus to his imagination. The *Iliad* could contain the coming together of Achilles and Priam because they are tragic, both under the sentence of death. But Aeneas is not tragic: he has won. For him to speak magnanimously to Latinus would be an anti-climax and would probably sound sanctimonious. Virgil's solution was masterly. First he provides the last and best of his scenes among the gods. Jupiter tells Juno that she must no longer resist the destined outcome; she submits and accepts the future: 'Let there be a Roman stock, strong in Italian manhood.' She becomes, as it were, Virgilian, grasping the poet's special feeling for the blend of Rome and Italy. But her hatred of Troy remains and she asks for the Trojan name, costume and language to perish. Jupiter consents, courteously declaring himself defeated.

The beauty of this is that it works on two levels. In terms of the domestic politics of Olympus, a great goddess must not be humiliated, and Jupiter's graciousness saves her face. In terms of larger destiny, it turns out that Juno's resistance has served the purposes of providence after all. We want Aeneas to win, so that the Roman race may be born. As Italian readers, we want Italian customs and traditions to survive. Jupiter's apparent concession ensures that both these hopes are fulfilled. It is indeed ironic that Aeneas' very victory thus ensures the destruction of things that matter deeply to him, but the grander purpose is achieved. It is the poem's one brilliant plot twist.

When Juno was introduced, the first deity in the poem, as the bitter enemy of Rome's ancestor, it created a dissonance, for every reader knew that she was a great Roman goddess, one of the three guardians of the city housed in the great temple on the Capitol, Rome's historic and sacred heart. This dissonance must be resolved before the poem can end, and the resolution here has a majestic finality. Virgil ties up the loose ends: he has told us that the two peoples, Trojans and Italians, will be bound together in eternal peace; he has now brought Juno on side; and this leaves him free to storm prestissimo to the poem's sudden conclusion, which is at once abrupt and complete.

The amount that happens in the last two dozen lines is extraordinary: no other work presents so much incident and so many new ideas so close to the finish. Aeneas has Turnus helpless before him; he thinks of mercy but then recalls Pallas. Kindled with anger and the spirit of vengeance, he thrusts his weapon into Turnus, declaring that it is Pallas who kills him. And immediately the poem ends. This is a troubling, searching ending, and it is right that we should ponder long and hard the moral significance of Aeneas' act. But at the same time there is a larger perspective. Virgil's genius was to invert the *Iliad*'s conclusion. That showed on the surface reconciliation and the restoration of natural rituals and appetites, but underneath nothing had changed. The *Aeneid* ends with no reconciliation described, but we know that it is to come, and underneath everything has changed. We feel at once the shock of the present moment and the further hope.

There is another doubleness in Virgil. On the one hand he is a very 'civilized' poet, literary, self-conscious, controlled. But he is also intuitive and instinctive: he finds dark and wonderful places, and no other Latin writer comes near to his sense of mystery and his power to evoke the undescribable. The golden bough which Aeneas plucks in an ancient wood before descending to the dead might stand as an emblem of this – an invention which everyone admires and no one has been able to explain. A story told that, not long before his death, Virgil asked for the *Aeneid* to be destroyed, should anything happen to him. There is no knowing whether it is true, but once more its interest lies in the fact that it was told. Virgil was a perfectionist who had written an imperfect poem, and although he left it unrevised, with some lines incomplete, some of its imperfections could not have been eradicated. Yet they are part of the poem's fascination. It conveys both a sense of struggle and a sense of sovereign mastery. It wears a classic authority, and yet no epic poem seems more personal.

CHAPTER 9

The
Augustan
Age

For Quintilian – whose treatise on how to educate an orator, written in the second half of the first century AD, included a survey of Greek and Latin literature – there were four Roman elegists: Gallus, Tibullus, Propertius and Ovid. This canon formed early: already Ovid had ranked himself with these others as the leaders in this genre of verse. For whatever reason Catullus is not of the company. There was something, it seems, that Gallus did first, which qualified him to be the canon's earliest member. His work has not survived, and so we can only speculate. Perhaps it was simply that Catullus wrote not enough in the elegiac metre, or too much in other forms; but someone must have been the first to write a series of elegiac poems from which we piece together, irregularly, the story of the ups and downs of a love affair, with glimpses of other people involved in it. That is what we find in the later, Augustan elegists. Someone must have originated it, and most likely it was Gallus.

The career of Gallus (c.70–c.27 BC) was stellar and then tragic. Octavian appointed him the first prefect of Egypt, but in some way he overreached himself, fell from favour and took his own life. The Augustan elegists, by contrast, eschewed public life. They were gentlemen of the Apennines, from the local nobilities of middle Italy. Ovid was always rich and independent, but in Tibullus and Propertius there is an element of the *déclassé*; they were losers, pretty clearly, from the years of civil war.

Tibullus (*c*.50–19) was from the start under the patronage of the grandee Messalla. His verse is marked by a kind of discursiveness and a kind of mildness. If he can be with his beloved, he says, he will not mind if people call him idle and ineffectual, and indeed he does make poetry out of weakness. The greater part of his first poem lays out the charming, humble existence that he hopes to pass in the countryside. More than fifty lines have passed before he addresses his patron, contrasting Messalla's military career with his own life as a lover, and then, almost accidentally as it seems, he starts speaking to his Delia. He is especially interested in the lover's fantasy, and how it may sit at odds with reality. In this first poem he declares that he hopes to be looking at her when he dies, but then hope hardens into certainty: 'You will weep,' he tells Delia, and she will mingle kisses with her tears. No one, he adds, will leave the funeral dry-eyed. His third poem imagines his future return to her after a long absence: may he arrive suddenly, unannounced, and seem to her as though sent from heaven. Then, as though this moment were already come, he tells her to run to him just as she is, her long hair dishevelled and with naked foot. We feel the innocent vanity in this, but a touch of poignancy too. Tibullus studies the lover's desire to arrange the object of his love as he would wish, but we know that we cannot fix the future in this way. In the fifth poem, after a breach with

Delia, he recalls the rural idyll that he had imagined for their life together, but, he concludes, imagination is all it was.

Later, he enlarges his story by falling in love with two other people, a second girl, Nemesis, and a boy, Marathus (a homosexual variation not taken up by the other elegists). Little details flesh out the story: Nemesis' sister fell out of a window; a horrid old man is also after the boy. And he had perhaps yet another love object: the poetry of Virgil, and especially the second Eclogue. For he was evidently fascinated by the psychological to-and-fro in Corydon's mind. This is plainest in a poem addressed to Marathus; the boy is clearly not present, and the argument is going on in the poet's own head. At one moment he is lofty and forgiving, at another bitter. He tells the rival lover (again, a purely imagined presence) that his sister-in-law is a slut and his wife is going the same way. Cheering up a little, he observes that she is decent enough, but naturally shrinks from her husband's aged and gouty embraces. But then he recalls that this is the man with whom his own boy has lain. He ends, like Corydon, with a spurt of childish defiance: he will fall for another lad, and then Marathus will be sorry.

Tibullus died young; we have sixteen poems, and no evidence that there were ever more. Quintilian thought him the most polished and elegant of the elegists; 'Some', he added, 'prefer Propertius'. Now Propertius (born c.50) was another gentleman of the heartland, from one of the leading families of Assisi in Umbria. In his first book of poems he writes to young noblemen on equal terms, but from the second book onward he addresses Maecenas as a patron, although the relationship seems to have been looser than that of the others in the circle. Some history of decline in his family's fortunes must lie behind this. In him we meet a figure who will reappear later in western literature, the *poète maudit*, the poet as lost soul or moral outlaw – or maybe we should say that he would rather fancy himself in that role. He begins his very first poem with his mistress's name, thus ensuring that *Cynthia* will be the title for the book as a whole. 'Cynthia first . . .' – the opening phrase indicates that she dominates both his life and his verse. He calls his affair 'worthlessness'; he says that she has taught him to shun nice girls and to live a life without aim; and he describes himself as 'good for nothing', his situation as slavery.

Propertius hopes, so he says, to 'give up his last breath to this worthlessness'. So does he enjoy his servitude, or does he hate himself for it? Does he regret the worthlessness, or is he a rebel against the conventional respectability that gives this name to a style of life that he enthusiastically embraces? Part of the fascination is that he seems not to know himself: we are shown the tossings and turnings of a restless and un-certain spirit. There is a touch of death wish, which, perhaps, he knows himself to be more than half a pose. Many, he adds, have perished in a long love gladly; in their number may the earth cover him too. And he imagines the young visiting his tomb and calling him the 'great poet of our own love'.

He also gives us the lover as aesthete, presenting himself as a man whose sensibility is steeped in literature and visual art and who brings his care for such things to his experience of Cynthia. The aesthete is to the fore at the beginning of one of his masterpieces, the third poem of Book 1. He begins with a series of pictures: like Ariadne as Theseus' ship left her abandoned, like Andromeda in slumber after being rescued from the rocks, like an exhausted Bacchant collapsed on the grass – such did Cynthia seem to him asleep. But then the poet smashes the lovely serenity that he has created, as he lurches into the scene, drunk and randy. He thinks of possessing her as she lies unconscious, but then thinks again, remembering her fierce tongue, and instead turns sentimental, laying his garland on her, rearranging her hair and putting apples in her hands – the aesthetic impulse again – until a moonbeam wakens her. She angrily reproaches him for unfaithfulness, and there the poem ends.

The beauty of this lies in its openness. Did they make up their quarrel, or did they not? Did the night end in lovemaking, or in bitterness? We do not know. We are simply offered the fragment of a story, a small lighted space, with darkness before and beyond it. Some of Propertius' motifs are likely to have derived from Greek epigram: the moonlight through the shutters, the narrator having his wicked way with a sleeping girl. But these elements are now incorporated into a more complex and unfolding narrative. And the woman now counts: her fierceness checks his sexual urge. Like Tibullus, he has an idea of how he would like her to look and be, but the real living woman will not remain the passive picture that he has sought to make of her.

In perhaps best of all his poems, the fifteenth of Book 2, triumph is mingled with darkness and defiance. He exults in the 'shining night' that he has enjoyed, the teasing, the nakedness, the shared delight, and he meditates future possibilities – bruises and ripped clothing. The eyes, he insists, are the guides of love: he does not care to do what he cannot see. But then his thought moves to another night – that long night which day will not follow. He ends by passionately urging his beloved not to lose the fruit of life: if she gives him all her kisses, they will not be enough. 'As the leaves drop from withering garlands, which you see strewn about, swimming in the cups, so for us, lovers who now breathe big, tomorrow's day may perhaps close our destinies.' Leaves suggest the brevity of our existence, as they have since Mimnermus, but they now float on the vivifying surface of the wine – a detail that is both visually acute and emotionally expressive. It is late in the party, but the party has been very good. For these final lines are a paean of praise to the goodness of life, and although death casts its shadow, the very last word is 'day'. There is a strength in this that we might not have expected from the wilting amorist presented in his earliest works.

Sometimes he is more straightforwardly outrageous. In one poem, looking back on another night of rough lovemaking – bites and scratches again – he declares that sex ought to have the spice of violence, and he scorns those whose love life goes smoothly. Paris enjoyed his passion all the more, he adds, when he came to it straight from the battlefield of Troy; while the Greeks are winning, while that barbarian Hector remains on the field to fight for his country's survival, he fights the biggest battle of all on Helen's breast. This is deliberately provocative and, for that matter, deliberately unserious: no one can seriously put Paris's inconstancy above his brother's gallantry.

In his third book Propertius turned in a new direction, or at least he purported to. He begins it by invoking two Greek poets, Callimachus and Philetas, and he will several times again present these two together, like bacon and eggs. We know very little about Philetas, who was active in the late fourth century, and Propertius may not have known much himself. The way that he recurrently presents them as a pair, undifferentiated, suggests that he was not deeply interested in either. His Hellenistic noises are a bit of a tease, a light-hearted variation on more earnest poets' allusion to the Greeks who inspired them. If Virgil and Horace can do it, he seems to say, so can I. And indeed Callimachus contributes little to Propertius' third book after the third poem.

In the first two poems Propertius indicates that this book will be a mixture of new topics and the old theme of love, and so it transpires. At the close of the book he announces that his affair with Cynthia is finally over, but in terms that lead us perhaps to question that finality, and in the event it will not quite be the end of her. His fourth and last book does have a new theme. It is here that he calls himself 'the Roman Callimachus', but this allusion now refers not to tone but to subject matter: he will write about the origins of Roman rites and customs, as Callimachus had written about those of Greece. More than half of the twelve poems in the book are related to this project.

Here Propertius' real pattern was Virgil. It is here that he describes the particular landscape of the Umbrian valley, as Virgil had described the particular landscape of the River

Mincius. He writes, he says, 'so that Umbria may swell with pride at my books, Umbria, home of the Roman Callimachus'. In those three proper names he encapsulates the three things that vivify him: literature, locality and nation. His inspiration was above all Book 8 of the *Aeneid*. In the very first lines of his own book he evokes the grassy hill that was the site of Rome before Aeneas came, the earthenware gods who have now made way for golden temples, and (of course) Evander's cows where the temple of Apollo now stands on the Palatine Hill. He is now incorporating Virgil's blend of humour, affection and patriotism into his own imagination.

There are only three Cynthia poems in this last book, but they include the two longest that he wrote about her, each of which is magnificent. The second is a wild, rumbustious comedy, an unexpected way for us to meet Cynthia for the last time. The first is set at a later date, for Cynthia has died, and her ghost visits him in a dream. For a while she is angry and bitter, but she ends with defiant passion: 'Now other women may possess you; soon I alone will hold you': they will mingle together, bone rubbing against bone. Here is the death fantasy again, but with a new kind of power and a physicality that lasts beyond the grave.

Propertius completed Book 4 around 15 BC, and we know nothing about him after that. Perhaps he died, perhaps he simply fell silent. There are poets who feel compelled to go on writing whether or not inspiration hits them, and there are those who write only when they have something new to say. Propertius seems to have belonged to the latter class. His oeuvre is small, less than ninety poems, but they seldom fail to be interesting; and just a few times he touched great heights.

Like those other Augustan loyalists, Virgil and Livy, Horace (65–8 BC) was born a long way from Rome, in Venusia (modern Venosa), among the mountains a little way short of the heel of Italy. He was a man of the margins in another way also, in that his father had formerly been a slave, and he was sneered at for that, as he tells us himself. His early life was insecure. After the killing of Julius Caesar, he joined the forces of the assassins, Brutus and Cassius, and fought on the losing side at the Battle of Philippi in 42: in wry allusion to Archilochus, he talks of 'having left his shield behind (not good)'. After what may have been a pretty desperate period, Maecenas accepted him into his circle, and from then on he was safe.

The early products of this patronage are not what we might have expected: they were 'epodes' and satires. 'Epodes' means merely poems written in lines of differing metrical form: Horace's affect a deliberate coarseness; his models are Archilochus and Hipponax. Most striking, perhaps, are two very obscene pieces about the disgustingness of sexual relations with old women. Two more are about witches, one of them presenting the torture and murder of a child; another poem expatiates on garlic and bad breath. Others are curses or vituperations of unnamed enemies, oddly unconvincing, as though being nasty were more of a duty than a pleasure. A few of these poems handle public issues, or look forward to the themes of Horace's later lyrics, but on the whole there is little here to foreshadow the glories to come.

He called his two books of satires *Sermones*, that is, *Conversations* or *Discourses* (the French *causerie* might give the flavour best). In his earlier satires especially he seems to have aimed at a mixture of rollicking vigour, sharpness and abruptness, following his model Lucilius – the most prominent writer in this genre, more than a century before – until he developed a conversational fluidity that was personal and new. Literature itself was a theme suitable for *satura*, and two poems in the first book discuss Lucilius; they are concerned with his style, and they are pretty critical. He wrote too much – he could write five hundred verses in an hour standing on one leg – and he would have improved his technique were he living at the present day. Horace returns to Lucilius in his second book, but now he is concerned with content rather than technique, and the tone is quite different. The virtue of Lucilius, he now thinks, is that one can see the old fellow's whole life as though on a tablet; and he seems to be confiding to us those private matters that one would only communicate to friends. The idea is that individuality is interesting simply for itself, and that intimate ordinariness has its own value. Montaigne loved his best friend simply 'because it was him, because it was me', and there is a similar spirit here: Lucilius' worth lay in showing his readers Lucilius.

Horace tells us more about himself than any other ancient poet. In the sixth satire of the first book he is already giving fragments of autobiography – his father's ambitions for him, his boyhood in Rome, how Virgil and Varius introduced him to Maecenas – but he ends with something more inconsequential – an account of how he spends a day in town, walking around, browsing in the food market, listening to fortune-tellers, dining on greens and pancakes. What we have here is the depiction of utter ordinariness without event, and this was quite new. Theocritus' bourgeois ladies were bustling through the streets of Alexandria for a special reason: they were off to hear a sacred concert. But Horace's ramble is entirely without story or special significance: he is making verse out of any old day. In the sixth poem of the second book he begins with an expression of gratitude for his country estate, a gift from Maecenas, and a prayer to Mercury that his blessings may last through life. The tone, informal but quietly elevated, lightly humorous with a touch of self-deprecation but seriously meant, exhibits a special poise. A humble style of story, suitable for *satura*, was the animal fable, and Horace ends with the story of the town mouse and the country mouse. He finds in this poem a new kind of personal and philosophical reflectiveness, which he was to pick up again later in his *Letters*; but for the time being he set it aside.

Lyric verse is sometimes thought to be a young man's game, but Horace was in his thirties when he turned to it exclusively. In the course of a decade or so he wrote nearly ninety such poems, which he collected into three books in 23 BC. They are conventionally known in English as odes, but Horace called them simply *Songs*. His favourite lyric metre was the alcaic, which he transformed. In almost every place where Alcaeus had allowed himself the choice of a short or a long syllable, he uses a long one. In particular, he always places three successive long syllables in the middle of the third line, and more often than not this place is filled by a single word. So although he breaks none of Alcaeus' rules, every stanza of his in this metre is heavier than any that we have from Alcaeus himself. Horace's stanza is nobly shaped, with the weighty third line giving way to the easier rhythm of the fourth (dum-di-di-dum-di-di-dum-di-dum-dum). He used the metre for many kinds of poem, but its new weightiness made it especially suitable for his more public and elevated utterances.

At the start of his third book he put together six big poems on political and national themes, nicknamed 'the Roman Odes' by modern scholars. Their theme and style, sometimes rugged and abrupt, look to Pindar. In his fourth, later book of *Songs* he was to speak about Pindar directly. The Greek poet is like a mountain river swollen by rain, seething, deep-voiced, pouring forth verses free of rule. A second simile describes Horace himself: he is small and makes songs that have been much worked over, like the bee that with constant toil collects its nectar from the thyme around the woods and waters of Tivoli. He thus advertises his self-consciousness as a poet, his awareness of being secondary, collecting his material from one place and another, like the foraging insect. In his public songs there is a tension between his aspiration to be a Pindar for his age and his sense that he cannot be. It is present in the form of his verse: the monodist's metre, the choral poet's themes. In two of his grandest lyrics he pulls himself back at the end, telling his sportive Muse to return to the lighter matters where she naturally belongs.

We need not take this self-deprecation to be entirely insincere. The Roman Odes are remarkable performances, but

the best of Horace is not here. Many of his songs are amatory, and here he can easily be misunderstood. Some are
indeed light-hearted, fragments of sex comedy, as it were, but
it is wrong to suppose that Horace thought love was unim-
portant, a thing belonging to the margins of life that should
be set aside once youth is past. Read attentively, his verse
celebrates passion, but in a different style from the other
poets of the time. The elegists wrote first-person fictions:
that is, the speaker of their poems is to be understood to be
Tibullus or Propertius or whoever. This does not mean that
a poem of (say) Propertius necessarily reports an event in
the actual life of the historical Propertius; it means that the
'I' who speaks is Propertius within the fiction of the poem. In
the elegists we can expect there to be consistency and coher-
ence between poems in how the author represents himself
and others.

With Horace this is no longer the case. In some of his
songs the speaker must be Horace, because he refers to events
unique to the life of Horace. In others we seem to be in a
timeless Greek or Graeco-Roman world; we may be unsure
whether the speaker is to be identified with the poet or not,
and we do not need to know. The Lydia or Chloe of one poem
may not be the Lydia or Chloe of another, and in some cases
cannot be. We are closer to the aesthetic of Virgil's *Bucolics*
than to that of the elegists. Tibullus and Propertius offer a
kind of realism; Horace advertises a kind of artifice.

One song is unique in being a duet between a man and a
woman. We hear in it of Lydia, of Thracian Chloe and of
Calais, son of Ornytus from Thurium. This is not a slice of
Roman life; rather, we are in that timeless Grecian world,

with the geography almost as mixed up as in Virgil's pastoral. The same pattern comes three times: the man speaks four lines, and each time the woman replies, echoing, capping and varying his words. In brief compass a story emerges: the pair have once been lovers, but each now has a new partner, to whom each claims a passionate attachment. But then the man begins to probe: suppose he were to push away his new love and open the door again to the old. The woman ends the poem by confessing that although her own new man is lovelier than a star, and her interlocutor is feckless and foul-tempered, she would love to live with him, she would die with him gladly.

This is literature that aspires to the condition of opera, symmetrical, melodious, overtly artificial. And yet it tells of lives gone wrong. Seemingly the two are still in love with one another, but it seems equally that nothing can be done about it: 'I *would* love . . . I *would* die . . .' As with the lovers in one of Robert Browning's poems, poised like Horace between humour and heartbreak,

> This could but have happened once,
>> And we missed it, lost it for ever.

Human mess and muddle are presented with flawless, luminous control. We might notice too that contained within this story of disordered hearts is the ideal of passionate love, all the way to a shared death. This is the product of a mature art: the poem is all the more moving for its reticence and compactness.

Its style of feeling is sharply different from the emotionalism in which the elegists indulged. Horace addressed two poems to such writers. The first of these is to Albius, who may or may not be the poet (Albius) Tibullus; Horace urges him not to grieve too much for Glycera and to stop droning on in lugubrious elegies about how she has dropped him for a younger man: the goddess Venus is a cruel tease, and such is the way of the world. The other poem is to his friend Valgius. Horace tells him that he is always going on and on about the dead youth Mystes in tearful verses; instead he should pull himself together and write about the glorious deeds of Augustus. This is not, to be frank, one of the great man's finer moments, but along with the song to Albius it tells us a good deal about his outlook on poetry. What he seems to have disliked in the elegists was emotional self-indulgence, a deficiency in manliness and restraint. It is partly an aesthetic, partly a moral attitude, a question of both how poetry should be written and how life should be lived.

In one of his glossiest poems he looks upon a pair of lovers, Lydia and Telephus; once more we seem to be in that timeless Grecian world. He observes the boy's rosy neck and waxen arms, and describes how his gracefully violent love-making has bruised the girl's white shoulders and his tooth has left a bite mark on her lips. The poet watches with jealousy, but his expression has an elegant and slightly chilly sensuality, like a Bronzino painting. Yet this artificial and mannered piece ends with the declaration that thrice and more than thrice happy are those whose bond is unbroken and whose love will end only with death. As with the duet poem, this expression of longing for a passionate fidelity is the more affecting for the cool vessel within which it is contained.

Horace was tough-minded. A song of consolation to Virgil on the death of a friend ends, 'Hard. But endurance makes lighter whatever it is forbidden to remedy.' There is hardness too in his song on the death of Cleopatra. He begins, 'Now for the drinking', a significant adjustment of one of Alcaeus' openings, 'Now for getting drunk'. Both poets celebrate the death of a tyrant, but whereas the Greek gets smashed, the Roman calls for a fine banquet at which noble vintages are served. Some lines of lusty abuse follow, but then comes a cold and remote simile: Caesar Octavian put her to frightened flight like a hunter after a hare in snowy Thessaly. The poem modulates from invective to a tribute to the queen: she was too high-born to accept a humiliating death, unlike a woman she did not fear the sword, she looked calmly on the ruins of her palace, dared to handle poisonous snakes, and so on. The praise is carefully limited and equivocal. As with Clytemnestra or Lady Macbeth, we may be invited to both admiration and horror at this woman unsexed and unnatural; and Horace ends with that most resonantly Roman word, 'triumph'. The tough-mindedness remains.

In his songs Horace both reveals and conceals himself. In the amatory pieces the middle-aged tone – is he finished with chasing the girls? Well, perhaps not quite – seems personal, but then we cannot always quite be sure that the narrative voice is the poet's own. In one of the Roman Odes he combines details unique to himself with fancies that we cannot believe (pigeons dropped leaves to protect him while sleeping as a boy, because he was to be a poet). We are to be aware of both the man himself and the vatic robes that wrap him round. An avuncular tone infuses the song in which he invites a young friend to look at a wintry landscape and Mount Soracte covered in snow; throw logs on the fire, he commands, pour the wine and leave the future to the gods. Then his mind moves from country to town, and from winter to summer. While youth is green and hoary age not come, it is the time for twilight whispers, the girl's laughter from a quiet corner betraying her, the token snatched from a finger that resists, but not too much. Green and white, summer and winter, youth and age – another poet might have made too much of this, but this song combines detachment and intimacy, solemnity and humour, philosophy and vivid scene-painting to make a blend that is specially his own.

Horace ended his third book of *Songs* with a proud envoi that was to be much echoed and imitated, by Ovid and Shakespeare among others: 'I have completed a monument more enduring than bronze, higher than the royal bulk of the pyramids . . .' Then he went back to hexameter verse, and wrote a book of *Letters* (conventionally *Epistles* in English, but that has a high-falutin tone which the Latin *Epistulae* lacks). Here he developed with even more assurance the conversational tone, both serious and humorous, that he had first found in his satires. At the same time he was inventing a new genre, the verse letter: all these poems, except the last, are addressed to real people, and friendship is among his themes. His subject, he says, is philosophy, and we should understand that to mean manners in the widest sense – a spectrum from moral earnestness at one end to 'how to get on in society' at the other, with the conduct of a gentleman somewhere in the middle. At the same time, Horace gives an indirect but living picture of himself, his life and his tastes.

There is a danger that a person who offers moral advice will seem smugly superior; Horace escapes it by adding just the right amount of self-mockery.

The book's masterpiece is the seventh letter, to Maecenas. It gives the longest glimpse into that intimate but combative friendship. Horace reproaches his patron for demanding his constant attendance: if he wants Horace to be rushing after him, then give him back his youthful energy, black hair and the laughter they shared about saucy Cinara. The letter then tells the story of a rich man who spotted a bloke sitting under an awning cleaning out his fingernails with a little knife (this exact and inelegant occupation is as delicately realized as anything in Horace). The grandee is so enchanted by the sight that he takes the man up and settles him as a farmer. But the scheme fails, and the unhappy man begs to return to his city life. It is the story of the town mouse and country mouse again, but the other way round, and reminds us that for all the noise Horace makes about loving the country he is also one of the great enjoyers of urban existence.

In this poem a new name has appeared: Cinara. It comes again when Horace tells the bailiff who manages his estate that he has known him a long time, from back in the days when he pleased Cinara. She reappears in the last book of *Songs*. In other words, she enters his verse only after she is dead: she represents loss, and the poet's increasing age. Did she exist? Whether she was real or a fiction, or something between the two, she shows us how calculating is Horace's self-disclosure, even in the more open hexameter poems. However, at the end of these *Letters*, in a piece addressed to his own book, he does present himself exactly as he is; his model is Virgil's picture of the poet as individual at the close of the *Georgics*, but he carries the individualism much further. For he describes himself: he is the man born to a freedman father (here he repeats the phrase which he had twice used in a satire, many years before) who has risen to mingle with the greatest in Rome. He is short of stature, strikingly white-haired, with a dark complexion, short-tempered but quick to cool down; and he ends by giving his exact age, month as well as year. Given this information, we should be able to pick him out at an identity parade; and there is no other author in antiquity of whom this is true.

He wrote three further verse letters: one to Augustus, in which he addressed the emperor directly for the first time; one to his friend Florus, which contains his straightest piece of autobiography; and one to the members of the prominent Piso family, better known as *The Art of Poetry*, whose precepts were to exercise a huge influence from the Renaissance onward. Late in life, he returned to lyric with fifteen poems, his fourth book of *Songs*. Some of these are courtly or patriotic pieces, as competent as ever, but now a little stiffer. Among the personal poems, a few have an autumnal air. One addresses Phyllis, 'the last of my loves, for I shall not now grow warm for another woman'. Another urges a businessman to relax from his money-making and have some fun before the dark fire comes: he should mix a little foolishness with his good sense; it is pleasant to be silly at times. The first poem in the book expresses the poet's pain at feeling the torments of love again after a long time without them; let Venus be merciful, for he is not the man he was when good Cinara reigned over him. The piece then seems to turn aside to other themes, but at the end the poet reveals that it is a lovely boy who now haunts his thoughts and dreams. We may feel that it was a little early for Horace to make this melancholy turn, but the ancients had little conception of middle life: a man proceeded from youth to age, with nothing much in between. And Horace was indeed near his end, dying at the age of fifty-five.

Despite all that has been lost, we can still acquire a good sense of the shape of literary development, as far as poetry is concerned, from the time of Lucretius on into the reign of Augustus. With history-writing the picture is more patchy. The earliest Latin history book to survive is Julius Caesar's (100–44 BC) memoir of his campaigns of conquest in Gaul. His battle narratives are perhaps the clearest and most persuasive in any Roman historian. Like Xenophon in the *Anabasis*, he wrote of himself in the third person, and the very favourable picture that the work gives of his character and ability is presented with apparent objectivity. His prose is lucid, plain and economical; from the soldierly manner we might not easily realize that few men before the twentieth century caused so much human misery. Cicero compared his style to naked figures, straight, elegant, denuded of literary ornament – a fair judgement, even if he meant to flatter. Caesar later gave his account of the civil war against Pompey. At the climax of this, he departed from his habitual sobriety to describe a series of portents. In a Greek temple of Minerva, a statue of Victory turned to look out through the doors – away from the goddess, that is, towards Caesar himself. This is not modest, and it is not plausible, but it does show a sense of artistic form.

Of Sallust's (86–35 BC) principal work, the *Histories*, only a few extracts remain, but two shorter monographs survive, the *War against Catiline* and the *War against Jugurtha*. His inspiration was Thucydides, even in his choice of style. We may recall Dionysius of Halicarnassus' description of the austere style, exemplified by Thucydides. The philosopher Seneca was to describe Sallust's manner in similar terms: the affectation of 'epigrams truncated and words dropped in before expectation and obscure brevity'. It is a clever style, rough and abrupt, and seasoned with archaisms. Like Thucydides, Sallust stresses the importance of his subject: he has written about the Jugurthine War because of its scale, and because it marked the beginnings of that struggle against the nobility which has led to the devastation of Italy – a rather curious claim. Likewise, he has chosen Catiline's conspiracy because it was an exceptionally memorable crime, and exceptionally dangerous. He emulates Thucydides too in having a big idea: the convulsions of the Roman state have been caused by moral decline. Energy and frugality made Rome great, but greatness brought wealth; wealth brought avarice and indolence, and worldliness was admired above virtue. The Romans have often been censured for their tendency to give moralizing explanations of historical process – in part unfairly. In a world without experts and statistics, without -ologies and -isms, other explanations were hard to find. For that matter, much of the analysis of modern historians – in terms of economics, sociology, class

struggle, or whatever – may still be moral at root. None the
less, Sallust's idea of decline is too sweeping and too systematic; it cannot match Thucydides' fierce dispassion. But he is
vivid and forceful. At the heart of *Catiline* are speeches by
Julius Caesar and Cato, the one arguing for leniency towards
the captured conspirators, the other against, and these too
carry on one of Thucydides' methods.

Conceivably the great historian of the age was Asinius
Pollio (76 BC–AD 4). Like Thucydides he had been a statesman and a general. In the 30s he withdrew from public life,
but he had had literary interests before. Catullus praised him,
Virgil wrote the fourth Eclogue in his honour and he is the
addressee of perhaps the most political of all Horace's songs.
He composed poems, tragedies and speeches, but his fame
rested on his *Histories*, which narrated the civil war between
Pompey and Julius Caesar and carried the story on a few
years after Caesar's assassination. Horace stresses that Pollio
opened his tale of civil strife in the year that Metellus was
consul – that is, in 60. In other words, he dug back to the
roots of the conflict more than a decade before open war
broke out. Pollio told of 'the causes of war and the evils and
the way things happened' – the poet's phrases suggest both
an analytic mind and a moral indignation. His *Histories* and
verses have perished; what survives, as he would never have
suspected, are three letters sent to Cicero in the year 43.
They give an impression of toughness and humanity. As
it happens, the longest fragment of the *Histories* that we
have is a summary assessment of Cicero, firm and balanced.
He expresses the wish that Cicero might have shown more
restraint when successful, more spirit in adversity; but

his fault was that whatever his circumstances, he could not imagine them changing. It is a shrewd judgement: when Cicero was up, he was cocky, and when he was down, he despaired.

Pollio was also a critic of other historians, and perhaps a severe one: he censured Sallust for his archaisms and Livy for provincialism. Livy (59 BC–AD 17) came from Padua, another of those northerners from across the Po. His enormous history, *From the Foundation of the City*, proceeded from Rome's origins to his own day in 142 books – the equivalent of between twenty and thirty modern volumes; about a quarter of it survives. His aim was avowedly patriotic: to memorialize the leading nation in the world. He had a romantic passion for the past: while his readers, he said, would probably be more interested in recent times, he liked to study distant eras as an escape from the evils of the present. He notes with regret that people nowadays generally suppose that the gods do not send portents. As for himself, in writing about the days of yore his mind somehow 'becomes ancient'. The sages of olden times thought that portents mattered, and his veneration for them leads him to include these things in his history. We have come a long way from Thucydides, but not, one may feel, in a forward direction.

Livy knew that the stories of Rome's prehistory were legendary, but included them nevertheless, on the grounds that antiquity is allowed to mingle the human and the divine and give the origins of cities a more sanctified character. How reliable he supposed his information about Rome's middle centuries to be is less clear. He was not a researcher: in each part of his work he relied on one or more previous historians and reworked their narratives. Like Sallust, he believed in the moral decline of Rome, but the later books in which he traced that fall are not extant. His style is rich, fluent and well varied; Quintilian admired its 'milky abundance'. There are some memorable passages of drama and pathos: the news of a city fallen or a battle lost, or the people of Alba expelled from the town that had been their home for four hundred years. But across the work as a whole the reiteration of vaguely described battles and fictitious speeches can become wearisome. We should perhaps bear in mind that for his first readers this was a serial publication; what seems to us repetition may have been enjoyed as another instalment of the national story. However, the most intellectually ambitious historians of antiquity studied periods close to their own time: these were the only periods for which information was ample and reliable enough to make serious analysis possible. For better or worse, that was not Livy's game.

Ovid (43 BC–AD 17) stands a little apart from the other Augustan poets – younger, richer, more flippant and more prolific. He had not yet reached his teens when Augustus' victory at Actium effectively put an end to the years of civil war, and we do not meet in him that sense of having come through a great ordeal which is present in all the other writers of his time. He was also the only one of these poets to go on into the last crabbed years of Augustus' reign, with disastrous consequences, for in AD 9 the emperor exiled him to Tomis, on the western shore of the Black Sea. The cause seems to have been some court intrigue, but on Ovid's own account a poem or poems were also a charge against him.

This has encouraged some readers to find him more shocking than he is.

Ovid's first work was *Loves*, three books of erotic elegy which at first present themselves as a send-up of the genre. 'I was preparing to sing of arms and violent wars,' he begins, 'in a metre fitting the theme' – 'Arms' is the very first word of the work, as it is of the *Aeneid*. But Cupid came and stole away a foot – in other words, he was trying to write hexameters, and the god turned them into elegiac couplets. So he needs to fall in love, and Cupid must fix that too. Once this is done, he asks for the chains to be loaded on, and depicts himself dragged as a prisoner in love's triumphal procession. The slavery of love, enjoyed and resented by Propertius, has become farce.

Not until the fifth poem does he give a name to his beloved: Corinna. But the woman's identity no longer signifies, as it had for Tibullus and Propertius. For example, in the third book he picks up a girl at the races. Is it Corinna or not? It does not seem to matter. Often he is designedly anti-realist. He tells the Dawn to delay and not to interrupt his night of love. She seemed to hear, he says, for she blushed; and yet she still rose at the usual time. He urges the door-keeper to let him in: a small request, for he is so wasted with love that the door needs only to be opened a crack (like the parlourmaid who got into trouble: 'But ma'am, it was only a very little baby'). He echoes Propertius in opening a poem by comparing his mistress to three mythological heroines, but dissolves the thing into absurdity – he is worried that Jupiter will go for her as a bull or eagle or in another of his disguises.

Yet Ovid is not simply a prankster, and his concern is not only with literature but with life. In contrast to the enervation affected by Propertius, he asserts that love should be fun. 'Every lover is a soldier,' he declares in an especially exuberant poem, and he rings some merry changes on that old metaphor, revelling in the excitement of it all. He tells his mistress how they can fool her husband: for instance, she can pass the cup to him at dinner, and he will drink from the place where her lips have been. Deceit and play are part of the great game of love, with an edge of cruelty too. Two poems deal with harsher topics: impotence and abortion.

Another piece stands out for its greater sense of realism. He evokes the heat of midday and a room with the shutters half closed to create a twilight suitable for seduction. Corinna comes; the poet tears her clothes off, as she puts up some unconvincing resistance. She stands naked before him and he coolly assesses the parts of her body, from the shoulders downward. And then – 'Who does not know the rest?' Here the woman has again become what the earlier elegists had found that she was not, an object. But is this an elegantly amoral picture of chilly lust, or is the 'I' of the poem laughing at his pose of practised amorist? It is hard to say. Ovid is not deep, but he is quite often a little more elusive than one expects.

In his *Heroines* he gave women their own voice. These are letters imagined to have been written by mythological women to their lovers (in three cases the men write, and the women write back). The idea is engaging, but Ovid did not have much gift for ventriloquism, and the collection is not as varied as one might have hoped, but a good deal of it is entertaining, and a few things are touching. *The Lover's Art* shows him at his most frivolous. This mock-didactic poem (still written in elegiac couplets, the 'wrong' metre for the didactic genre) instructs the reader how to succeed with the opposite sex; its subject is almost entirely the art of seduction, with bedroom technique handled only briefly at the end of each of the first two books. To those willing to take them, it offers the pleasures of pure irresponsibility.

Its construction is casual and rickety. From time to time Ovid varies his subject by digressing into a mythological story, commonly introduced on the flimsiest of grounds (wine is a good way of softening up a girl, so here is a story about Bacchus, the wine god). A passage in praise of Augustus' grandson is stuffed in without any serious attempt to disguise that it is a later addition; and Ovid tacked on a third book, addressed to the ladies this time, again without bothering to conceal that it was an afterthought. In another poem this would matter; here it seems part of the general insouciance. For all the supposed naughtiness of its subject, *The Lover's Art* is a curiously innocent performance. Like *Loves*, it joins reality and fantasy in counterpoint, but does so differently: whereas the earlier work had had little sense of place, this is full of Roman topography: it is grounded in the urban fabric and the metropolitan life of the modern city. Yet on this base rests an idea of unbounded Don Juan promiscuity that is pure fantasy.

What Ovid really loves, one may feel, is not so much the ladies as the life of Rome. If the girl is walking in a colonnade, he says, join her in the stroll, go ahead, go behind, hurry, dawdle, slip between the pillars, touch your flank to hers. It is a kind of dance, with courtship, architecture and idleness charmingly intertwined. We may fancy – perhaps Ovid means us to fancy – that he is more interested in the game itself than in its ostensible purpose. In the poem's most strongly felt passage he declares that he is delighted to have been born in the present age, not because of its wealth and luxury, but because it is cultivated, and the old rusticity has faded away. Ovid is the celebrant of a happy modernity; the unexpected disaster that was to overcome him has tended to obscure that fact.

Ovid designed the *Metamorphoses* to be his masterpiece, and his bid for immortality. Here he turned from his usual elegiac couplet to the hexameter, and to the difficult task of writing an epic after Virgil; in fifteen books, it is the longest Augustan poem. His solution was to shatter the unity which Aristotle had declared to be the mark of epic into a dazzle of fragments; instead of one story, he provides more than two hundred, linked by the fact that each contains a metamorphosis, with one or more of the characters being turned into animals, birds or trees, or a woman into a man. This was an original answer to the question of what to put into a big poem, but it also suited his temperament. He had little taste, and perhaps little talent, for the large scale: his longer works are in one way or another episodic. Thus his *Fasti* (the word means a religious or ritual calendar) versifies the festivals and observances of half the year, a book per month; the scheme formed a peg on which he could hang disparate myths and other material. The *Metamorphoses* has some loose structural principles. It begins with the creation of the world, and the later books move rapidly through Roman history, ending with the present day, but most of the poem has little chronology. The amours of the gods appear in the earlier books; scattered across the middle books are a series of acratic heroines; but the main compositional principle is metamorphosis, change itself.

The work was also original, among the larger poems of antiquity, in eschewing moral purpose and high seriousness (except at odd moments, for the sake of change). It is an entertainment, and, as in a variety show, there is room for the occasional sentimental number, or a horror story. But the predominant tone is comic. Even in the graver passages it is usually not too long before a joke pops up. It is hard to be sure how much Ovid is in control of his own effects. Is it that he cannot resist a clever turn of phrase, as some readers already thought in antiquity? Or is it the ethos of the poem that cheerfulness should keep breaking in? But perhaps this uncertainty is part of the tease.

The *Metamorphoses* was very widely read in the Middle Ages and after, and it thus became for many centuries Europe's chief source for classical mythology: Ovid's, essentially, are the gods who crowd those Renaissance canvases and sprawl across those Baroque ceilings. It is easy, therefore, to get the impression that classical mythology was normally like this, but it was not. Ovid's way of handling the gods was new. We have seen Aristophanes making fun of them, but still with the sense at the back of it all that they are real and powerful beings. Ovid turns them into counters in a game; he invites the reader, as a sophisticate like himself, to look down upon them, a little as Theocritus invited his friend to look down on Polyphemus, but with less human sympathy.

The game is to suck all the numen out of them. An Olympian god is turned into an awkwardly boastful swain, a goddess into a naive ingénue.

Some of the humour is cheerfully broad. When Daphne is fleeing from Apollo, he suggests to her that if she runs more slowly he will pursue more slowly too; it is as though the pursuit were a game played for the reader's amusement. (Ovid also notices that she looks even prettier in flight.) Apollo also boasts of the important places where he is worshipped and points out that Jupiter is his father. Jupiter himself, courting the maiden Io, observes that he is not one of your plebeian gods but the one who holds the sceptre and launches the thunderbolts. Sometimes the humour is slyer: when one of the nymphs, ravished by a god, becomes pregnant, the virgin goddess Diana is too innocent to realize what has happened. Ovid adds wryly, 'The nymphs are said to have noticed.'

His account of Daedalus and Icarus shows his narrative at its most engaging. The tale of the youth who flew too high, so that the wax of his wings melted and he fell to his death, lends itself to either of two morals: on disobedience (his father, Daedalus, had told him not to), or on pride (flying too high). For a moment it seems that Ovid will take the moral path: Daedalus tells his son to take the middle course, for whereas the sun is a danger if he goes too high, if he goes too low over the sea the spray will weigh the wings down. This sounds like a metaphor for the idea of virtue as the mean between two opposite virtues. But Ovid gestures at this possibility only to toss it aside. He makes Icarus a child, an innocent: the picture of him getting in his inventor father's way as he works on the wings is charmingly done. And Icarus flies high because he is 'touched with desire for heaven'; that is sheer glorious aspiration, and we can hardly resist it. But as we are preparing to shed a tear Ovid suddenly turns the tale into a just so story (why the partridge flies low to the ground), and Daedalus turns from a sympathetic victim into a past murderer. There was a partridge in a bush by the place where he was burying his son; and by a strange coincidence it had previously been his nephew, Partridge, whom he had killed from jealousy by throwing him from the Acropolis in Athens, which is why the bird avoids heights. The switch from heroic myth to animal fable, from sentiment to quaintness, is deliberately incongruous. It is easy to think of a smoother way of moving from Icarus to Partridge, but Ovid prefers the comic deflation.

Sometimes he explores the actual process of metamorphosis. The youth Hermaphroditus bathes in the waters of Salmacis, who is both nymph and fountain. She flows back and forth around him, like a serpent, and their bodies fuse – becoming hermaphrodite. This slithery scene is beautiful and sinister. Meleager will die when a piece of wood perishes; the wood is burned, and his spirit slips slowly into the thin air as the ash slowly veils the glowing ember. That is exactly how an ember goes out – Ovid has looked intently – and the sound of the verse is veiled to match its meaning.

Best of all, perhaps, is the tale of Pygmalion. In earlier versions this had been a myth of perversion: Pygmalion was a king who copulated with a statue. The story of the artist who falls in love with his own creation is first found here, and may be Ovid's own invention. Two of the classical myths that have had most appeal in modern times make their first appearances in the Augustan poets (the other, as we have seen, is the story of Orpheus and Eurydice in Virgil's *Georgics*), and in each case it would be agreeable to think that the Roman poet is the inventor, although the truth is unknowable. Pygmalion's kiss, a seeming warmth in return, a hand on the breast, the pressure of a thumb and the veins pulsing in response – it is all beautifully done.

The *Metamorphoses* can be overrated. Ovid's inspiration sometimes runs thin, especially in the last third of the poem. His passages of natural description are rather unimaginative, and he has less variety of tone and style than one might have hoped; Virgil's range is far greater. However, the ending is splendid, even if its leading idea was pilfered from Horace. After fifteen books about mutability, we confront something that will not change. Neither age nor fire nor Jupiter's anger will be able to destroy this work, the poet boasts; his name will be imperishable, he will be read wherever the Roman sway extends, and live in fame through all the centuries to come. *Vivam*, 'I shall live': that is as forceful as any final word in classical literature.

In exile he wrote five books of *Sorrows* (*Tristia*) and four books of *Letters from Pontus*. The second book of *Sorrows* consists of a single poem, a defence of his life and verse, rather a sparky performance. But Augustus did not relent, nor did his successor Tiberius, and Ovid remained in Tomis until his death in AD 17. It was around this time that Manilius wrote his *Astronomy*, a didactic poem about astrology of more than four thousand lines. We know nothing about him beyond his name and date. Much of the poem is given over to complicated arithmetical calculations concerning the zodiac, ingeniously contrived to fit into hexameter verse. Like Lucretius, he refers to his struggle with the recalcitrance of his subject matter, but there is a difference: the difficulty is now technical rather than intellectual.

As a Stoic, Manilius opposed the Epicurean philosophy of Lucretius, but the influence of his poetry can be felt throughout. When he digresses from his didactic theme, Manilius shows a real poetic gift, with a knack for the noble line and the pointed phrase; for example, a long declamation on the immutable and divinely ordained pattern and motion of the stars is a fine set-piece in the Lucretian manner. But we still miss Lucretius' depth and passion, as we do the moral imagination of the *Georgics*. Also from the first half of the first century, but entirely different, is Phaedrus. He was a freed slave, and his subject too was humble: the animal fables of Aesop put into verse. In Horace such tales were incorporated into larger satires or letters; Phaedrus was the first Latin writer, as far as we know, to give them independent status. Clear, lively, humorous, sometimes snappish, these pieces perhaps get us as close to genuine popular culture in the Roman world as anything before the *Acts of the Christian Martyrs*.

After the Augustans

In the traditional view the reign of Augustus, ending in AD 14, was the golden age of Latin literature. There was then a gap until the appearance of a silver age, beginning under the emperor Nero (who came to the throne in 54) – a revival of quality, but less brilliant than that earlier flowering. In its essentials, this picture seems fair enough, although it is most persuasive if we end the story a few years before the end of the first century, when the satirist Juvenal and the historian Tacitus appear on the scene. It is interesting to listen to the Romans themselves on this subject. Velleius Paterculus, a retired soldier, wrote in the 20s a history of Rome, in the course of which he considered the pattern of literary history, and asked why the periods in which a particular genre flourished most brilliantly were so short. There are two elements to his answer. The first is that talent is stimulated by emulation: an original writer finds new possibilities, and other writers become eager to explore them. We should not confuse emulation with imitation: the idea here is that one writer acts on another not as a model but as a catalyst. The second element is that genres become exhausted. The great period of every literary form is short: the good ideas are used up, the seam is worked out and the writer of genuine talent and ambition will be looking for new territory to exploit.

This is an interesting argument, partly because it does seem rather persuasive, but also because of the historical moment that produced it. For the first time there were two shadows looming over the aspirant author, not only the Greek achievement but a great age of Latin literature as well. Velleius was writing at a point when there was no poet alive who seemed important in his own time, or later. The idea was also around in the first century AD that oratory was in decline. Petronius' novel, the *Satyrica*, contains a declamation against declamation: the speaker argues that display oratory is about nothing real and therefore lacks sinew. Later came Tacitus' only non-historical work, the *Dialogue on the Orators*, in which all but one of the speakers assume the fact of decline; again the vacuity of declamation is blamed, with its cultivation of epigram and petty cleverness, and the loss of a Republic whose leading men had fought genuinely fierce battles in the courts and on the political stage. History was in no better case, in Tacitus' view: once Augustus had come to power, he wrote in his *Histories*, the eloquence and freedom with which earlier writers had told the Roman story were at an end, and 'the great talents ceased'.

Petronius was writing in and Tacitus looking back on a period, at its height in the 50s and 60s, which cultivated irony, wit and point to an extreme: the aim was to cram each sentence with an epigram, irony or paradox. This taste encouraged a staccato manner. 'Seneca writeth as a boar doth piss,' said a seventeenth-century don – that is, by jerks. He and his nephew, the epic poet Lucan, were the masters of this manner. But they introduce us to a novel phenomenon: the 'bad good' or 'good bad' writer. Of course there had been authors before who had large flaws and authors who were much better in some parts than in others; what was new was a kind of writing in which the author's badness seems so much part and parcel of his merit that they cannot easily be separated.

Seneca (*c.*2 BC–AD 65) was first and last a Stoic philosopher, but as mentor to the young Nero he was for a while, before his fall from favour, one of the most influential men in the Roman empire. Few philosophers have had so good a chance to exercise real power. He also wrote tragedies. There are seven complete plays and a large part of an eighth, which seems never to have been completed. Two other plays, by unknown authors, have come down under his name. One is the longest classical drama, *Hercules on Oeta*, the work of a prolix imitator. The other is *Octavia*, the only surviving example of a Roman historical drama, in which Seneca himself appears as a character.

Seneca's tragedies are strange creations. Their lack of concern for stagecraft (for instance, the business of getting people on and off set) suggests that they were meant for reading or recitation rather than performance in a theatre. That circumstance may have encouraged him to push the sententious style to an extreme. The plays are melodramatic and exaggerated, and the characters are almost all praters and poseurs; how far he intended them to come out that way is perhaps a mystery. Psychological realism is almost totally absent. When Thyestes discovers that he has eaten his children, for example, he finds all sorts of clever, paradoxical things to say – everything except what someone might actually say after realizing that he was digesting his progeny. When the Greeks prepare to slaughter Hector's young son, in the *Trojan Women*, the army gathers for the sadistic enjoyment of the spectacle. But then Seneca changes gear: everyone is moved to tears by the sight of the boy, who alone is perfectly calm – and perfectly incredible.

Seneca's angle can be seen most clearly when we can compare his plays with Greek tragedies on the same subject. Euripides' Medea leaves with the bodies of her children; Seneca's Medea, in a final gesture of contempt, tosses the corpses down to Jason. Euripides' ending speaks a psychological truth: she has killed her children in part because she wants to keep them for herself, dead or alive, and she wants Jason not to have them: he shall not have even the consolation of being able to bury them. Seneca, by contrast, has sacrificed psychological verity to *grand guignol*. We saw that Euripides' Hippolytus was a religious adept, devoted to Artemis and to a noble if intolerant ideal of purity. Seneca's Hippolytus is an urban neurotic. In a speech of more than eighty lines he declaims upon the virtues of country life, the corruption of cities and the vileness of the age, culminating in a rant about the wickedness of women, the chief cause of evil. The Nurse briefly protests, whereupon Hippolytus launches into a further tirade against the female sex: 'I loathe them all, shudder at them, flee them, abhor them.' Even by Seneca's standards, the man is a crazy extremist.

At the play's end Hippolytus is brought on in pieces and his father attempts a kind of jigsaw puzzle: the right hand belongs here, this must be a piece of his left side, where should this piece go, what a lot of pieces are missing. There is a section missing from Euripides' *Bacchants* in which Agave seems to have handled the fragments of her son's body, and we may suppose that passage to have had a grotesque power, but we do not get this here. The kindest thing that we can say is that Seneca was aiming for the sardonic macabre, but even in these terms he has failed. A good number of his epigrams have snap, and sometimes the gothic horror has its own fascination, but in the end it is hard to avoid the conclusion: a man must have real talent to write works as bad as these.

Seneca included a parody of his own tragic manner in his *Apocolocyntosis* ('Pumpkinification'), a rather inventive Menippean satire, in a mixture of prose and verse, on the posthumous deification of the emperor Claudius in 54. His scientific studies, the *Natural Questions*, find some room for philosophy, but he expounded this chiefly in a series of essays, mostly fairly short, except for the massive treatise *On Benefits*. Their theme is practical morality, the subjects including anger, mercy, peace of mind and the shortness of life. Three are consolations addressed to individuals who have been bereaved. Consolation is a difficult business: it is hard not to moralize, and it is a genre in which artifice and insincerity are especially unfitting. Sulpicius Rufus could do it, and Horace, but Seneca does not escape the pitfalls. In all these pieces there is much fine phrase-making, but the content does not get beyond the commonplace, and the author's sense of superiority can become wearing. The Stoic philosopher was supposed to look down from the citadel of wisdom upon the unenlightened, and Seneca is certainly very ready to despise the mass of mankind. Yet despite the relentlessly high moral tone, the modern reader may find some of his advice rather worldly. Riches are inessential, but the wise man will prefer to be rich, and although he can go on foot, he will prefer to get into a carriage. Nor can the poor look to him for aid: 'To some I will not give, although there is need, because, even if I give, there will still be need.' He can spare compassion, however, for the suffering of the very rich, who are left no freedom by the mob of needy petitioners pressing around them.

The *Moral Letters* are his most attractive work. All 124 are addressed to one Lucilius. A few have a small flavour of occasion: Seneca answers a query from his friend, notices that ships have just arrived, or complains about the noise from the neighbours. But even these gestures are slight, and he makes hardly any attempt to make these seem like real letters: essentially they are short essays, some on the moral topics that he handles in his treatises, others on literary or cultural matters. One discusses the treatment of slaves; the manner is more rhetorical than epistolary: '"They are slaves." No, men . . . "They are slaves." No, fellow slaves, if you think of fortune's rights over both sorts of people.'

This letter has been admired, reasonably enough, for its humanity; but there is a problem. Homer's view of slavery, and the Greek tragedians', is clear and sane: that it is sheer disaster for the slave. But once philosophers started to look at the issue, they lost that clarity. Aristotle was right to see that slavery needed to be justified, wrong in the justification that he found: that some people are naturally servile. The idea that we are all alike the slaves of fortune creates a further difficulty, for it suggests that actual slavery does not much matter. And the last problem is one recurrent in this author, self-complacency: it is hard not to feel that he is more interested in the nobility of his own sentiments than the people whom he pities. The best letters are perhaps those on cultural themes. For example, one on the relationship between an author's style and character (from which Seneca's judgement on Sallust was quoted above) is wide in reference, perceptive and finely expressed.

Lucan (AD 39–65) was only twenty-five when he was forced to kill himself after getting involved in a conspiracy against Nero. He was already a prolific poet, but only one work remains, the unfinished *Civil War*, relating the conflict between Pompey and Julius Caesar in the 40s BC. There are ten books (twelve were probably intended), with Caesar's decisive victory at the Battle of Pharsalus in Book 7 as the central climax. If Homer is 'primary' epic (the supposedly natural product of a supposedly primitive age) and the *Aeneid* is 'secondary' epic (the self-conscious recreation of primary epic's form and the loading of it with universal import), then the *Civil War* might be called 'tertiary' epic: it turns the epic poem satiric, anti-heroic and personal. And it is the *ne plus ultra* of the sententious style: there is a touch of epigram in almost every line. It is a poem without gods: 'We lie in saying that Jupiter reigns,' he declaims in the midst of the great battle. And it is without heroes: Pompey is inadequate, Julius Caesar a monster, and only the secondary figure of Cato represents decency. In the climactic battle there are no individual acts of valour of the usual kind, but a welter of indiscriminate slaughter.

The poem is openly rhetorical: tossing aside the epic poet's traditional even-handedness, Lucan insists that his aim is to persuade posterity which was the right side. Constantly he harangues and interrogates his characters. 'What was this madness, citizens . . . ?' he is already asking in the eighth line, and before fifty lines are up he has also addressed Rome, King Pyrrhus of Epirus and Julius Caesar. The first line brings the first bitter jest: 'Wars more than civil across the Thessalian plains and rights given to crime I sing . . .' The war was 'more than civil' because the chief combatants were notionally relations, Pompey having been married to Julius Caesar's daughter, now dead.

Lucan had a brilliant talent for epigram, exploiting the terseness of Latin to the full (his wit is difficult to translate: the denial of Jupiter quoted above is only three words in the original). And his conception is impressive: a relentlessly bleak, acid, angry narrative, diversified only by fantasies of baroque horror. But the execution is not equal to the conception: no classical author of comparable talent is so often and so massively bad. He spends most of the time screeching at the top of his voice: a prophetic cavern, necromancy, serpents in the Sahara, Cleopatra's palace – all are described with such frantic hyperbole that they become dull and incredible. Above all, there is a fatal mismatch between the desire to write a historical epic, bearing a political message, and the indulgence in preposterous fantasy. Even Caesar's enemies conceded that he was suave and conciliatory; when Lucan has him gloating lustfully over the corpses of Pharsalus, he forfeits the claim to be taken seriously. Caesar is sometimes presented as a madman (which is dull enough), but when he defies a stupendous storm at sea he seems perversely brave, and when he then comes safely to shore after all, there is mere bathos.

Lucan has his fine moments. One such is Cato's obituary speech on Pompey. It begins with a noble plainness: 'A citizen has died . . .', and Cato proceeds to give a measured assessment, combining praise and reservation. Pompey was far inferior to earlier generations in recognizing the limits that law should put on power, but useful in so lawless a time as this. He was 'ruler of the senate, but of a sovereign senate'. Here Lucan uses epigram, for once, in the service of balance, with a sense of the historical situation. The seventh book begins with a typical silliness: the Sun was so upset about the coming battle that it rose later than usual. But it continues with perhaps the only passage in the poem that is genuinely tragic: in his last hours of good fortune Pompey dreams of being back at Rome, hailed by the people in the theatre that he had built – an idea well suited to this theatrical author. 'Break not his sleep,' the poet tells the watchmen. The speech of the eunuch Pothinus to Ptolemy, the boy king of Egypt, begins as an effective argument for cynical expediency, but unhappily Lucan will not leave it there, and before he has concluded the man has turned into a pantomime villain. We happen to know that the *Civil War* was the work of a very young man. That allows us to wonder whether he would have modified his faults had he lived longer (who would have guessed that the author of *Titus Andronicus* would go on to write *The Tempest*?).

Another writer active in Rome at this time wrote in Greek. An obscure Jewish cultist and preacher, and only an occasional author, he had made his way circuitously to the capital from his home town in the eastern Mediterranean, arriving as a prisoner. His very existence was unknown to the literati, who would have been surprised to learn that he was to become arguably the most influential of all classical authors. Posterity knows him as St Paul.

By convention Christian writings are not counted as classical literature. Paul of Tarsus, a Jew from the coast of Anatolia in the first century, is not a classical author; Lucian of Samosata in the second century, of unknown ethnicity, from a far more distant place on the banks of the Euphrates, is. This cannot be defended on the grounds that these works were not known at the time. No one would exclude Thomas Traherne from seventeenth-century or Gerard Manley Hopkins from Victorian literature because they were only read later; and anyway, some people were indeed devouring these texts at the time, only not the people who fill the history books.

The literary qualities of the New Testament have also been underestimated. One reason may be that many New Testament scholars are committed to its religious value, and feel that to press its literary value might be taken for partiality. And some people enjoy the idea that revelation should have come in the simple language of simple men; indeed, that notion can be traced back to the New Testament itself, where Jesus thanks God for hiding the truth from the wise and revealing it to babes. But in reality, in a world where most people were illiterate, no author was exactly a simple man, and some at least of the New Testament texts are highly sophisticated. They are written in *koine*, the 'common tongue', the form of Greek spoken across the eastern Mediterranean at this time. But this was a period when writers with literary pretensions were liable to be 'Atticizers' – that is, they used Greek as it had been in Athens several centuries earlier. This has infected much scholarship with the feeling that anything written in *koine* must be inferior stuff. But the gospels are written in plain Greek in the sense that this book is written in plain English: they use the language of their time. And since the gospels are straightforward narrative, they do not need elaborate syntax or vocabulary.

Paul's immense effect is based on a remarkably small oeuvre. We have thirteen letters claiming his authorship; seven of these are certainly authentic, three are clearly by another hand, and the remaining three are under different degrees of suspicion. They are varied in tone and subject, even within a single letter. Some are intently theological (there is a sense in which Paul invented theology), some deal with matters of behaviour and practical morality, and some passages are prayer-like or exalted. The letter to the Galatians is fast, passionate and angry; no other classical text radiates quite this white heat of unmediated emotion. Paul's philosophical message is revolutionary, for he proclaims the moral equality of all human beings: in Christ there is no longer slave and free. That leaves Seneca's well-meaning condescension far behind. Only once does Paul narrate any event in Jesus' life, when he briefly describes the institution of the eucharist; storytelling was for the gospels.

The title of these works is not 'Life of Jesus' but *Euangelion*, 'good news', and probably they are different enough from other ancient biographies to be regarded as a genre of their own. Even the shortest and simplest of the four gospels to be accepted into the New Testament, that of Mark, is a remarkable narrative. If Christianity had perished, and this were the only one of its documents to have survived, we might appreciate that better. Three of the four are related, and have become known as the synoptic gospels (that is, the ones that 'see together'). Luke and Matthew both contain the greater part of the material in Mark, and also share material that is not in Mark. Luke and Matthew have each a source of its own, not shared with another gospel. In addition, these two gospels each have a source unique to itself for the narrative of Jesus' birth. Luke's narrative, in particular, has a flavour different from the rest of his gospel. The most familiar explanation is that Matthew and Luke drew on Mark and on another unknown source, besides having sources peculiar to themselves. This is likely to be right in broad terms, though there may have been some cross-fertilization.

The narrative of Jesus' birth is the world's most popular story. Its familiar form today is a mixture of Luke and Matthew, with a few additions from apocryphal gospels or much later elaboration. The two gospel accounts of Jesus' birth are unrelated. They agree on only two points: that he was virginally conceived; and that although he came from Nazareth he was born in Bethlehem (for which they give different and incompatible reasons). Luke's account is more than three times the length of Matthew's, and contains most of the favourite episodes, apart from Matthew's wise men: the angel's appearance to Mary, the angels and the shepherds, 'no room at the inn'. He also has his characters break out into rapturous hymn-like utterances: Mary's 'Magnificat', and the songs of redemption uttered by her brother-in-law Zechariah and the old priest Simeon. The combination in his telling of folk-tale-like simplicity and transcendence, plain narrative and rhapsody, is unique, and quite different from the rest of the gospel. Whether its special flavour is due to Luke or his source is unknowable.

In the synoptic gospels Jesus tells parables, very short exemplary stories. This is the earliest known appearance of parables in the repertoire of Jewish spiritual teaching, and so they may have been Jesus' innovation. Some are humorous or quirky, some disturbing, some moving and profound. The very best of them are in Luke alone, such as the parables of the Good Samaritan and, greatest of all, the Prodigal Son. This last is also the longest – at a little under four hundred words, about half as long again as the Gettysburg Address. It begins as the tale of a young man gone wrong, until his father starts to emerge as the more affecting and complex figure. Then the prodigal's elder brother enters the narrative, and for a while it looks as if, with his envious respectability, he is going to be the butt of the story, but there is another twist at the end. The telling is vivid, the moral exploration profound, and it is all done in an extraordinarily brief compass. Who devised the story? The most economical hypothesis is that it derives from Jesus himself. 'A greater than Elijah is here', but it may be – hardly less surprising – that we have here a greater than Chekhov too.

Whereas Matthew and Luke were content much of the time to copy down existing material with rather little alteration, in John we are at once aware of a shaping intelligence.

The book is constructed around seven miracles, which he calls 'signs'. These alternate with vatic discourses in which Jesus makes exalted claims for himself ('I am the way, the truth and the life'). There are no parables. John assumes the existence of the synoptic gospels, or something like them. Instead of a birth narrative, he opens with a discourse about the eternal Word, referring to the virginal conception in only one phrase. Instead of describing the institution of the eucharist at the Last Supper, he has Jesus deliver a farewell sermon, and saturates other parts of the text with eucharistic imagery ('I am the bread of life', 'I am the true vine'). Even on the cross Jesus stills seems in command. John omits the cry of desolation which is in two other gospels ('My God, my God, why have you forsaken me?'); instead, Jesus entrusts his mother to his favoured disciple, and dies with the declaration 'It is finished', in Greek a single word, signifying completion as much as termination.

It is tempting, therefore, to see John as a great thinker who has virtually abandoned biography in favour of theology. Like (on one account) the speeches of Thucydides, he has made Jesus say 'the needed things', concerned not with what he said in actuality but with what his life most deeply signified. Yet this is not quite the whole story, for John is also, among other things, a very fine storyteller. His account of the resurrection is by far the best of the four, and some of its details – such as the other disciple outrunning Peter in the dash to the tomb, and the conversation between Mary Magdalen and the risen Jesus when she mistakes him for the gardener – are among the most telling and affecting moments in all ancient narrative. The culminating sign – when Jesus raises Lazarus from the dead – is also the most vivid and detailed narration of a miracle in any of the gospels. With this in mind, we can see that the discourse with which John begins is storytelling also. The Book of Genesis opens, 'In the beginning God created the heaven and the earth' – and that is clearly the start of a story. John echoes this: 'In the beginning was the Word.' His account of the Word made flesh is storytelling of a new kind, a unique fusion of philosophy, narrative and proclamation.

Towards the end of the century, under the reign of Domitian, Statius (c.50–c.95) appeared to be the leading poet of the day. Some of his works have perished, notably a panegyric on the emperor's wars in Germany, which was to be satirized by Juvenal. Two epics remain, and the verses which he collected into five books that he called Silvae ('Timbers' – 'bits of material' seems to be the idea). These are mostly occasional poems; six are addressed to Domitian, and show the expected sycophancy; others are written for rich friends and patrons, congratulating or commiserating or praising their palatial villas. Statius seems keen himself not to claim too much for these performances, saying that he turned them out at the rate of as much as a hundred lines a day. A shorter piece mourns the death of a friend's parrot; the description of its cage agreeably parodies the set-piece descriptions of palaces in Latin poetry. Shortest of all, and entirely different in character from anything else in these books, is an insomniac's address to Sleep, elegant and lightly touching.

By contrast the Thebaid ('Theban Story') was long pondered, an epic in twelve books on the war between Oedipus' sons after his death. Statius' style is fluid and graceful (he uses more short syllables than any other Latin writer in hexameters), and there are atmospheric moments, for example the half gods, Clouds, Rivers and Winds, hushed and gathered in Jupiter's golden palace, the ceiling's convexity tremulously radiant, the portals glowing with a mysterious light. He has many pleasing pieces of natural description too, although he draws a little too often on the pathetic fallacy, which Virgil had used with such masterly restraint and depth of feeling. But there is no character whom we can find interesting, and as he comes to the climactic battle he can find nothing better than frantic hyperbole in the Lucan manner.

The most startling passage comes at the very end. 'Will you last?' he asks his poem anxiously – this product of twelve years' labour. 'Live, I beseech you; yet do not challenge the divine *Aeneid*, but follow at a distance, ever worshipping its footsteps.' In other genres it was proper for the poet to be modest (or mock-modest) – Horace deprecating the 'pedestrian Muse' of his satires, Virgil presenting the *Georgics* as the product of ignoble ease – but the epic bard was expected to be self-confident and impersonal; so this is a very unusual note. It is earnest, honest and a little touching; but it does suggest that the burden of the past was weighing heavier than ever.

It was sporting of Statius to give voice to his self-doubt, for he cuts close to the bone. The hard truth is that the *Thebaid* has no sufficient reason to exist: it is just another epic poem. This can be seen from the very first word. The *Iliad* had begun 'Wrath', the *Odyssey* 'Man', Virgil 'Arms-and-the-man', Lucan 'Wars'. Statius begins 'Fraternal battle'.

'Fraternal' – an adjective: it is so much weaker. The old seams were worked out, and even the theme of incestuous warfare had already been handled more fiercely by Lucan. The two epic poems by other authors which survive from this period fall under the same condemnation: the unfinished *Argonautica* of Valerius Flaccus and the *Punica* ('War against Carthage') of Silius Italicus, the longest poem in classical Latin.

After the *Thebaid* Statius began an *Achilleid*, a 'Story of Achilles'. This offers us something unique in classical verse, an extended account of childhood experience, carried out with considerable charm. Statius had written only one book and the beginning of a second when he died. It is tantalizing not to have more, but perhaps fortunate, as the work would probably have grown more conventional as it proceeded, and it is hard to see how he could have dealt with Achilles' adult career without seeming a pale shadow of Homer and Virgil. As it stands, this fragment is his most attractive and original work.

The best poet of Statius' moment was, by contrast, one who worked on the small scale: Martial (*c*.40–*c*.104). His longest piece reaches fifty lines; most are very much shorter; many are of two lines only. He is the master of the epigram, as that word is usually understood today: the pithy, witty piece with a twist in the tail. His tone is typically satirical; many of his verses are bawdy or obscene – that was in the nature of the game. The modern epigrammatist needs rhyme to achieve the required sharpness and neatness; Martial used the neatness of the elegiac couplet. There is some dross among his pieces (flatteries of the emperor Domitian, for example), and with more than fourteen hundred poems to his name, he could not always avoid repetition, but his standard of invention is high, and few classical authors are so often funny. As well as elegiacs, he also used those low or scurrilous metres, the hendecasyllable (Catullus' favourite) and the 'limping iambic'. His verses in these forms are usually too discursive to be called epigrams; mostly amiable, they have the flavour a little of Catullus' 'man about town' pieces, a little of Horace's *Conversations*.

Like other epigrams, Martial's are best sampled over time, not read through continuously. And yet the whole is greater than the parts, for across his works he gives us a sense of his world and his place in it. If you read about Oedipus and Thyestes (he writes), about Hylas and Endymion and all that mythology, you are reading empty stuff – this is the note that we heard from Virgil in the *Georgics*. Instead, 'read this, of which life can say, "It is mine." You will not find here Centaurs, Gorgons or Harpies: my page smells of man.' He does not, like Horace, give us glimpses of his interior life, but he gives us a great many externals. We even learn that he has unruly hair and hairy legs and cheeks – a typical Spaniard. He tells us where he lives, at one time by the Tibur column where the temples of Flora and Jupiter stand face to face, at another in a garret up three flights of stairs 'by the Pear Tree' on the Quirinal Hill. He also has a little countrified place on the Janiculum Hill, across the river, from which one can take in the whole of Rome. He shows us the texture of his immediate neighbourhood: Atrectus' bookshop with the small ads on the doorposts, the statue of Orpheus by the pool, up the hill from the market where he buys eggs and greengrocery. In fact, he gives us more of the topography of Rome than any other classical author, perhaps as much for those who had never been to it as for those who knew it well: as a man from Spain he was likely to be especially conscious that a poet's readership would lie increasingly among people who had never seen the metropolis. In one place he boasts, not too seriously, that he is read among the Germans and the Goths.

'My page smells of man' – that was a metaphor, but a telling one, for he is more interested in smell than any other classical author. A dried-up marsh, salt-water fishponds, a humping billy-goat, a tired veteran's boot, human and animal fear – any one of these smells better than Bassa's breath. To be sure, other Latin writers, from Cicero to Horace, had written satirically about personal odours, if not as inventively. More subtle are Martial's evocations of delicate aromas. Like the scent of an apple as a girl bites into it, like grass newly grazed by sheep, like turf sprinkled lightly with summer rain, like a garland that has rested on perfumed tresses – such are the kisses of the boy Diadumenus. There is slightness, moistness, acuity of perception in these smells. The wafting of weary balsam from yesterday's vases, the last breath from a jet of saffron, apples ripening in their winter box, silks from a royal lady's presses, amber warmed in a girl's hand, a jar of vintage wine broken open a long way off – all these are in the fragrance of another boy's morning kisses.

Again we feel not only the delicacy of the smells, but their evanescence; and they are at a distance, in time or space. One poem touchingly commemorates the little slave girl Erotion, dead at the age of five or six. Her breath too was fragrant as a rose bed or new honey or amber snatched from the hand. But this poem then turns in a surprising direction: Paetus complains that he has suffered much more, for he has recently buried his rich and aristocratic wife. She has left him a millionaire, the poet comments, and yet the poor fellow can bear to go on living. Martial reminds us that he is a satirist, not a sentimentalist.

This period produced another letter writer, Pliny the Younger (c.61–c.112), in whom we can see elements of Cicero, Horace and Seneca. Like Cicero's, these are letters addressed to a range of real correspondents, and they were probably sent to the addressees in the first place, but it is equally obvious that they were designed for later publication. Like Seneca's, each one essentially handles a single theme, although it is half hidden behind the veil of the epistolary manner. Pliny is interested in showing us the externals of a cultivated (and immensely rich) gentleman's life: one letter describes how he spends the day at his summer place in Tuscany, in a mixture of ease, exercise and literary work, another gives a very detailed account of his colossal villa on the sea near Rome. Like Horace, he is also in the business of indirect self-presentation, emerging as humane and civilized. It is deftly done, but he could not quite solve the problem, which only Horace solved, of representing oneself favourably without visible self-admiration. The letters are collected into ten books, the last of which is entirely different from the rest. At the end of his life he was sent out to Asia Minor as governor of the province of Bithynia, from where he sent missives to the emperor Trajan asking for instructions and advice. The book preserves these and Trajan's businesslike replies. One letter has fortuitously acquired great importance as the first pagan account of Christianity.

Pliny's other surviving work is his *Panegyric*, a long oration buttering Trajan up with lavish praise. After every allowance has been made for the conventions of the time, it remains impossible to like. Most of it is tedious, but it does contain one remarkable passage in which Trajan's presence in his palace, a broad calm in the midst of Rome's bustle, is contrasted with the bad emperor Domitian's earlier existence there, skulking fearfully in the small back rooms. The atmospheric evocation of a spacious, almost numinous interior provides a moment of unexpected poetry.

A great deal of Greek prose remains from the later first and second centuries. The most attractive of the display orators who flourished at this time is Dio of Prusa (*c*.45–*c*.115), also known as Dio Chrysostom ('Golden-Mouth'). Many of his pieces are in effect essays in practical morality. The best known of them gives a picture of the life of hunters and pastoralists on the island of Euboea, where the speaker claims to have been hospitably treated. The later part of the speech discusses the plight of the urban poor, with a stress on the moral importance of the humblest people not common in pagan texts. Another speech, delivered in front of Phidias' giant statue of Zeus at Olympia, one of the seven wonders of the world, combines analysis with an almost rapturous feeling for the beauty of the divine, as it considers in what senses images in human form do and do not represent the nature of god.

Dio was contemporary with Plutarch (*c.*45–*c.*125), who has been described as one of the most attractive writers of antiquity. The accolade is owed less to any one of his writings than to the totality of them: it is natural to warm to the energy which led him to discuss such a wide variety of topics, and we may seem to sense in him an almost puppyish enthusiasm. His works fall into two classes. He wrote essays, known collectively to later Europe by the Latin name *Moralia* ('Manners and Morals' might give the flavour of that title in English). Most of them are on topics in ethics and practical morality, some on matters of antiquarian concern. They mostly make agreeable reading, without suggesting a mind of great power.

Plutarch's other line of work was biography; like all ancient biographies, his are short by modern standards. He saw this as a distinctive genre: 'I am writing not histories but lives.' He compares himself to a portrait painter, who gives most attention to the face and the expression of the eyes, bothering little with the rest of the body. So his concern is not with great battles and glorious deeds, but with the details that reveal the mind of a man, his character, his virtues and vices. It is little things, he says, that can be most telling, a remark or a joke, for example.

Most of Plutarch's lives come in pairs: he tells the story of a famous Greek, then of a famous Roman, adding at the end a few pages of comparison between the two. His method varied a good deal from life to life. It had to, since his subjects ranged from recent men, about whom a good deal might genuinely be known, to legendary figures like Theseus and Romulus, who did not even exist. He varied his treatment even when dealing with men from the same period, where the quality of the evidence was pretty much the same. Thus his life of Julius Caesar has a strongly political character and depicts the Roman conflict in terms of a struggle between the people and the few (arguably an analysis that suits the Greek city-states better than Rome), while his life of Mark Antony deplores and delights in the romantic story of an *égoïsme à deux*. The difference can be seen reflected in the two plays that Shakespeare made from them. *Antony* is the crown of Plutarch's achievement. It is one of his 'negative lives', the history of a talented man who went wrong, but it also revels in the theatricality of Antony and Cleopatra's floridly self-destructive amour. The early chapters give a vivid picture of a tough and not altogether likeable person, but once Cleopatra appears on the scene, she becomes as prominent in the story as he, and after his death she has a long coda all to herself, telling the tale of how she outwitted Octavian's attempt to capture her, dying by her own hand. Before Antony's death, Plutarch presents her as a schemer, enslaving Antony for her own ends; now she becomes a heroine. There is a little awkwardness in this, easily forgiven in the strength of the telling. Again, the shape and colour of all this is retained in Shakespeare's tragedy; and his famous picture of Cleopatra on the Nile ('The barge she sat in, like a burnished throne . . .') is in fact a fairly close paraphrase of one of Plutarch's set-pieces.

Plutarch was a conscientious writer; he did not, like many lesser historians, simply latch on to one or two sources and more or less reproduce what they told him, but researched as widely as he could. But any biographer, however good, was severely restricted. Even when the evidence was better than usual, anecdote was at best unreliable, and there was no true way of knowing what the subject was really like. So Plutarch was 'not writing histories' not only in the sense that his genre was different but also because he lacked the information for a serious account of the actuality. It is significant that the finest biography of antiquity, Tacitus' *Agricola*, was written by a man who for once had known its subject intimately. Plutarch's depictions of people in a way have more in common with fiction than with philosophic history; indeed, as studies of character they performed for his original readers one of the functions that readers look for in the literary novel today.

The first century is also the likeliest date of a Greek critic who has already appeared in this book, author of a treatise *On Height*. His name is lost; a scribe wrote that it might be 'Dionysius or Longinus', this was then misunderstood as the name Dionysius Longinus, and he has been generally known as Longinus ever since. *On Height* is *De Sublimitate* in Latin, and his work has usually been called *On the Sublime* in English. Longinus' concept of height includes what we would call sublimity, but has a larger range: it includes great thought, emotional power, effective use of metaphor and other figures, and skill in style, rhythm and choice of language. Height is a yardstick by which quality can be judged, both technique and inspiration, and Longinus is the best practical literary critic to have survived from antiquity. He quotes from the beginning of Genesis, and the citation of a Jewish text is so unusual that he may himself have been a Jew.

*

If we were to stop the clock around AD 90, the history of Latin literature might seem to have a clear shape, rather similar to Greek. There is a summit of dazzling achievement, then a dip, then a second, smaller summit, in a period conscious of its belatedness, and of the shadow of a greater past looming over it. But this picture is disturbed by the appearance, near the end of the first century, of two writers of genius: Tacitus and Juvenal. Although very different from each other, there is something that they share: a kind of saturnine grandeur and dark brilliance. In that shared note they found perhaps the best response to both the political circumstances of their time and their place in the development of literary history.

In Tacitus (c.56–c.118) the potential of the Latin silver age was belatedly achieved. He inherited its taste for epigram but combined this with a capacity that Seneca and Lucan had lacked: the power of self-restraint, of knowing when to stop. His first work, probably, was a life of his father-in-law, the general Julius Agricola. At its centre is Agricola's work in governing and pacifying Britain, and here Tacitus combined admiration for his subject with a remarkably detached and independent view of the effects of Romanization. He shows that Agricola had a civilizing mission, encouraging the Britons to build houses, forums and temples and educating their leaders in the liberal arts. The natives even took to the toga, and regarded it as a sign of distinction. But Tacitus saw that this was an equivocal gift, as he explained with his usual sardonic brevity. Gradually they were lured by those enticements to weakness, colonnades, baths and the elegances of the dinner-table. In their naivety they called it culture, whereas it was part of their enslavement. In similar vein Tacitus allows a British chieftain to turn upon the Romans one of his most famous phrases: 'They make a devastation and call it peace.'

Towards the end of the work Tacitus first showed his talent for dark yet poetic narrative. Agricola returns to Rome, and to the jealous emperor Domitian. He slips by night into the city, by night to the Palatine Hill and the imperial presence. He then lies low, but falls ill and dies soon after, whether by foul play or from natural causes, Tacitus says that he does not know. His final assessment of Agricola is both magisterial and charmingly personal. Its anger against Domitian is evident and yet austerely controlled. It uses point and epigram, but combines it with a lapidary authority. In these paragraphs he lifted Latin prose to a new level of eloquence and emotional force.

His monograph *Germany* again took him to the edges of the empire and beyond; this was an essay in ethnography, an attempt to understand the customs and society of barbarians – their religion, for example – in their own terms. His first work of narrative on a large scale was the *Histories*. This related Roman history from 69 to 96, but only the early part of it, covering the years 69 and 70, survives, with the consequence that we lack Tacitus' account of events when he was himself at the centre of affairs (he was a consul in 97). The extant narrative is divided between warfare at a distance and the action in Rome itself. This was a period of civil war and chaos, with five emperors in little more than a year, and all but the last of them coming to sticky ends. Tacitus describes all this with brilliant savagery and force. No writer presents the city of Rome with a greater intensity: it becomes almost a character in the drama. The last days of the emperor Vitellius, for example: he flees from the Forum to the imperial palace on the Palatine Hill, where he is terrified by the emptiness and solitude, then flees again to the Aventine Hill, where he is seized, dragged half naked through the streets, slaughtered, and hauled with a hook into the Tiber.

For his last work, the *Annals*, Tacitus went back in time, narrating the reigns of the first four emperors after Augustus, from the accession of Tiberius in 14 to the death of Nero in 68. This too comes down to us incomplete: missing are part of Tiberius' later reign, all of Caligula's, the early part of Claudius' and the later part of Nero's. Tacitus' style, abrupt, compressed, alert and asymmetrical, is throughout superbly accomplished. Latin has neither the definite nor the indefinite article, and it can dispense with many of the pronouns and other little auxiliary words that English requires; it can thus achieve a tightness and terseness that other languages cannot match. Tacitus exploits the genius of his language to the full, and many of his best phrases are very hard to translate. His style is inseparable from his content: the aphoristic tautness, the penetrating drops of acid, are a way of thinking and feeling as much as a manner of writing. He uses his language mostly to cast a cold eye on power, ambition and folly, but he could be poignant too, as when he briefly relates how after Tiberius' formerly all-powerful minister Sejanus fell, his children were murdered. As they were dragged to prison, the boy knew what to expect, but the girl understood so little that she kept asking what she had done wrong; she could be beaten (she said), as children are, and she would not do it again. The historian adds contemporary report that, because the execution of a virgin was unheard of, the executioner raped her beside the noose, before both children were strangled. When one thinks what Lucan would have made of this, Tacitus' terseness stands out all the more. There is no sentence in Latin prose more harrowing than these.

At the start of the *Annals*, Tacitus claims that whereas previous accounts of this period have been obsequious or vengeful, he will write 'without anger or partiality, of which I am far from having cause'. But he waits until his fourth book, more than half way through the narrative of Tiberius' reign, to give a summary of his own methods and purpose. All states, he says, are ruled by the people, by an aristocracy or by a single man. That analysis chimes with Polybius, but he differs in his conclusion: the mixed constitution is difficult to achieve, and even then cannot last long. When studying a democracy, he argues, the need is to understand the populace and how it is manipulated; with an oligarchy, to understand the minds of the leading men; and where one man rules, the petty details about him signify. Some of his content, he observes, may be thought slight and trivial, but matters which seem slight at first glance may have momentous consequences. This recalls Plutarch's concern for the little telling details, something that in his view belonged to biography as distinct from history. For Tacitus, however, they are useful for the historical lessons that they may provide, but they offer 'the least possible entertainment'. This recalls Thucydides' dour observation that the lack of fable in his work may make it less attractive, but Tacitus adds a newly truculent tone. The historians of an earlier epoch, he declares, could write about wars and conquests, or the political struggles of a free people, whereas 'my own toil is narrow and inglorious'. They could describe the geography of other lands, the changes and chances of battle, a general's glorious death; he must recount cruelty, betrayal, the ruin of the innocent – an unvarying and wearisome recital. So Tacitus brings together two claims: that his theme is drabber than that of other historians'; and that it is monotonous.

There is some rhetorical sleight in this. We cannot quite believe that Tacitus would rather be writing like Livy, and we may doubt whether he expects us to. Indeed, when he does recount campaigning in Germany, his heart seems to be less in it. As with the doggedness of Lucretius, his bitter concentration on his grim theme has its own aesthetic power, achieved not despite the bleakness and narrowness but through those very qualities. We know that this is what he really wants to do, and he knows that we know. There is a sense in which Tacitus flatters his readers: he supposes that we too have a knowingness, and the ability to spot his nuances and ironies.

His study of the operation of autocracy is at its most intense in his account of Tiberius' reign, which occupies the first six books. When Tiberius dies, Tacitus sums up his character and career. In antiquity the prevalent although not the only conception of human character was that each person is born with a fixed disposition. Circumstances may or may not allow it full expression, but essentially it is innate. Tacitus' idea is that the ruling principle of Tiberius' life was the vice of dissimulation. So as he nears his deathbed, 'Now his body, now his strength, not yet his dissimulation were deserting him.' But his will remained rigid, his face and conversation firm, for Tacitus continues to find something impressive in this bad man. His final verdict is that Tiberius' behaviour declined in stages through his life, as the various restraints upon him fell away, with the successive deaths of Augustus, his nephews, his mother and Sejanus, until the true ugliness of his nature stood revealed. But, a little earlier, he put into the mouth of one of the emperor's contemporaries another interpretation: that Tiberius, for all his long experience of public life, had been changed and subverted by the effect of absolute power.

This sounds like the understanding favoured today, that character is malleable and may be altered by circumstance. So although Tacitus asserts his own view in lapidary summary, he allows, in passing, for another possibility. That is the act of a responsible historian. His own analysis, however, seems to face a difficulty: if Sejanus was the evil genius who drove Tiberius downward, as Tacitus has earlier claimed, how can his death have lowered him still further? Tacitus wriggles out of the problem with a brilliant epigram: 'His cruelty was detestable but his lusts hidden as long as he loved Sejanus – or feared him.' That tiny twist at the sentence's end glances at psychological complexity, the dark places of the mind. Many modern historians think that Tacitus underestimated Tiberius' reasons of policy, diplomacy and (in his earlier life) sheer necessity for hiding his feelings. But while his judgement may be debatable, it was not unconsidered.

Because his idea is that Tiberius' behaviour continually deteriorated, and because he sees one vice as directing it, he allows him some merits, especially in the earlier part of his reign. He was not superstitious; he was reasonably firm against the temptations of money; he could resist flattery. In later life he retired to the island of Capri, to indulge, so rumour said, in various sexual depravities. Suetonius (born *c.*70), who wrote short biographies of the first twelve emperors, provides the details. The crucial part of Tacitus' history is missing, but probably he did not make much of this tittle-tattle. However, might this limited kindness to some parts of Tiberius' character be part of a deeper cunning?

Among Plutarch's essays is one *On the Malice of Herodotus*, whom he presents as a sneaky rhetorician. He lists the techniques that a malicious writer employs: he uses severer language when gentler terms would suffice; he drags in discreditable material where it is irrelevant, and leaves out material creditable to his subject; where two accounts are possible, he prefers the more unfavourable one; sometimes he tells a damaging story, and then says that he does not actually believe it himself; he mixes a little praise in with the blame in order to sound more plausible. As an account of Herodotus' method this is strikingly imperceptive, but that is exactly where its interest lies. Plutarch has applied to the historian the standards of his own time, describing the rhetorical techniques of praise and blame: how to blacken your tyrant. And we can see all these techniques in Tacitus.

Does this refute his claim to write 'without anger or partiality'? Not quite. Tacitus could have answered that the orator's job is to put his case as persuasively as he can, and in this respect history is a branch of rhetoric (in fact a contemporary Greek sophist, Rufus of Perinthus, said just that). Of course the historian should make his own judgements, and provided he does not falsify the facts it is up to the reader to distinguish fact from interpretation, and to use his own judgement in turn. Where we can test Tacitus against evidence from other places, he looks reliable. Indeed, those who accuse him of rhetorical manipulation pay him a back-handed compliment, for they draw their own evidence mostly from his text. He gives us the material with which to contest his conclusions. True, we may need to keep alert, but he expects no less of us.

And there is another consideration: Tacitus loathes Tiberius, but he is half in love with him too. Uniquely in the *Annals*, he describes how he looked: tall, bent and exceptionally thin, bald on top, his face covered with sores and patched with plaster. This sort of thing belonged, if anywhere, in biography rather than philosophical history. Is it not the last unfairness, some might say, that his sinister appearance should be used against him? But we do better to feel that Tacitus is enthralled by this man, whose presence is so powerful that even his physical being forces itself on to the page. This is the most extended study of an individual in classical prose, and the place where antiquity comes nearest to our own idea of the literary novel. It can be tempting, therefore, to see Tacitus as a literary master, who matters more aesthetically than historically. But that would be a mistake. Rather, his genius was to bring an aesthetic imagination to the service of an intellectual quest.

Rome did not achieve a continuous tradition of verse satire; each of the four principal satirists – Lucilius, Horace, Persius and Juvenal – stands isolated. Persius (34–62) wrote in the reign of Nero; there are only six poems, along with a short prologue in 'limping iambics'. He admired the slyness of Horace, the acuity concealed in play, but that was not his own way. Instead he is splenetic, tight and tortuous; he imagines his old tutor telling him that he is clever at sharp juxtapositions, and he despises contemporary verse for lacking balls and the taste of bitten fingernails. He was greatly admired in the Renaissance, and Donne's *Satires* give some sense of his odd, edgy tone. Juvenal (active *c*.100–130) is the last of the four verse satirists, and quite different from the other three. His style is richer, and the personal, confiding tone that was affected by Lucilius and Horace is replaced by a grand impersonality. The voice is vehement, but we do not know where it is coming from. That effect recalls Lucretius, and indeed Juvenal's poems and the satiric parts of Lucretius are more like one another than they are like anything else.

The first satire begins with an explosion of crossness: 'Am I always to be only a listener?' It is as though we are in the middle of a poetry reading. He is fed up with all these literary recitals, and he will get his revenge. Then he plunges us into the rush of Rome: the lawyer Matho's litter passes, full of Matho, a supergrass follows, sycophants shove us out of their way. Stand at a crossing, and you will want to fill a large notebook with the crooks that you see. 'If nature denies me, indignation makes my verse – such verse as it can, as I write, or Cluvienus.' We do not know who Cluvienus is, and we do not need to – clearly some hack. The idea is that the ugliness of modern life drives him in the satiric direction; it is as if he had a frustrated aspiration to something nobler. In a later poem he wonders if the reader will think that he has stepped outside the bounds of his genre and begun to sound like Sophocles (to which the answer is indeed no). It is hard to find traces of the earlier satirists in him, but there are Virgilian resonances.

Indignation need not mean anger, and it need not mean moral indignation: many of the figures whom he sets before us are indeed vicious, but much of his satire is directed at vulgarity and tastelessness: indignation is the large sense that 'things shouldn't be like this'. Towards one of his most sordid characters he adopts an ironic mildness: Naevolus in Satire 9 is a male prostitute who specializes in pleasuring pathics. Juvenal interviews him, he complains what a tough time he has, and the satirist replies with sympathy and sweet reason. We are left to supply the disgust ourselves. The denunciation of Rome in Satire 3 is not presented as his own but put into the mouth of the imaginary Umbricius, who is leaving town, driven out by the impossibility of earning an honest living there. Unlike Juvenal, he is a native of the city itself, and there is a melancholy to his exile. Touching too is Umbricius' picture of the penurious Cordus, who lived in a garret beneath the tiles where the gentle doves used to lay their eggs, with a few ornaments and a box of books that the philistine mice would nibble, not knowing Greek. 'Cordus had nothing, who denies it?' – but he has lost that nothing in a fire. There is poignancy here, but an affectionate humour plays about it. As Juvenal introduces Umbricius, he provides his own list of the horrors of Rome: fires, buildings collapsing, a thousand savage dangers, and poets still reciting in August. Those dangers were real enough – we hear of them in many other places – but Juvenal ends his list with a lightly humorous anti-climax. The scowl is there, but an easy smile breaks in.

At different times Juvenal has been interpreted as a prophetic voice denouncing the sins of his generation, as an easy opportunist and, more recently, as a self-mocking ironist who sets up a moralizing persona whose hypocrisies we are meant to see through. All these views miss the point: Juvenal is a declaimer. We have found Petronius and Tacitus condemning declamation for its damaging effect on oratory. Juvenal laughs at it himself. He looks back to his schoolboy exercises in declamation when he 'gave advice to Sulla', recommending to the dictator, a figure from a rather distant past, that he should retire and sleep more soundly. 'Go, madman,' he tells Rome's great enemy Hannibal, 'and rush over the savage Alps, to become the schoolboys' favourite and a declamation piece.' But declamation gave him the structure for several of his poems.

This is clearest in Satire 8, which begins with a question – what is the use of family trees? – and proceeds to argue that noble birth is a bad thing, because it makes a man likely to look inferior to his ancestors. The topic for declamation is proposed in the first words, and duly answered. The enormous Satire 6 is an argument against marriage. It begins with a picture of the days of Saturn, the golden age when Chastity and Justice still dwelt on earth. Women then were not like Lesbia or Cynthia, the ladies of love poetry, but suckled big babies at their breasts, often looking shaggier than their acorn-belching husbands. This is not simple-minded idealization of the past, but an ironic view. The poem runs through different kinds of women: some are monstrously cruel or promiscuous, but others are merely tiresome: the affected music-lover, the lady interested in politics, the literary enthusiast, the aristocrat who makes her husband seem small. And suppose you did find the perfect wife – who could bear perfection? It would be wrong to write this powerful and inventive satire off as seven hundred lines of misogyny. Men are to blame also: the man who casts his wife off as soon as she begins to lose her looks, all those men who find virtue simply boring. The poet is an advocate making a particular case as strongly as he can; as far as anything said in the satire goes he could have written another seven hundred lines warning women about the awfulness of men.

In a less overt way declamation also provides the structure for Satire 10, his grandest performance. The implicit topic is the question, 'What should one pray for?' and the poem goes through the things conventionally supposed to be blessings – power, military glory, beauty, long life – demonstrating how each can bring misfortune with illustrations from contemporary life, history and myth. Old age, for example, brings impotence, and Juvenal describes the member lying flaccid for all its owner's nightlong efforts – but in language reminiscent of Virgil. Virgil is again in his mind as he evokes the magnificence of King Priam of Troy – happy had his life only been shorter – and then describes his slaughter, like a poor old ox at the altar. There is a majestic, bitter pity to this, contempt mixed with a kind of angry compassion.

For all that some of his poems may seem to sprawl, Juvenal is a concentrated writer and a brilliantly inventive phrase-maker, the language alert and alive with point and detail in almost every line. He is also a master of technique: no one had used the hexameter so expressively since Virgil. This can be seen, in a small way, by observing how his most famous phrases gain from the context in which they occur. For example, he will let the telling word or phrase spill over into the start of a new line, where it stands highlighted: '"Draw the bolt, keep her in." But who will guard the actual | guards?' In sonorous threnody he declares that the Roman people, who once had the power to bestow office, power and armies, now 'anxiously wants only two things, | bread and circuses'. In the tenth Satire he draws the argument to a conclusion, in the proper declaimer's way: 'Is there nothing, then, that men should pray for?' Well, there is something: 'a healthy mind in a healthy body'. In its place this is not quite the public-school ideal that it may seem. If you must pray for something, he has said, and want to go through all that business with entrails and sausages – religious ritual disdainfully described – then pray for this. The sentiment is grudging: hope at least that your mind and body work. And yet a nobility remains: the poem ends by looking towards the virtue that prefers labour to luxury and rises superior to anger and desire. A powerful tension pulls between lofty Stoicism and satiric belittlement.

One of Juvenal's satiric techniques is literalism. 'Weigh up Hannibal,' he demands; how many pounds does the great commander come to? Alexander the Great chafed at the limits of the world, but he will have to be content with the space inside a sarcophagus. This literalism is allied to visuality. How does a Roman triumph actually look? It displays damage and unhappiness: broken armour and chariots, miserable captives. If Hannibal had entered Rome victorious, what would that have been? A one-eyed man atop an elephant. Juvenal has a superb eye for detail, often mingled with fantasy: the music-lover's rings glittering as her hand moves across the sounding-board; the 'watching windows' of Rome at night, which both depicts the candlelight and gets inside the jumpy pedestrian's skin; the pike, 'fat from the gushing sewer', penetrating the heart of the city subterraneously. The man before a corrupt military board faces 'a soldier's boot and big calves drawn up to great benches', and we share his nervous, downward gaze. Grimy schoolbooks are assimilated to their authors, Horace discoloured and Virgil black with soot. Sometimes there is sheer loveliness: the 'apples on the mere scent of which you might feed, such as the eternal autumn of the Phaeacians knew, or which you might believe stolen from the African sisters . . .' But these are served to the host and his favoured friends at a grand banquet; a piece of rotting fruit is what you get on the lowest table. Juvenal did more than any other ancient writer to give the modern world its idea of satire; he is the most satiric of poets, but the most poetic of satirists too.

Two Novels

The ancient world did not practise the kind of literary realist novel that has been so important in western culture since the eighteenth century. The earliest work of prose fiction, as we have seen, was Xenophon's *Education of Cyrus*, but its historical mode did not attract other writers. Much later the Greeks developed the romance novel: in these stories a boy and girl fall in love, are separated, and endure hardships and adventures before the eventual happy ending; pirates, brigands, exotic travel, prison, torture and the threat of rape are the standard ingredients of these works. Five examples survive complete, dating from between the first and the third or fourth centuries AD. One of these, unusually short, has a gentleness and innocence that mark it out from the others. This is Longus' *Pastoral Tale of Daphnis and Chloe* (late second or early third century), which retains a genuine if faintly anaemic charm. It is of great historical importance for bequeathing to later Europe the idea of pastoral romance in prose: it is, for example, the ancestor of Sir Philip Sidney's *Arcadia* and Thomas Lodge's *Rosalind*, which was in turn the model on which Shakespeare based *As You Like It*.

Shorter still, and entirely different in character, is perhaps the most imaginative and compelling work of prose fiction in

Greek, from the late first century: the *Revelation* of John (of whom we know nothing beyond what we can learn from his book – certainly not the author of the fourth gospel), which became the last book of the Bible. For a fiction it is, an account of imaginary events supposedly experienced by the author himself, told in the first person, like Dante's *Divine Comedy*. Its affinities are with Jewish apocalyptic writing, but it far surpasses the other examples known to us. We can also compare the *Shepherd*, a second-century Christian account of visions by a narrator who gives his name as Hermas – much more pallid and discursive. It is notoriously difficult to describe convincingly a world beyond death, and especially to describe paradise. John's brilliant insight was to focus on God himself and the act of worship, so that the minds of the inhabitants of heaven are directed not to their own bliss, but outwards, towards another. The eschatological horrors in the centre of the work are its most famous part, but even more remarkable is the final picture of the new Jerusalem descending from above, a vision of irradiated peace and joy. The travel of the story towards the light of an ultimate revelation or consummation is hardly to be matched elsewhere in classical literature (and seldom perhaps at any time) outside one or two of its greatest works: the *Iliad*, for example, the *Oresteia* and the *Republic*.

Only two Latin novels survive, and only one complete, but each is a masterpiece and each is unique, like nothing much except itself. The first of these is Petronius' *Satyrica* (the commonly used title *Satyricon* comes from a misunderstanding; it is a Greek genitive plural: X books 'of *Satyrica*').

The title, 'A Satyr-like Tale', invites the expectation of rau-
cousness, bawdy and sexual incontinence. The work appears
to date from Nero's time, and it is attractive to suppose that
its author was the very Petronius who was famous as Nero's
'arbiter of taste'. Tacitus' character sketch of this able and
cynical voluptuary does not mention that he wrote anything,
and if he was indeed the author of the *Satyrica* that silence
becomes significant: the novel, that low genre, was below the
dignity of philosophic history. But the question of authorship
remains uncertain. One section, 'Trimalchio's Dinner', survives complete, along with a few other quite substantial
chunks. The novel may have been very long, in which case we
have only a small part of the whole.

It is told in the first person by Encolpius, in whom are
combined two types popular in the twentieth century but
rare in antiquity, the anti-hero and the dodgy narrator: cultivated and sophisticated, he is also a parasite and thief, and
his are the cold, clever eyes through which we view the
action. The story seems to have charted his wanderings with
his unfaithful catamite Giton and his rival Ascyltus (all three
names are sexually suggestive). He has problems with impotence, and the plot seems to have him persecuted by the
phallic god Priapus in parody of Odysseus' persecution by
Poseidon in Homer. Some, perhaps much, of the work was
highly obscene, and the social comedy of Trimalchio's dinner
may have been an untypical part of it. Another character is
the bad poet Eumolpus, but with the opportunism of farce
Petronius allows him to tell the comically macabre story of
the widow of Ephesus in dashing style. This is one of classical

literature's best short stories: in its ability to unfold a vivid tale, with a twist or two, in a small compass, it resembles the parable of the Prodigal Son, although in nothing else.

Trimalchio is a former slave who has become immensely rich. Petronius makes his wealth preposterously large: he contemplates buying land in Sicily so that he can travel from Naples to Africa entirely on his own property (one thinks of P. G. Wodehouse's American tycoon, who had put in an offer for Kent and Sussex, and was waiting to see if it had been accepted). But Petronius is observant as well as fantastical, and as a rounded study of character Trimalchio is unique in ancient prose fiction. He is a mess of contradictions, but that is his nature; he wants to take up an attitude, but cannot decide which. At one moment he is harsh to his slaves, at another he takes the high-minded philosophical view that we heard from Seneca: slaves are human and have drunk the same milk as others. His confusion is illustrated by the silver skeleton that he has brought in: he declaims sentimentally about the littleness of man, while the expensive material asserts his importance. One should talk literature at dinner, he says, but the epitaph that he has written for himself is proudly philistine: 'Virtuous, brave and true, he began humbly, left thirty million sesterces, and never listened to a philosopher.'

Sometimes Petronius allows him to be wittier than he ought to be – unless we suppose that his wit is unintentional: dilating foolishly on astrology he remarks that those born under the sign of the ram have 'a hard head, a shameless brow and sharp horns. Many professors are born under this sign . . .' Mostly he is a comic butt: he is superstitious and mawkish, his puns are puerile and his showing-off vulgar: he uses a silver chamber-pot in public, and wipes his hands on a slave's head. He has a hundred cups, he says, portraying 'Cassandra's dead children' so skilfully 'that you would think they were alive'. He craves affection: he has told his slaves that he means to free them in his will 'so that my household may love me now as though I were dead'. Throwing his dog a bit of bread, he remarks, 'No one in my house loves me more.' Later, drunk and maudlin, he rehearses his funeral: his shroud is brought in, and lying on a heap of cushions he announces, 'Pretend I'm dead. Say something nice.' Encolpius finds Trimalchio nauseous and contemptible, but the modern reader is likely to find something endearing in him. What did Petronius intend? Maybe he wants us to disagree with the narrator, but maybe this is one of those cases where an author's creative vitality has overridden his conscious design and produced something richer than he meant.

The story is also enlivened by the conversation of the humbler guests, fast, dour and gossipy. In some cases we do not know enough about colloquial speech to be sure whether a neat phrase is a cliché or a lively invention: 'He has joined the majority', for example, of a man who has died. Here we first meet the trope that Dickens was to give to Sam Weller: '"There's bits like this and bits like that," as the yokel said when he lost his spotted pig.' Some of the talk is meant to be tiresome, although Petronius has the skill to make tediousness entertaining. One speaker seems precariously poised between sentimentality and an eloquent nihilism: 'Dear, dear, we are but walking bladders. We are worth less than flies . . . no more than bubbles.' Encolpius and the others think him a bore, and yet an expressive bleakness remains, as in Trimalchio's own story of seeing the Sibyl hanging in a bottle, who when the children asked her what she wanted, answered, 'I want to die.'

The *Satyrica* is not wholly without literary ancestry. Horace had satirized the preposterous dinner-party, and Juvenal was to do so again; and it may have owed something to Menippean satire. Essentially, though, it seems completely original. There is ice at the heart of it; perhaps we can call it satire, but satire tends to have a moral standpoint, and Petronius is rumbustiously averse to all that. We should keep the airbrush away from him: the *Satyrica* may be unique among the larger works of antiquity in its ferocious indifference to propriety.

The only Latin novel to have come down to us entire is the *Golden Ass* of Apuleius, who was born in Madauros, in what is now Algeria, around AD 125. Other works of his remain, notably the *Apology*, a vivid, learned and eccentric speech in his own defence against a charge of magic, and *Florida*, a collection of showy extracts from his declamations. But his ticket to immortality is the novel which he probably called *Metamorphoses*, though the more familiar name was in use by the fourth century.

The basic plot comes from a lost Greek story, of which an abridged version survives: when a magic experiment goes wrong, the narrator, Lucius, is turned into a donkey and undergoes many vicissitudes before eventually resuming human form. Much of the work consists of stories told by the people whom he encounters: the longest of these, the tale of Cupid and Psyche, takes up a fifth of the novel. At the end, Apuleius departed entirely from his model: after coming back to human shape, Lucius sees a vision of the goddess Isis, passes through a mystic initiation, and takes up residence in the temple of Isis in Rome as a kind of monk.

The work begins at speed, and in the middle of a sentence: 'But I will weave together varied tales for you . . .' We seem to be accosted by a huckster, who presses us to look at his Egyptian papyrus. This speaker then explains that he is a Greek, later self-taught in Latin, which is why his lingo may sound peculiar. But this is of course a feint, and he is soon comparing his art to that of the circus rider who leaps from one horse to another – a stylistic virtuoso, in other words. Tacitus and Apuleius are indeed the two greatest masters of Latin prose style, and each developed a highly idiosyncratic manner, but they could hardly be more unlike. Tacitus is terse and asymmetrical, Apuleius symmetrical and effusive. He liked loosely hanging clauses, echoing phrases, rocking rhythms and hints of rhyme. His diction is a unique farrago of archaisms, colloquialisms, new coinages and sheer fantastication; his narrative combines driving energy with elusive beauty. Comedy and mannerism combine: when Lucius asks a cackling crone for directions, she replies with a bad joke, but he proceeds, straight-faced, with elaborate orotundity: 'Jesting put aside, my good old lady, tell me, pray, what manner of man he is and in what abode he lodges.' And when he falls for a feisty slave girl as she stirs the stew in a seductive manner, the picture is both charming and absurd. Counterpointing the adventure are brilliant set-piece descriptions: winged statues that seem to be in flight, with a mossy grotto behind them, filled with glowing shadow; a head of hair, glistening gold in the light and shaded the colour of honey.

Apuleius delivers the entertainment that he promises at the outset, and yet much of the work is sombre or grotesque. The ass is constantly beaten, cudgelled and subjected to all sorts of dangers and indignities, including the threat of castration and being forced to copulate in his animal form with women. People are drenched in urine or spattered with excrement; many of the characters, the virtuous as well as the wicked, die in gruesome ways. Sex and sanctity, coarseness and refinement, horror, bawdy and romance are strangely blended, the whole held together by the verve of the style and the storytelling.

In the tale of Cupid and Psyche, Apuleius becomes even more rococo, exquisite and enchanting. Incongruously, the story is related by an old woman who is cook to a gang of bandits; we can compare the incongruous melodiousness with which Proteus tells of Orpheus and Eurydice in Virgil's *Georgics*. Here he achieves an extraordinary fusion of different tones. On one level this is a fairy-story: 'In a certain country there were a king and queen,' it begins. Sure enough, Psyche is the youngest and loveliest of their three daughters, and she has two wicked sisters, like Cinderella. On another level, this is a myth in the style of Plato: the union of *psyche*, 'the soul', with *cupido*, 'bodily desire'. It is also a romance in the fashion of the Greek novels, in which the heroine undergoes many sufferings before everything eventually comes right. It also contains comedy in the Ovidian manner, with goddesses behaving as though constrained by the etiquette of modern society.

In the middle of the story Psyche is visited nightly by an unseen lover, who warns her that she must never try to look upon him; if she disobeys she will never see him again. But, led astray by her sisters, she purposes to kill him, brings a lamp to the bedside and beholds the god Cupid. There follow perhaps the most sheerly beautiful sentences ever written in Latin prose, a translator's despair, but it may be worth trying a fairly literal version:

> She sees the festive tresses of his golden head drunken with ambrosia, the clusters of ringlets that roam over his milky neck and rosy cheeks beauteously trammelled, some hanging a little before, some hanging a little behind, at whose excess of brilliance, flashing like lightning, the very light of the lamp wavered. Along the shoulders of the flying god dewy feathers glisten, their flower sparkling, and although his wings are settling to rest, the ends of the featherlets, tender and delicate, wanton restlessly in tremulous dance.

This is indeed a bravura display, a cadenza of gorgeous euphuism, inebriated, like Cupid's hair, with its own beauty. For 'hanging before' and 'hanging behind' Apuleius invents a couple of words, *antependulus* and *retropendulus*; and *decoriter*, the word here translated 'beauteously', is also unique to him. But there is more here than surface show: Apuleius is looking hard. The feathers flower, the flowers twinkle, the twinkle is dewy: the language is both fantastic and precisely observed. It searches for details, such as the tiny flicker of movement at the edges of the down. Psyche's enraptured gaze brings us to the story's erotic climax, and yet it fixes itself not on something sexual, or even human, but on feathers. So physical desire is both glorified and transcended: human passion, natural beauty and divine epiphany become one. This is, astonishingly, one of Latin literature's most religious moments. And it is sacramental: a curl of hair and the moistness of a feather are both intensely present in their material reality and by the same token the means by which the god's supernatural numen is revealed.

Scholars have been puzzled by the last part of the novel – in which Lucius is spiritually transformed – because it is supposedly so much at variance with the rest of the work. Perhaps the problem is more one for critics than for readers: the *Golden Ass* resembles the *Georgics* in having an ending which is quite different from what has gone before and yet is strangely satisfying. In any case the change of outlook may be less than is often said. Apuleius does not revel in the bawdy side of his story as Petronius does: for all his brio, the narrative has a dark colour, and we emerge at the end into a great light. And if we have appreciated the religiousness that is part of the extraordinary fusion of tones that he has brought to the tale of Cupid and Psyche, we may feel that Lucius' conversion has been in a way prepared. The procession in honour of Isis, in the earlier part of the last book, is exuberant and carnivalesque; religion and hilarity can still walk hand in hand. This leads on to Lucius' mystic revelation and spiritual transformation. It is unique as an account of religious conversion within a pagan cult; hitherto, Christianity apart, the conversion experience had only been available, so far as our evidence allows, to a philosophical allegiance, as with Lucretius. Apuleius may have been imitating the Christians; or maybe we have here a glimpse into a realm of pagan religious experience otherwise hidden from us. But from wherever he drew his material, he created a style, a tone, a world, that are all his own.

Epilogue

Western civilization is founded on the ancient Mediterranean and on the culture of three peoples, Greeks, Romans and Jews – so much is a commonplace. And the highest achievements of classical literature are very great. A recent history of philosophy observes that any competent list of the greatest western philosophers must include four names; Plato and Aristotle are the first two of them. A list of the six greatest poets of Europe should surely include Homer, Aeschylus and Virgil. If we had to pick the greatest historian of all, the choice should probably fall on Thucydides. The ancients pioneered most of the major literary genres, although one obvious exception is the novel as we understand it. The confessional memoir appeared in late antiquity, with the *Confessions* of St Augustine (354–430), as did the sermon.

But since the ancients invented so much (and not only in literature), we may wonder about what they did not invent. Why did they not invent the wheelbarrow or the windmill or pedal locomotion? And why not printing? That omission limited authorship in various ways. There could be no journalism. There are no diaries. We have little or no genuinely popular literature, because although entertainments might be written for a popular audience, they would not survive unless scribes copied them and went on copying them. The fact that books were expensive may have inhibited the growth of minor genres. There is no detective fiction (the brief story of Bel in the Apocrypha can hardly count) or science fiction (the journey to the moon in Lucian is comic fantasy) or children's literature (animal fables were for adults).

So classical literature left plenty of new fields for later authors to explore (it would be dispiriting if it had not), but we should not conclude from this that it was restricted in style, method or outlook. We are entangled by language. The word 'classical' has several common meanings; this book has used one of them – a descriptive term covering Greek and Roman antiquity up to somewhere around the middle of the first millennium AD. But the word takes its origin from the idea of a body of work possessing special authority and from the fact that the Greeks and Romans were long regarded as the people who should teach us how to write, sculpt, build and think. In another sense 'classical' is contrasted with 'romantic', with the notion that classical literature is the kind that most values control, rules, tradition, discipline and formal beauty.

We should try to keep the different meanings of 'classical' distinct, but they easily bleed into one another. It should be clear from this book that plenty of ancient literature is 'romantic', in any of the senses of another elusive word. At the end of a survey of classical antiquity we may also be struck by how original are all its greatest writers. This is worth stressing, as the idea is around that the ancients were not much concerned with originality. It is commonly said that these authors were keenly conscious of the genres in which they worked, and of the rules or at least the expectations that each genre brought with it. There is a kernel of truth in this, but the 'rules' of genre should be understood as a description of those ways of writing which authors found congenial and rewarding, not as a set of pre-existent commands that authors felt obliged to obey. (One might compare a modern genre, the Hollywood epic, which has some familiar rules or conventions, but only because directors and audiences have liked them, not because some cultural authority has imposed them.) Whenever rules hardened into commands (and this did happen sometimes in antiquity), it was a sign that the creative spark was fading. As we have seen, Latin literature as a whole was secondary, written under the shadow of Greece, but the best Latin writers are the ones who found ways of being original despite this.

And these are the truths that the great spirits of later centuries understood. Shakespeare and Milton, the architects of the Renaissance and Baroque eras, Titian and Tintoretto did not find that their classical sources inhibited them; rather, they stimulated them towards new possibilities. The ancient Greeks and Romans are our parents, and on the whole they have been good parents. The healthy fledgling quits the nest, and it is among the achievements of the best ancient authors that, properly appreciated, they have enabled us to fly free.

Notes

CHAPTER 1: HOMER

7   each handle a single action: *Poetics* 8.

7   Achilles' explosion: *Iliad* 9.308–429.

8   would not allow Homer into his ideal republic . . . : *Republic* 10.606d–607a.

9   made his men gods . . . : *On Height* 9.7.

9   Diomedes actually manages to wound . . . : *Iliad* 5.335–7 and 5.858–9.

10   compares the scene to a chariot race . . . : *Iliad* 22.162–6.

10   shield that the god Hephaestus makes for Achilles . . . : *Iliad* 18.478–613.

11   'As the generation of leaves . . .': *Iliad* 6.146–8.

12   speaker of words and a doer of deeds . . . : *Iliad* 9.443.

12   best of the Achaeans in battle, but . . . : *Iliad* 18.105–6.

12   singing about the famous deeds of men . . . : *Iliad* 9.186–9.

12   a bird collecting morsels . . . : *Iliad* 9.323–4.

12   a little girl running . . . : *Iliad* 16.7–10.

13   embroidering a tapestry . . . : *Iliad* 3.125–8.

13   the gods have put an implacable spirit . . . : *Iliad* 9.636–8.

13   'Let him be tamed . . .': *Iliad* 9.158–61.

13   refuses to marry Agamemnon's daughter . . . : *Iliad* 9.392.

14   'always to be the best . . .': *Iliad* 11.784.

14   a speech of Sarpedon to Glaucus . . . : *Iliad* 12.310–28.

15   Agamemnon uses the language of fault . . . : *Iliad* 19.85–9 and 19.137–8.

15   'I have lost him': *Iliad* 18.82.

15   he 'was not to help' Patroclus . . . : *Iliad* 18.98–115.

15   Hector talking to himself . . . : *Iliad* 22.99–130.

16   gift of second sight . . . : *Iliad* 22.359–60.

16   if he continues to fight at Troy . . . : e.g. *Iliad* 18.115–21.

16   Patroclus' ghost appears to him . . . : *Iliad* 23.65.

16   'the Destinies have put . . .': *Iliad* 24.49.

16   one must bury whoever dies . . . : *Iliad* 19.228–9.

17   provokes Achilles to smile . . . : *Iliad* 23.555.

17   marvels as Priam appears before him . . . : *Iliad* 24.483.

17   threatening to kill the king . . . : *Iliad* 24.566–70.

17   The two men weep . . . : *Iliad* 24.509–12.

17   speaks to Priam with a new pity . . . : *Iliad* 24.518–51.

18   encourages Priam to eat: *Iliad* 24.601–19.

18   Priam asks for a truce . . . : *Iliad* 24.660–67.

18   Achilles is last seen . . . : *Iliad* 24.675–6.

18   his wife, his mother and Helen lament . . . : *Iliad* 24.723–81.

19   'a glorious banquet in the halls of Priam': *Iliad* 24.802–3.

21   an ancient scholar observed . . . : Aristophanes of Byzantium on *Odyssey* 23.296.

21   'All strangers and beggars . . .': *Odyssey* 6.207–8.

21   'giving, such as mine': *Odyssey* 14.57–9.

21   'I know and understand . . .': *Odyssey* 18.228–9.

21   order her to her room . . . : *Odyssey* 21.350–55.

22   '*Argo* known to everybody': *Odyssey* 12.69–70.

22   Their world is half magical . . . : *Odyssey* 7.114–19, 7.201–3 and 8.557–61.

23   Alcinous proposes some sporting contests . . . : *Odyssey* 8.100–103.

23   Alcinous observes blandly . . . : *Odyssey* 8.246–9.

23   'Thus the leaders and rulers . . .': *Odyssey* 13.185–9.

23   Calypso dwells in a cave . . . : *Odyssey* 5.55–74.

24   compares her to Artemis . . . : *Odyssey* 6.102–9.

24   if she is a mortal or a goddess: *Odyssey* 6.149–51.

24   Odysseus first sees her . . . : *Odyssey* 6.85–8 and 6.113.

24   ostensibly to wash . . . : *Odyssey* 6.57–65.

24   another thought in mind . . . : *Odyssey* 6.66–7.

24   Nausicaa and her girls playing ball . . . : *Odyssey* 6.99–101.

24   Standing at a distance, she speaks . . . : *Odyssey* 8.457–68.

25   the trickster has been tricked . . . : *Odyssey* 13.287–95.

25   Zeus delivers the first speech . . . : *Odyssey* 1.32–43.

25   In the country of the good king . . . : *Odyssey* 19.109–14.

26   he comes from Ithaca . . . : *Odyssey* 9.19–28.

26   Odysseus tells Nausicaa . . . : *Odyssey* 6.182–5.

27   his dog and his old nanny . . . : *Odyssey* 17.300–304 and 19.379–94.

27   inspired to . . . make their hearts flutter . . . : *Odyssey* 18.158–62.

CHAPTER 2: ARCHAIC GREECE

31   slices cut from the great banquet of Homer: Athenaeus,
      Scholar-Diners 8.347e.

32   the thirteenth of the month is a bad day . . . : *Works and Days* 780–81
      and 790–91.

32   Drink freely from the wine jar . . . : *Works and Days* 368–9.

32   the story of Prometheus . . . : *Works and Days* 42–59; *Theogony* 507–72.

32   The story of the ages . . . : *Works and Days* 109–201.

33   his father migrated . . . lives himself in Ascra . . . : *Works and Days* 633–40.

33   never been to sea . . . : *Works and Days* 650–53.

33   how the Muses visited him . . . : *Theogony* 22–34.

34   Homer . . . appeals to the Muses . . . : *Iliad* 2.484–92.

37   Rabirius . . . was the best . . . : *History of Rome* 2.36.3.

37   the wisest of men . . . : e.g. Plato, *Apology* 21d.

46   Longinus called Stesichorus . . . : *On Height* 13.3.

46   Quintilian echoed . . . : *Orator's Training* 10.1.62.

48   'the souls of wretched mortals . . .': *Songs* 5.63–7.

50   Horace compared him . . . : *Songs* 4.2.5–8.

50   Longinus classed Pindar . . . : *On Height* 33.5.

CHAPTER 3: THE RISE OF TRAGEDY AND HISTORY

58   Aristotle argued . . . : *Poetics* 13.

61   The chorus quote the king's own words . . . : *Agamemnon* 206–17.

61   two sacrificial virgins in Euripides . . . : *Hecuba* 546–70 and *Iphigenia at
      Aulis* 1551–83 (this section of the play not by Euripides).

61   in language of appalling beauty . . . : *Agamemnon* 228–47.

63   Clytemnestra orders purple cloths . . . : *Agamemnon* 907–57.

63   a magnificent speech of triumph . . . : *Agamemnon* 1372–98.

64   'The sea is there . . .': *Agamemnon* 958–60.

64   'Ototototoi, alas, ah, Apollo, Apollo': *Agamemnon* 1072–3.

65   But her last words . . . : *Agamemnon* 1322–30.

66   'chicks of the eagle': *Libation Bearers* 247 and 256.

66   she first calls for an axe . . . : *Libation Bearers* 889.

67   Athena calls on the 'Athenian people' . . . : *Kindly Ones* 681.

68   the ghost of Clytemnestra . . . : *Kindly Ones* 94–116.

CHAPTER 4: THE LATER FIFTH CENTURY

CHAPTER 5: THE FOURTH CENTURY

125   revealed . . . by a priestess, Diotima . . . : *Symposium* 201d–212c.
125   'procreation in the beautiful' : *Symposium* 206c–e.
127   the Myth of Er . . . : *Republic* 10.614–21.

CHAPTER 6: THE HELLENISTIC AGE

133   We heard of this your love . . . : *Origins* fragment 75.
136   Catullus translated a piece of his court poetry . . . : *Poems* 66.
136   Virgil toyed wittily . . . : *Bucolics* 6.3–8.
136   dismissed him in his *Georgics*: *Georgics* 3.4–8.
136   follow in the footsteps of Callimachus . . . : *Elegies* 3.1.1.
136   called himself 'the Roman Callimachus' . . . : *Elegies* 4.1.64.
136   Ovid's judgement . . . : *Loves* 1.15.14.
136   a dialogue mostly between two bourgeois ladies . . . : *Idylls* 15.
137   'Where are my bay leaves? . . .': *Idylls* 2.
141   unique character of the River Thermodon . . . : *Argonautica* 2.972–84.
141   his picture of the treacherous Syrtis . . . : *Argonautica* 4.1237–49.
142   Hylas, the youth beloved of Heracles . . . : *Argonautica* 1.1222–39.
142   as a sunbeam quivers in a house . . . : *Argonautica* 3.755–9.
143   Jason promises her future fame . . . : *Argonautica* 3.1006–12.
143   She wants to die, but . . . : *Argonautica* 3.806–16.
144   St Paul is made to quote from it . . . : Acts of the Apostles 17.28.
146   brilliance of display . . . : *History* 6.56.6–11.

CHAPTER 7: THE ROMAN REPUBLIC

151   'O Solon, Solon' . . . : *Timaeus* 22b.
152   Cicero could say that Latin . . . : *For Archias* 23.
153   'Captive Greece . . .': *Letters* 2.1.156–7.
154   Homer appearing to him in a dream . . . : *Annals* book 1 (2–11 in Skutsch's edition).
155   supreme in *ingenium* . . . : *Sorrows* 2.424.
155   An anecdote from very late antiquity . . . : Cassiodorus, *Institutes* 1.1.8.
156   the dream of Ilia . . . : *Annals* book 1 (34–50 Skutsch).
156   Agamemnon's dream in the *Iliad* . . . : *Iliad* 2.16–22.

160 Juvenal joked . . . : *Satires* 10.123–4.

161 two fatherlands . . . : *Laws* 2.5.

162 'What a wag . . .': Plutarch, *Comparison of Demosthenes and Cicero* 1.

163 various personae . . . : *For Caelius* 33–8.

163 Piso's grandfather was a Gaul . . . : *Against Piso* 34, 53 and fragment.

163 dancing and the company of Greeks: *Against Piso* 22.

163 a licence for self-indulgence: *Against Piso* 37.

164 the letter of consolation . . . : Cicero, *Letters to Friends* 4.5.

167 human life formerly lay on the ground . . . : *Nature of Things* 1.62–79.

167–8 'To such a pitch of evils . . .': *Nature of Things* 1.101.

168 'Death therefore is nothing . . .': *Nature of Things* 3.830.

168 father sky precipitates . . . : *Nature of Things* 1.250–51.

168 'we see fertile cities blooming . . .': *Nature of Things* 1.255.

168 'We are all sprung . . .': *Nature of Things* 2.991–1001.

168 repeats . . . that the earth is rightly called 'mother' . . . : *Nature of Things* 5.795–6 and 5.821–2.

169 In a very beautiful passage . . . : *Nature of Things* 2.67–79.

170 'By the changes of the parts . . .': *Meditations* 12.23.

170 'the great kinship of man . . .': *Meditations* 12.26.

170 Virgil is the only man . . . : *Georgics* 2.490–92.

171 'a divine pleasure and shudder . . .': *Nature of Things* 3.28–9.

172 The figure of Nature appears . . . : *Nature of Things* 3.931–63.

172 a kind of spiritual exercise . . . : *Nature of Things* 3.1024–52.

172 *homoeomeria* . . . : *Nature of Things* 1.830 and 1.834.

173 When we look up at the stars . . . : *Nature of Things* 5.1204–10.

173 In the diatribe on death . . . : *Nature of Things* 3.894–903.

174 the effects of attrition . . . : *Nature of Things* 1.311–18.

174 children deliberately making themselves . . . : *Nature of Things* 4.400–403.

174 He captures the split second . . . : *Nature of Things* 2.263–5.

174 iridescence of a dove's neck . . . : *Nature of Things* 2.801–4.

174 He watches colour changing . . . : *Nature of Things* 2.828–30.

174 an awning flapping . . . : *Nature of Things* 4.75–80.

174 hoariness and glossiness . . . : *Nature of Things* 2.766–7.

174 optical illusions . . . : *Nature of Things* 4.420–52.

174 Looking at a puddle . . . : *Nature of Things* 4.414–20.

174 sun, moon and stars . . . : *Nature of Things* 2.1030–39.

174 The blight of modern life . . . : *Nature of Things* 3.1060–67.

174 early mankind used to . . . : *Nature of Things* 5.1403–4.

178 'I hate and love' . . . : *Poems* 85.

178 Lesbia's infidelity . . . : *Poems* 75.

178 The longest of all . . . : *Poems* 76.

179 his visit to the tomb . . . : *Poems* 101.

179 Twice Catullus mentions the metre . . . : *Poems* 12 and 42.

180 death of her pet sparrow . . . : *Poems* 3.

180 'You ask, Lesbia . . .': *Poems* 7.

180 'Let us live, my Lesbia . . .': *Poems* 5.

181 In one place he uses it . . . : *Poems* 8.

183 two wedding poems . . . : *Poems* 61 and 62.

183 one of his two experiments . . . : *Poems* 11.

184 the naked sea-nymphs emerging . . . : *Poems* 64.14–18.

184 Peleus' palace glittering . . . : *Poems* 64.43–9.

184 the beauty of her distress . . . : *Poems* 64.60–67.

184 a long, plangent lament . . . : *Poems* 64.132–201.

184 Bacchus coming to her rescue . . . : *Poems* 64.251–3.

185 'Such were the *shapes*' . . . : *Poems* 64.265.

185 It falls into three unequal parts . . . : *Poems* 68.1–40, 68.41–148 and 68.149–60.

185 Lesbia's arrival for an assignation . . . : *Poems* 68.70–72.

CHAPTER 8: VIRGIL

189 *neoteroi* . . . : *Letters to Atticus* 7.2.1.

189 nine years in the making: *Poems* 95.

189 An allusion in Virgil's *Bucolics* . . . : *Bucolics* 6.47 and 6.52.

190 'Something greater than the *Iliad* . . .': *Elegies* 2.34.66.

191 He even advertises the fact . . . : *Bucolics* 4.1 and 6.1–2.

192 'both Arcadians' . . . : *Bucolics* 7.4.

192 the satyr Silenus sings . . . : *Bucolics* 6.64–73.

192 'I saw you when little . . .': *Bucolics* 8.37–41.

192 Two shepherds refer to the absent Menalcas . . . : *Bucolics* 9.23–5, 9.27–9, 9.39–43 and 9.46–50.

193 a shepherd takes on a woman's role: *Bucolics* 8.64–109.

193 Corydon describes the gifts . . . : *Bucolics* 2.51–3.

194–5 he talks about his creative character . . . : *Georgics* 2.475–94.

195 his plan for a future poem . . . : *Georgics* 3.10–39.

195 his native Mantua . . . : *Georgics* 3.13–15.

195 Horace on . . . Bandusia . . . : *Songs* 3.13.

195 Propertius on . . . Assisi . . . : *Elegies* 4.1.121–6.

195 'Earths are on my hands': *Georgics* 2.45.

195 Those mythological stories . . . are all hackneyed . . . : *Georgics* 3.4–8.

195 a memorable cameo . . . : *Bucolics* 6.43–4.

196 everyday farmyard nuisances . . . : *Georgics* 1.118–59.

196 He is discussing, in standard didactic tone . . . : *Georgics* 2.109–35.

197 'But,' he says . . . : *Georgics* 2.136.

197 'So many towns piled up . . .': *Georgics* 2.156–7.

197 culminating in the great men of Rome . . . : *Georgics* 2.167–72.

197 'Hail, great mother of crops . . .': *Georgics* 2.173–4.

197 he is the man who sings . . . : *Georgics* 2.176.

198 'glory of the divine countryside': *Georgics* 1.168.

198 pests like ants and moles . . . : *Georgics* 1.181–6.

198 the raven stalking solitary . . . : *Georgics* 1.388–9.

198 rhapsody about the shepherd's life . . . : *Georgics* 3.22–38.

198 the blessings of country life . . . : *Georgics* 2.458–540.

200 hopes that no small glory . . . : *Georgics* 4.6.

200 The bee-keeper is to hurl rocks . . . : *Georgics* 4.26.

200 labours of the Cyclopes . . . : *Georgics* 4.170–75.

200 'little Quirites': *Georgics* 4.201.

200 Medes and Egyptians . . . : *Georgics* 4.210–12.

200 In a splendid set-piece . . . : *Georgics* 4.67–87.

200 Skittishly, he pretends . . . : *Georgics* 4.116–24.

201 Orpheus and Eurydice . . . : *Georgics* 4.450–527.

204 'lifting on his shoulder the fame and fate . . .': *Aeneid* 8.731.

205 Virgil, accused of plagiarism . . . : *Life of Virgil* 46.

205 Aeneas' enemies call him a Paris . . . : *Aeneid* 4.215 and 7.321.

205 The Sibyl tells Aeneas . . . : *Aeneid* 6.89.

206 how to fit Augustus into the poem . . . : *Aeneid* 1.286–96, 6.791–805, 8.678–84 and 8.714–24.

206 'I have established a noble city . . .': *Aeneid* 4.655.

206 'with great love of the earth': *Aeneid* 1.171–2.

207 'shuddersome with woods . . .': *Aeneid* 7.170–72.

207 the Trojans see the River Tiber . . . : *Aeneid* 7.29–36.

207 hearing her song and the howling . . . : *Aeneid* 7.8–20.

207 Tiber is miraculously stilled . . . : *Aeneid* 8.86–101.

207 'cattle wandering all over . . .': *Aeneid* 8.360–61.

208 'She calls it marriage . . .': *Aeneid* 4.172.

208 Instead he speaks of Juno . . . : *Aeneid* 4.160–70.

209 Creusa's wraith speaks . . . : *Aeneid* 2.776–89.

210 'dear little Aeneas' . . . : *Aeneid* 4.328–9.

210 'like to the light winds . . .': *Aeneid* 2.792–4.

210 The lines are repeated . . . : *Aeneid* 6.700–702.

210 the dead souls are likened to leaves . . . : *Aeneid* 6.309–12.

210 'They were going darkly . . .': *Aeneid* 6.268–72.

210 'shapes terrible to behold': *Aeneid* 6.273–81.

211 Anchises ends his speech . . . : *Aeneid* 6.847–53.

211 Aeneas conducts human sacrifice . . . : *Aeneid* 11.81–2.

212 Aeneas wishes that he had died . . . : *Aeneid* 1.94–101.

212 contemplates abandoning his mission: *Aeneid* 5.700–703.

212 this terrible desire for life: *Aeneid* 6.721.

212 he tells his son . . . : *Aeneid* 12.435–6.

213 'we squander the hours in weeping': *Aeneid* 6.539.

213 last and best of his scenes among the gods . . . : *Aeneid* 12.791–842.

215 The golden bough . . . : *Aeneid* 6.136–48 and 6.187–211.

215 Virgil asked for the *Aeneid* to be destroyed . . . : *Life of Virgil* 39.

CHAPTER 9: THE AUGUSTAN AGE

219 For Quintilian . . . : *Orator's Training* 10.1.93.

219 already Ovid had ranked himself . . . : *Lover's Art* 3.333–40 and 3.535–8; *Sorrows* 2.467.

220 If he can be with his beloved . . . : *Elegies* 1.1.58.

220 he addresses his patron . . . : *Elegies* 1.1.53.

220 starts speaking to his Delia: *Elegies* 1.1.57.

220 he hopes to be looking at her . . . : *Elegies* 1.1.59–66.

220 may he arrive suddenly, unannounced . . . : *Elegies* 1.3.89–90.

220 he tells her to run to him . . . : *Elegies* 1.3.91–2.

221 he recalls the rural idyll . . . : *Elegies* 1.5.19–36.

221 Nemesis' sister fell out of a window . . . : *Elegies* 2.6.39–40.

221 a horrid old man . . . : *Elegies* 1.9.

221 a poem addressed to Marathus . . . : *Elegies* 1.9.

221 the most polished and elegant of the elegists . . . : *Orator's Training* 10.1.93.

222 'give up his last breath . . .': *Elegies* 1.6.25–6.

222 Many, he adds, have perished . . . : *Elegies* 1.6.27–8.

222 the young visiting his tomb . . . : *Elegies* 1.7.23–4.

224 another night of rough lovemaking . . . : *Elegies* 3.8.

226 'so that Umbria may swell . . .': *Elegies* 4.1.63–4.

226 the two longest that he wrote about her . . . : *Elegies* 4.7 and 4.8.

227 in wry allusion to Archilochus . . . : *Songs* 2.7.

227 two very obscene pieces . . . : *Epodes* 8 and 12.

227 Two more are about witches . . . : *Epodes* 5, 17 and 3.

228 two poems in the first book discuss Lucilius . . . : *Conversations* 1.4 and 1.10.

228 returns to Lucilius in his second book . . . : *Conversations* 2.1.

230 The Greek poet is like a mountain river . . . : *Songs* 4.2.5–27.

230 A second simile describes Horace . . . : *Songs* 4.2.27–32.

230 In two of his grandest lyrics . . . : *Songs* 2.1 and 3.3.

231 a duet between a man and a woman: *Songs* 3.9.

233 Horace addressed two poems to such writers . . . : *Songs* 1.33 and 2.9.

233 Lydia and Telephus . . . : *Songs* 1.13.

234 A song of consolation to Virgil . . . : *Songs* 1.24.

234 song on the death of Cleopatra . . . : *Songs* 1.37.

234 In one of the Roman Odes . . . : *Songs* 3.4.

234 An avuncular tone . . . : *Songs* 1.9.

235 'I have completed a monument . . .': *Songs* 3.30.

236 when Horace tells the bailiff . . . : *Letters* 1.14.

237 One addresses Phyllis . . . : *Songs* 4.11.

237 Another urges a businessman . . . : *Songs* 4.12.

238 Cicero compared his style . . . : *Brutus* 262.

238 In a Greek temple of Minerva . . . : *Civil War* 3.105.

239 Seneca was to describe . . . : *Moral Letters* 114.17.

240 Catullus praised him: *Poems* 12.

240 perhaps the most political of all Horace's songs: *Songs* 2.1.

240 three letters sent to Cicero . . . : Cicero, *Letters to Friends* 10.31–3.

241 he censured Sallust . . . and Livy . . . : Suetonius, *On Grammarians* 10; Quintilian, *Orator's Training* 1.5.56 and 8.1.3.

241 His aim was avowedly patriotic . . . : *From the Foundation of the City*, preface.

241 He notes with regret . . . : *From the Foundation of the City* 43.13.

241 Livy knew that the stories of Rome's prehistory . . . : *From the Foundation of the City*, preface.

242 'milky abundance': *Orator's Training* 10.1.32.

242   the people of Alba expelled . . . : *From the Foundation of the City* 1.29.

242   a poem or poems were also a charge . . . : e.g. *Sorrows* 2.207.

243   picks up a girl at the races . . . : *Loves* 3.2.

243   tells the Dawn to delay . . . : *Loves* 1.13.

243   urges the doorkeeper . . . : *Loves* 1.6.

243   echoes Propertius . . . : *Loves* 1.10.

244   'Every lover is a soldier' . . . : *Loves* 1.9.

244   how they can fool her husband . . . : *Loves* 1.4.

244   Two poems deal with harsher topics . . . : *Loves* 3.7(6) and 2.13(14).

244   Another piece stands out . . . : *Loves* 1.5.

245   wine is a good way . . . : *Lover's Art* 1.525–6.

245   praise of Augustus' grandson . . . : *Lover's Art* 1.176–228.

245   If the girl is walking . . . : *Lover's Art* 1.491–6.

246   delighted to have been born in the present age . . . : *Lover's Art* 3.121–8.

248   When Daphne is fleeing . . . : *Metamorphoses* 1.510–11.

248   looks even prettier in flight: *Metamorphoses* 1.527–30.

248   Apollo also boasts . . . : *Metamorphoses* 1.515–17.

248   Jupiter himself . . . : *Metamorphoses* 1.595–6.

248   'The nymphs are said . . .': *Metamorphoses* 2.452.

248   Daedalus and Icarus . . . : *Metamorphoses* 8.152–269.

249   The youth Hermaphroditus . . . : *Metamorphoses* 4.356–67.

249   Meleager will die . . . : *Metamorphoses* 8.522–5.

249   the tale of Pygmalion . . . : *Metamorphoses* 10.243–97.

251   a long declamation on the immutable . . . : *Astronomy* 1.474–531.

CHAPTER 10: AFTER THE AUGUSTANS

255   pattern of literary history . . . : *History of Rome* 1.16–18.

256   a declamation against declamation . . . : *Satyrica* 1–2.

256   'the great talents ceased': *Histories* 1.1.

257   When Thyestes discovers . . . : *Thyestes* 1035–51.

258   When the Greeks prepare . . . : *Trojan Women* 1068–1103.

258   Seneca's Medea, in a final gesture . . . : *Medea* 1024.

258   a speech of more than eighty lines . . . : *Phaedra* 483–573.

258   a kind of jigsaw puzzle . . . : *Phaedra* 1256–74.

260   the wise man will prefer to be rich . . . : *On the Happy Life* 22.

260   'To some I will not give . . .': *On the Happy Life* 24.

260 One discusses the treatment of slaves . . . : *Moral Letters* 47.

261 the relationship between an author's style . . . : *Moral Letters* 114.

261 'We lie in saying that Jupiter reigns': *Civil War* 7.447.

262 gloating lustfully over the corpses . . . : *Civil War* 7.786–96.

263 defies a stupendous storm . . . : *Civil War* 5.653–77.

263 Cato's obituary speech . . . : *Civil War* 9.190–214.

263 Pompey dreams of being back at Rome . . . : *Civil War* 7.7–24.

263 speech of the eunuch Pothinus . . . : *Civil War* 8.484–535.

265 the institution of the eucharist: 1 Corinthians 11.23–6.

267 the Prodigal Son . . . : Luke 15.11–32.

268 he has Jesus deliver a farewell sermon: John 13–17.

268 'I am the bread of life': John 6.35.

268 'I am the true vine': John 15.1.

268 'My God, my God . . .': Mark 15.34; Matthew 27.46.

268 'It is finished': John 19.30.

268 His account of the resurrection . . . : John 20.1–18.

268–9 when Jesus raises Lazarus . . . : John 11.1–46.

269 death of a friend's parrot . . . : *Silvae* 2.4.

269 an insomniac's address to Sleep . . . : *Silvae* 5.4.

270 half gods, Clouds, Rivers . . . : *Thebaid* 1.119–210.

270 'Will you last?' . . . : *Thebaid* 12.810–19.

270 deprecating the 'pedestrian Muse' . . . : *Conversations* 2.6.17.

272 If you read about Oedipus . . . : *Epigrams* 10.4.

272 unruly hair and hairy legs . . . : *Epigrams* 10.65.

272 by the Tibur column . . . : *Epigrams* 1.117.

272 'by the Pear Tree' . . . : *Epigrams* 10.20.

272 a little countrified place on the Janiculum . . . : *Epigrams* 8.61.

272 the texture of his immediate neighbourhood . . . : *Epigrams* 9.97.

273 read among the Germans . . . : *Epigrams* 4.64.

273 A dried-up marsh . . . : *Epigrams* 4.4.

273 Like the scent of an apple . . . : *Epigrams* 3.65.

273 wafting of weary balsam . . . : *Epigrams* 11.8.

273 the little slave girl Erotion . . . : *Epigrams* 5.37.

274 his summer place in Tuscany . . . : *Letters* 9.36.

274 his colossal villa on the sea . . . : *Letters* 2.17.

275 the first pagan account of Christianity: *Letters* 10.96.

275 Trajan's presence in his palace . . . : *Panegyric* 47–8.

275 hunters and pastoralists on . . . Euboea . . . : *Speeches* 7.

275 giant statue of Zeus at Olympia . . . : *Speeches* 12.

CHAPTER 11: TWO NOVELS

297   the widow of Ephesus . . . : *Satyrica* 111–2.

298   contemplates buying land . . . : *Satyrica* 48.

298   slaves are human . . . : *Satyrica* 71.

298   silver skeleton . . . : *Satyrica* 34.

298   One should talk literature . . . : *Satyrica* 39.

298   proudly philistine . . . : *Satyrica* 71.

298   dilating foolishly . . . : *Satyrica* 39

299   a silver chamber-pot . . . : *Satyrica* 27.

299   'Cassandra's dead children' . . . : *Satyrica* 52.

299   he has told his slaves . . . : *Satyrica* 71.

299   'No one in my house . . .': *Satyrica* 64.

299   'Pretend I'm dead . . .': *Satyrica* 78.

299   conversation of the humbler guests . . . : *Satyrica* 41–6.

300   Trimalchio's own story . . . : *Satyrica* 48.

300   the preposterous dinner-party . . . : Horace, *Conversations* 2.8; Juvenal, *Satires* 5.

301   Lucius asks a cackling crone . . . : *Golden Ass* 1.21.

301   a feisty slave girl . . . : *Golden Ass* 2.7.

302   winged statues . . . : *Golden Ass* 2.4.

302   a head of hair, glistening . . . : *Golden Ass* 2.8.

302   tale of Cupid and Psyche . . . : *Golden Ass* 4.28–6.24.

303   She sees the festive tresses . . .: *Golden Ass* 5.22.

Index

Economics:
The User's Guide
Ha-Joon Chang

What is economics?

What can – and can't – it explain about the world?

Why does it matter?

Ha-Joon Chang teaches economics at Cambridge University and writes a column for the *Guardian*. The *Observer* called his book *23 Things They Don't Tell You About Capitalism*, which was a no.1 best-seller, 'a witty and timely debunking of some of the biggest myths surrounding the global economy'. He won the Wassily Leontief Prize for advancing the frontiers of economic thought and is a vocal critic of the failures of our current economic system.

A PELICAN
INTRODUCTION

Greek and Roman Political Ideas
Melissa Lane

Where do our ideas about politics come from?

What can we learn from the Greeks and Romans?

How should we exercise power?

Melissa Lane teaches politics at Princeton University, and previously taught for fifteen years at Cambridge University, where she also studied as a Marshall and Truman scholar. The historian Richard Tuck called her book *Eco-Republic* 'a virtuoso performance by one of our best scholars of ancient philosophy'.

A PELICAN
INTRODUCTION

Human Evolution
Robin Dunbar

What makes us human?

How did we develop language, thought and culture?

Why did we survive, and other human species fail?

Robin Dunbar is an evolutionary anthropologist and Director of the Institute of Cognitive and Evolutionary Anthropology at Oxford University. His acclaimed books include *How Many Friends Does One Person Need?* and *Grooming, Gossip and the Evolution of Language*, described by Malcolm Gladwell as 'a marvellous work of popular science'.

A PELICAN
INTRODUCTION

Revolutionary Russia, 1891–1991

Orlando Figes

What caused the Russian Revolution?

Did it succeed or fail?

Do we still live with its consequences?

Orlando Figes teaches history at Birkbeck, University of London and is the author of many acclaimed books on Russian history, including *A People's Tragedy*, which *The Times Literary Supplement* named as one of the '100 most influential books since the war', *Natasha's Dance*, *The Whisperers*, *Crimea* and *Just Send Me Word*. The *Financial Times* called him 'the greatest storyteller of modern Russian historians'.

A PELICAN
INTRODUCTION

The Domesticated Brain
Bruce Hood

Why do we care what others think?

What keeps us bound together?

How does the brain shape our behaviour?

Bruce Hood is an award-winning psychologist who has taught and researched at Cambridge and Harvard universities and is currently Director of the Cognitive Development Centre at the University of Bristol. He delivered the Royal Institution's Christmas Lectures in 2011 and is the author of *The Self Illusion* and *Supersense*, described by *New Scientist* as 'important, crystal clear and utterly engaging'.

A PELICAN
INTRODUCTION